DEEP WATER

DEEP WATER

Moya Crawford

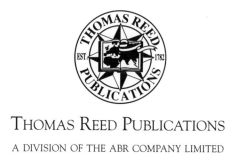

THOMAS REED PUBLICATIONS

A DIVISION OF THE ABR COMPANY LIMITED

Published by
Thomas Reed Publications
(a division of The ABR Company Limited)
The Barn, Ford Farm
Bradford Leigh, Bradford on Avon
Wiltshire BA15 2RP
United Kingdom

First published in Great Britain 1999

British Library Cataloguing in Publication Data
A CIP catalogue record for this book is available from the British Library

Printed in Hong Kong by Midas Printing Limited

ISBN 0 901281 83 2

Registered at Stationers' Hall

CONTENTS

To
Rob, Drew, Patrick and Rachel

ACKNOWLEDGEMENTS

I would like to thank Sukey Roxburgh and Jonathan Miller, for all the help and encouragement they have given during the writing of this book. I am delighted that it has been published by Thomas Reed Publications, as this imprint is well known to the international salvage industry. I would also like to thank John Beaton for his deft touch in editing.

AUTHOR'S NOTE

Deciding whether to use imperial or metric measurements has posed something of a problem in this work, as all the wrecks to which I refer, apart from the *François Vieljeux*, were built in feet, inches and tons. A compromise has been made by sticking to the pertinent system of measurement in all cases. As a slight quirk, even modern ships' tonnages are still expressed in tons.

1

ON SITE

It was dusk and there was a stiff breeze in the air. The tattered and smoke-stained Red Ensign whipped against its mast above the engine room funnel; disappearing briefly in the diesel fumes, as they curled upwards before being swept into the encroaching night. The ever-moving sea heaved, shoving past us, and the ship slowly rolled.

The main hoist winch was hauling in, droning away.

Almost without warning the massive grab appeared above the stern of the ship, lurching menacingly from side to side and I knew that this was the climax of seventeen years' hard work. Water cascaded from its battered steel frame, falling onto the aft deck and catching in the beam of the deck light, like falling shards of glass. Stealthily, as if it were an unwieldy monster with a life of its own, it was hauled inboard. In the wheelhouse switches were flicked and it shuddered open, the six curved limbs peeling outward to reveal almost talon-like claws as it disgorged its load and the wet, glistening copper sheets spread across the decking with the painful grind of metal against metal.

This was a world record smashed.

One thousand two hundred and fifty metres beneath us lies the wreck of the French cargo/container ship, *François Vieljeux*. To put this in perspective, she rests as deep in the water as Britain's tallest mountain Ben Nevis is high. We were taking cargo out of her holds through a space no more than five metres wide, the width of an average house roof. Nobody had achieved this before. We had tripled the existing depth record, beating government-sponsored foundations and multi-national companies alike. A small, family business, we lead the international field and yet operate in complete and utter obscurity.

Here, onsite, it is often quite conceivable that we are the sole humans alive. We toil away isolated, thirty miles offshore. Land is rarely visible even in daylight and into this lonely bivouac, with the sky as canvas and the ceaselessly moving ocean as a sort of false floor, only the occasional freighter or container ship breaks our horizon, as it plies the Atlantic coast of Spain. When darkness takes over such baulks are reduced to the fleeting white and red or green of navigation lights, accompanied by a blip on the radar screen. What is real is our ship, the *Redeemer*, her four crew and her four mooring buoys, to which she is tied like a spider in the centre of a scanty web. There is nothing more but passing schools of dolphins or the odd, opportunistic sea bird.

I notice my husband, Alec, give up his post at the controls, high up, through the dimly lit windows of the forward wheelhouse. He is illuminated by the glow of the video monitors. After a moment, he appears and skirts nimbly around the obstacles on the hatch. Tired, but surefooted as ever, he jumps over the vice with its clutter of tools to join me aft. Before he speaks he shouts a word of encouragement above the noise of the engine room below to the others, who have already begun to stow the spoils.

'Two tonnes, I reckon. Around forty sheets' and he lifts a thumb and grins boyishly in acknowledgement of a good haul. He is in such harmony with the ship and its equipment, that he has guessed the weight of the copper almost exactly as he lifted it to the surface from the reading on the pressure gauge that was before.

'Are there any wire bars?'

The answer, 'Three,' is shouted back.

'Great!' he confirms.

He now turns his attention to me, speaking quietly and more confidentially. His loose-fitting boilersuit, stained with oil is gathered at the waist with an old leather belt and his thick, calloused hands are a contrast to his pleasant, well-spoken voice.

'This is more like it, Moya' he says with a sigh of relief.

'Yes, I know,' I reply, smiling gently. Few words are required between us, Our eyes tell each other that we both appreciate how soul destroying our struggle has been. We stand together for a few moments in the shelter of the aft winch, in that easy silence that intimacy brings. The 'lads' sort the heavy sheets of copper, known as cathodes. Each is a metre square and weighs on average fifty kilograms. Some are as flat as the day they were formed, others have been crumpled by the force of the grab, as if they were made from cardboard. These are thrown to one side, where Frank, swarthy and pirate-like, is wielding the sledge hammer with resounding thuds. As they are beaten into reasonable shape, the two deckhands remove them to the gunwales, slinging them with wire in bundles of forty.

Alec watches intently for a few moments, hands languidly on hips and bearing the weight on one leg, in a characteristic pose. His body is lithe and muscular, belying his forty-six years and he sways instinctively in the continual motion of the ship. On his face is a look of deep concentration and then suddenly, as if realising that he was lost in thought, he puts his hand roughly, but affectionately on my shoulder and shakes it. 'I'd better get on.' The gesture is an apology and a dismissal in one.

'Right, lads,' he shouts, 'I'll lift the grab and put it over, again' and he turns and makes his way purposefully back.

How well I know this man and his ways. His temperament is incredibly even and he thinks that this makes him easy-going, which always rather amuses me. It is true that he seldom makes personal demands. I am not expected to organise his care and maintenance like so many wives, or pander to his whims, but on the other hand it is taken for granted that I shall cope with any level of technical or bureaucratic difficulty anywhere in the world.

When I am in the office in Scotland, the phone will ring and it will be Alec, speaking from *Redeemer* via a radio link. He will say, 'Moya, we have a slight problem here ...' This is a familiar understatement that makes my heart sink, for it is generally followed by such sentences as, 'the generator on the Lister has burnt out and we need spares immediately – we can't work without them,' or 'I've damaged my eye, it's been pierced by a piece of mooring wire and I need to go to hospital in Vigo as soon as we get in'. And there have been several occasions when I would have swapped an offhand demand for an ironed shirt, or a criticism of a dress, with the trust and confidence of, 'we've been arrested, can you get hold of somebody and sort the matter out?' He treats me as an equal in everything except physical strength, considering me a perfect counterpart whom he implicitly trusts. This is a very great compliment despite the responsibility it brings.

My attention returns to the deck. It is beginning to get cold and as it will be some while before the grab returns from the wreck to be emptied again I follow Alec inside and up the ladder to the wheelhouse where he is already at work. He is wedged uncomfortably on a backless seat in the corner, between the control panel and the starboard side, and is gazing intently at the monitor in front of him with hardly a blink. I position myself by his shoulder and watch too. Curiously, there is no impression of travel or speed as the grab descends, just the passing of time. The video camera is always switched on after half a minute, once it is in the sunless region, so that its lens is not damaged by natural rays. Bright underwater lights penetrate the gloom. The intensified black and white images are so clear and immediate that it is difficult to comprehend that they soon will be taken from over a kilometre below.

Plunging downward as fast as water resistance will allow resembles nothing more closely than driving through a winter storm. The lights are reflected back by the myriad plankton suspended in the water column and these illuminated white flecks seemingly career towards the screen, as blinding as flakes of snow. Every so often a fantastically shaped creature, a delicate membrane supported by sea water like an iridescent balloon, will zip through the view. There are a few fish here and there, but little else, until out of oblivion looms the superstructure of the wreck, cold, grey and foreboding. Seeing it gives me a jolt every time, but Alec knows it is coming and accordingly he has already begun to slow the descent of the grab. With his left hand, he reaches across the array of switches and levers, and engages the ones he wants without so much as a sideways glance.

'Right,' he says, preparing himself for the onerous task of manoeuvring into the narrow space of the hatch, 'we're here.'

He means it. As far as he is concerned, he is there. He and the grab are as one.

CHAPTER
2

FOULA

One evening some months before, I had been walking back from a drinks party at the yacht club at Monte Carlo beside the glimmering Mediterranean, when the oil executive's wife whom I was accompanying, asked, 'May I ask what do you do?'

It was obvious from the politeness of her question, that she thought I was in some suitably female employment, such as public relations or personnel.

I smiled gently, 'I run a small marine salvage company.'

She was visibly surprised, 'That's unusual ... How does a young woman like you find herself working in such a man's world?'

It was a frequent enough question, but having been vastly outnumbered by the opposite sex at the offshore technology conference her own spouse was also attending, my sense of the absurd got the better of me and I replied, mischievously, 'It's very simple. For a long time I only kept my job by sleeping with the managing director ...'

'Oh my dear, no-o-o!' she butted in before I could finish the sentence, leaving me to disappoint her by explaining ... 'He's my husband and now that I've replaced him as managing director, one might equally say he only keeps his job as technical director by sleeping with me ...'

There is an element of truth both ways. Our company has only survived because of our partnership.

Alexander Charles Crawford – I have known this salvor for well over twenty years, all but one of them in marriage. If I were still of a romantic disposition, I would write that I ran away to sea with him as a child bride, and strive to give the impression that he was a mariner possessed by the oceans like some latter-day Captain Ahab. This would indeed conjure up the youthful, reckless passion in which I threw my lot with his, forsaking my home and family for a life bound to the waves. It would also epitomise the occasions, particularly earlier on when we were inseparable and caught in storm or danger, that I literally had put my life in his hands. Certainly, such drama has been ours, yet underlying our union has always been such a bedrock of logic in the form of applied physics, that I feel bound to ignore this hyperbole. The reality is that our type of marine salvage, which concentrates on one specific wreck for a long period of time, has never held any sense of escape, more belonging; and although the marine world has always fascinated Alec and he is driven intellectually to unlock its secrets, I would describe him as single-minded, not compulsive.

This does not mean that he is not frequently impossible.

Sometimes, when he is going through a design phase and perhaps has talked about nothing but lifting speeds of winches, the diameter of umbilicals, voltage drop, electric motors, solid state relays and so on, during every conversation for days, even if we have begun talking by me mentioning the farm or the children, I tease him that he has a mixture of salt water and hydraulic oil in his veins. This is only half a joke because, the sea and engineering are such an integral part of his life, that if it were medically possible, I believe it would be true.

I heard of Alec Crawford several weeks before we happened across each other and have to admit ruefully to not wanting to meet him at all, at the time. The circumstances were so distinctly out of the ordinary, that they would be difficult to forget. The year was 1975. It was just a fortnight after my seventeenth birthday and I was being ferried to the island of Foula by one of its inhabitants in his small, open boat. This outcrop of rock, no more than three miles by two, sits far to the west of Shetland on the same latitude as the southern tip of Greenland to the west and St Petersburg to the east, surprisingly close to the Arctic Circle for a piece of Britain.

I was going there to take a summer job on a croft. All I had been given was the owner's telephone number and the information that she was an elderly woman, who had recently had a serious operation, making her unable to cope with her workload. I had contacted her from the lobby of a run-down hotel in Lerwick, where I had been mascarading as a waitress since leaving school the month before. Our conversation had been brief and to the point.

'Mrs Holbourn, my name's Moya Gerrard. A friend of mine from Yell teaches alongside Andy Gear, and I understand from him that you're looking for some help on your croft.'

'Yes,' came the reply in the strong local tongue, 'but does dee ken much about sheep?'

'A bit. I live in the Outer Hebrides and I've helped out with dipping and shearing. I'm also planning to study agriculture at Aberdeen, after starting a year's practical in September.'

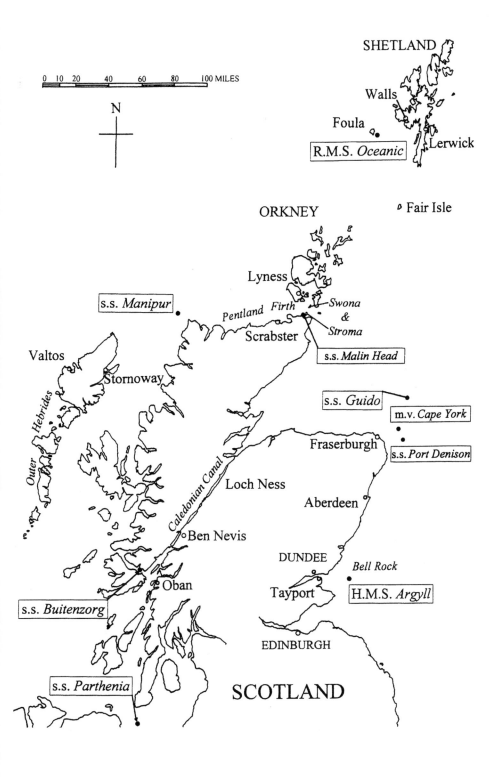

SHETLAND

Walls

Foula

R.M.S. *Oceanic*

Lerwick

Fair Isle

ORKNEY

Lyness

s.s. *Manipur*

Pentland Firth

Swona & Stroma

Scrabster

s.s. *Malin Head*

Valtos

Stornoway

Outer Hebrides

s.s. *Guido*

m.v. *Cape York*

Fraserburgh

s.s. *Port Denison*

Caledonian Canal

Loch Ness

Aberdeen

Ben Nevis

DUNDEE

Bell Rock

Oban

Tayport

H.M.S. *Argyll*

s.s. *Buitenzorg*

EDINBURGH

s.s. *Parthenia*

SCOTLAND

0 10 20   40   60   80   100 MILES

N

'Well, I can't offer much. Just a couple of pounds a week, and a bed and keep.'

'That's all right. I really want to visit Foula When would you like me to start? I was thinking about catching the ferry on the ninth of June.'

'That would suit me fine, lass.'

I was delighted with the appointment, because it was true – I really did want to visit Foula. This far flung isle had caught my imagination ever since I had been taken by fishing boat to camp on St Kilda, which lay even beyond our horizon on the west coast of Lewis. Despite being used to isolation in our home by the shore in Valtos, there was a magic and pathos about this small group of five rocks, that captivated me with their loneliness. Hirta, the main island, with its evacuated street-like village and the majesty of its sharply-etched cliffs, impressed me in particular, so that I read the *Life and Death of St Kilda* and every other book I could find. 'How could people eke out a living on such a small piece of land and be so cut off from the rest of the world?' I had wondered. 'Their perspective must have been unique.'

Foula was an island with such similarities to Hirta in topography and location that it was often mentioned in comparison and in retrospect, although I was not conscious of it at the time, my curiosity and a yen for wilderness drew me there.

Staying at school at the Nicholson Institute for just as long as it took to get my qualifications, I walked out of its gates in Stornoway without a backwards glance. Lessons had bored me all through the final year, made even more stale by the rigid Presbyterianism with which we were force fed. My breaking point had been in Higher Chemistry when we had been instructed in all seriousness, that we must not accept the validity of carbon dating, as it took no account of the Flood. Even the adolescent liberty of sharing digs with my friend Liz, as an alternative to the hostel in which the bulk of the country girls stayed, did little to relieve the tedium. Impatient for adventure and longing for freedom and space, the main cities of Edinburgh and Glasgow were snubbed and I pursued my notion of visiting Shetland.

Catching the steamer, *St Clair*, in Aberdeen, my journey began in the worst storms since Easter. The seas were menacingly heavy and this old-fashioned tub wallowed with a vengeance. In the fug-filled saloon a handful of hardy travellers drank and played cards. Periodically their drinks would bolt from one side of their table to the other in a particularly severe roll, and were whipped up and put to the lips before they spilt. 'Another pint of lager and a whisky chaser.' The ambience was spit and sawdust on a seesaw. It was my first solo expedition and sitting quietly in the corner, I relished every moment of it.

Venturing out onto the upper deck, the breaking swell shimmered in the moonlight as it peaked and frothed in the darkness all around. Reeling from handhold to handhold, grabbing at the rail on one side, fending myself off against the superstructure the next, the wind buffeted my face and the salt spray lay as a film of moisture on my hair and lips. The sensation was exhilarating, and I felt as intrepid as Captain Robert Falcon Scott, never once feeling sick.

When we eventually entered Bressay Sound, it had taken eighteen hours to complete a passage that was normally covered in twelve, and as Lerwick, the islands' capital hove into view, a striking composition of stone dwellings, shops and businesses unfolded. I had never seen anywhere like it before, the influence on shapes and designs was Nordic, not evenly faintly Scottish. Along the waterfront, many of the buildings formed the harbour wall, so that the water lapped under the high windows. Here there was a gable end painted with a giant boot, there an enormous boat builder's shed. Foreign names, like Laurensen or Malakoff, decorated various signs and the lorries and cabs that were waiting on the quay. Everywhere was a bustle of activity, and the brightly painted hulls of the fishing fleet added a foil of colour. Making my way down the gang plank and crossing the square, the flagstoned street seemingly rose to meet my feet, and then disappeared into hollows, as my subconscious continued to compensate for the rolling swell, so that I lurched unsteadily in the direction of my first employ. The shopfronts were full of hand-knitted jumpers, hats and shawls, traditional patterns in shades of brown, cream and grey intermingled with more colourful Norwegian and Icelandic patterns, but there was not a flash of tartan anywhere. This discrepancy was symbolic, for without leaving the United Kingdom, I had travelled abroad.

It took only a couple of shifts at the hotel I had chosen from the *Yellow Pages* as a means of being self-supporting, to assure me that I was not cut out to serve the general public. The work was thankless and its organisation shambolic. I had little aptitude and was given less training, as the place was continually short-staffed. One busy evening meal, rushing, I stopped and the soup I was delivering jettisoned into the customer's lap. She was very decent about it. On the other hand, the manager's father whose aperitif I forgot was not. Every day was much the same; long shifts, spent continually on your feet. The travelling salesmen stared at your breasts beneath your blouse, lingering over ordering and generally so many customers were surly, that being pleasant over breakfast, lunch, high tea and dinner, seemed a poor way to spend the summer. Not least when I had to explain, 'I'm terribly sorry, your lunch is going to be another half an hour, the Calor gas has run out.'

What made matters worse was that the establishment turned out to be a den of iniquity – Sodom and Gomorrah with two stars. The cook was pregnant with her second illegitimate child and had been thrown out by her father; the woman with whom I worked had a lover ten years her junior; the barmaid from Manchester was a happy hooker; and rumour had it that the barman, who had recently left, had welcomed the attention of those male customers who were not quite her type. In and out of this promiscuous maelstrom traipsed the unsuspecting guests, including the late Joe Grimond, the former leader of the Liberal party who was the local MP. I am sure he would have taken it all in his stride, had he known.

Unlike me.

Fortunately, I was considered to be such a nice girl, that I was put in an undecorated room in the main body of the hotel, well away from the happenings in the staff quarters across the road, and so rough was the public bar, I was not allowed to put my nose round the door, even when it was shut. Even thus protected, the bawdy gossip when everyone got together during teabreaks and meals, made my eyes widen and my jaw drop, as I found myself blushing and disappearing lower and lower behind the covers of some improving book.

'Here, a drunk battered so hard against our door last night, that he broke it down!'

'What happened then?'

The rude tale would unfold.

Young and homesick, I was out of my depth and consequently handed in my notice as soon as I had organised the Foula job. Heedless about money, this was the opportunity I had craved.

First, I spent a few days exploring the islands of Unst and Fetlar to the very north of the Shetland archipelago, and then on the arranged day, by catching a combination of buses and ferries, began to make my way to Walls. Getting off in the middle of nowhere at Voe, what had seemed a short distance on my map, turned out to be fifteen miles of undulating road. Weighed down with a heavy rucksack, that was half full of reading matter, I would never have made it on time had it not been for a succession of three unsolicited lifts. The last of these was offered by a fishermen who took me right along to the departure point, which turned out to be nothing more that a spit of stones covered with grass, down the end of short track. 'You're lucky,' he mentioned, 'most people think that the Foula mailboat goes from the Steamer's pier over there' and he pointed far across the inlet of water, 'but that's just a store.'

As I tumbled out onto the springy turf, I was soon to find that little about the Foula mailboat was predictable. My Shetland Islands Council timetable had assured me that the service left at two o'clock every Monday afternoon, weather permitting.

'Five to two – I've just made it. I'm so grateful,' but I could not see it anywhere. 'Do you think it's late?'

Seeing that I was gazing hopefully in the wrong direction, he pointed to the small, open boat, which I had overlooked, even though it was tied up beside us, on our lee, with its engine running.

'Looks as if yon's off to Foula' he nodded, indicating the blue Shetland model, in which there was a man stowing boxes and bags.

At about twenty feet in length, with no shelter of any sort, it resembled nothing more than a large rowing boat. My eye was not completely inexperienced in these matters and I was appalled, certain that this was hardly an appropriate public transport for the exposed trip out into the Atlantic. Why, the crofters on Lewis took sheep to the sheltered islets in craft bigger than this!

This opinion must have been written plainly across my face, because as I approached the skipper, a giant of a man dressed in a blue woollen guernsey, black jacket and cheese-cutter hat, remarked with authority, 'The mailboat is off being refitted. This is my boat. It's calm and if we leave shortly, we'll be perfectly safe.'

My reservations were strong, but the options seemed limited. If I refused, I would either have to wait and see if I could get a seat aboard the odd charter flight from Sumburgh, or not go at all. Speculating that as he had got here safely and seemed to be proficient, there was no reason to believe he should not make it back, I handed down my rucksack and he made a space for me on one of the hard wooden seats that ran breadthways. There, like Audrey Hepburn in a diminutive version of *The African Queen*, I sat hemmed in by numerous boxes of groceries, fence posts and sacks of Her Majesty's Mail. Within moments we had cast off. The day was glorious. A pair of porpoises leapt out of the glassy water as we cut a gentle, splashing bow wave down the voe, past Vaila Hall and out into the ocean; in a westwards journey that would take over three and a half hours, it was so far.

The time passed easily. Jim Gear, owner of the *Happy Voyager*, was ideal company being happy to converse. With one hand casually on the tiller, he chatted above the noise of the puttering engine amidships, covering life on the island, its history, the people and who did what and lived where; as a newcomer I could not have wished for a better guide. Soon I found out that I owed my imminent employment to his brother, who would be visiting later in the year. That the postmaster's name was Harry and he was also a Gear, and that Lisbeth Holbourn cleaned at the school and kept Loch Cottage as a holiday home, as well as running her crofts.

I had no qualms about anything until he mentioned with some pride, 'And we have two divers on the island, at the moment, as well. They're salvaging the White Star Liner, RMS *Oceanic* which sank on the reef of the Shaalds. She was a forerunner of the famous *Titanic*, and the largest ship in the world when she was built.

'I helped them find the wreck. My father used to show me the position when he took me out fishing as a boy ...'

I had never heard of the *Oceanic*, and that she lay just a few miles off our course raised absolutely no curiosity in me at all. In fact, I was taking in little about the ship, or the part Jim had played in finding her remains. What had struck me most forcibly was the prospect of there being divers on the island. 'Oh no! How awful!' I had thought. The crudest, most embarrassing men that ate at the hotel in Lerwick had been a bunch of construction divers, who came in for lunch every day. They had been loud, boisterous and full of innuendo.

'Hey love, what've you got on offer that can satisfy a man ...?'

I would reply, studiously frigid, 'I believe the steak and kidney pie's quite good' and return to plonk down their orders at arm's length.

As there was no reason to believe that these salvage divers would differ, I resolved instantly to have nothing to do with them. They were not going to spoil my stay on Foula and the best course of action would be to keep entirely out of their way.

Of course, in retrospect, this disgust was just tempting fate.

Gradually, as Foula grew from a hazy grey shadow on the horizon to a tangible lump, with distinctive peaks, Jim told me their names. 'Going from the South End, that's the Noop, Hamnafield, the Kame, the Sneug and Soberlie. There are two main groups of crofts now. One beneath the Noop, which is called the Sooth Toon and the other around the Voe, which lies beneath Hamnafield. There are about forty people on the island all told. We got as low as twenty-six at one time, but there was never any talk of evacuation.'

I thought about St Kilda and asked, 'Why not?'

'I don't know really. The people just did not want to leave and clung on. Foula is special, in a way.'

He was quite right. Rock, with a covering of sparse vegetation though it was, it exerted a certain force. Just as its very existence had attracted me and was about to change the course of the rest of my life.

As we neared, the shape in the distance, which had been flat like a stencil, developed into a three-dimensional mass. The clefts in the cliffs became apparent, as did the contours of the land. Colours began to stand out, the green of the parks for grazing and the brown of the peat banks.

Houses suddenly appeared from out of the impressive backdrop, like pop-up illustrations, white wispy smoke lacing from their chimneys. All came into focus and then the scenery loomed large, as the island's six hundred and fifty metre summit towered majestically in the sky, dominating all.

The noise of the nesting seabirds suddenly became obvious; the anxious cries of the kittiwakes and prattling of the fulmars. The long gentle swell broke with a soothing hush on the shoreline, and Jim cut the engine as we glided into the narrow haven and jut of concrete that formed Foula's only pier.

There was a small reception committee to meet us.

'Every one's keen for their Walls boxes and mail,' Jim explained, 'this being the first trip I've managed to make across to the Shetland Mainland in over six weeks.'

Given the air of cheery expectation with which he was greeted, there was no opportunity to ask more. I was eyed with polite curiosity as Jim helped me ashore and pointed out Mrs Holbourn's croft that stood close by on a knoll just up the road.

'The first boat to go to the mainland in six weeks ...' I had wondered even then, 'what if I had decided to turn up last week or the week before?' It was only a better acquaintance with the vagaries of the island's transport system that assured me of my luck, for I hardly think that even when the proper mailboat returned, it was sitting waiting ready to leave at two o'clock on a Monday afternoon, in all the rest of the summers I was there.

As impressive as Foula is, it is not its shape or its size, but its inhabitants that still mean most to me, and even though she is long dead, I cannot think of Lisbeth Holbourn without both affection and a smile. She received me all those years ago through a narrowly opened door, as if she had a chain on, her knee jostling against two fat, overgrown pet lambs, which though long off the bottle were still intent on getting in. This gave the impression that I was an undesirable and the conversation was interspersed with orders and instructions to the woolly, boisterous pair.

'Get dee out. Get dee out. Away!'

Inevitably, as she admitted me, they barged past, cornering through the porch and hallway at speed, to stand bleating noisily in the middle of the kitchen floor.

Shortish and full figured with a tremendous bust, she wore a flowery pinafore. Her taut, sun-tanned legs bowed out above her plimsolls, appearing surprisingly thin, and for all the world her shape reminded me of Mr Toad dressed up as the washerwoman.

'What is dee doing?' she demanded of the caddie lambs, as they were called, hustling them out with much noise and vigour.

'Well. My, my. What a welcoming!' she laughed. 'Sit dee in and I'll put on a pot of tea.' Coming up to sixty, she was not an attractive woman, nor even a handsome one, but her face, which was swarthy and dark, held enormous character. Thick, steely-piano wire hair shook in waves above jet black eyebrows and the rimmed, National Health spectacles she wore could never conceal the sparkle in her mahogany brown eyes, be it from mirth or anger. Her mouth was broad and deep red. In complexion and temperament she had warm, fiery, blood bequeathed to her from some long distant relation, a Spaniard from the Armada, perhaps. Imperfect, volatile, gregarious, and kind, Lisbeth was certainly not of Calvinist stock. When she laughed, as she frequently did, her whole body shook. When she lost her temper, it was as rapid as hitting the bell on a 'Test Your Strength' machine at the fair.

Large-hearted, overworked and disorganised, what she lacked in method, she more than compensated for in sheer guts. I was soon to find out that domesticity at Ham was a topsy-turvy affair, despite her best intentions and sharing her unruly life, which ran late for every schedule and season alike, is something that I shall always cherish. Despite her faults, she outshone many wealthier and more sophisticated people. Lisbeth was totally unhypocritical, and her sense of duty was as simple as it was solid.

Testament to this, was not only her care of Joanne Robertson, her ageing adoptive mother, but Tom Umphray, her next door neighbour. Both lived in the house, and whereas one could understand her dedication to the former, who had brought her up and given her affection, he was as boney and cantankerous, as she was round and sweet. Apparently, he had been carried into kitchen one day by the divers who worked on the *Oceanic* suffering from a mild stroke. They had found him prostrate in the road, a short distance from Lisbeth's, muttering about 'Yon King Hussein and them Arabs.' One had taken his legs, the other his torso and they had delivered him semi-conscious. He recovered, but was unable to look after himself. He had no relations. No one else wanted him and so like pass-the-parcel, an unwittingly malicious present, he stayed.

He and Joan hated each other with a venom rarely found outside a sibling relationship. Having lived their entire lives so closely together, they shared all the impatience of brother and sister and sat on the hard, high-backed Orkney benches either side of the enamelled kitchen stove, squabbling intermittently across the void of lino, like politicians in the House of Commons. Lisbeth, the Speaker, dealt with all this quite stoically, feigning deafness much of the time, but then occasionally she would be driven to exasperation and let forth. Tom was invariably the protagonist and she would shout, 'Tom! Stop prattling thy mouth and go out and take thy pipe and have a smoke on the pier!' To which he would raise himself up grumbling and shuffle off in slow motion, head bent, back bowed and hands in pockets in the style of an enormous question mark.

Parted from her husband, into her unremitting toil appeared a respite in the shape of the happy-go-lucky divers, who lived at the Haa.

For the first fortnight I never met them and it was from Lisbeth's general conversation, the tone of her voice, which began to change my views about their behaviour. It seemed from what she said that they had troubled themselves for her. Staying on late into the winter and returning in the spring long before it was weather to dive, they had time on their hands; when she had been worried about her sheep subsidy, they had written a letter to the Department of Agriculture; when cold weather and long nights had taken its toll on her flock, they had buried her dead ewes; they had brought her new harmonium from the mainland on their vessel, *Trygg* and had carted her peats; one of them, Alec, had even overhauled her much neglected generator. For all this, she was very grateful. Their quick minds and strong muscles came in useful, but what Lisbeth valued most about the Divers, as they were universally known, was their company. For her, it was a pleasure just having them around with their tales of work, their humour and activity.

This was obvious from the first time I saw them come in through the door, windswept, unkempt and smiling.

They did not have a phone of their own and the pretext was to contact their scrap merchant in Glasgow. What they did not let on, was they had planned the foray to get a better look at the new 'piece of skirt' working at Lizzie's, as they referred to me and her respectively. That I should be an attraction for any grown man, never occurred to me for one moment. Both were in their mid to late twenties.

Simon Martin was dark, tousle haired and bearded. Alec Crawford was slightly taller, clean shaven and fair. Happy and polite, Lisbeth was overjoyed to see them; her step lightened and she became positively girlish as they sat themselves down on the rickety wooden chairs and stayed for a cup of tea. It was like a small, impromptu party. Old Joanne and Tom equally brightened. Only I did not know what really to expect.

Working between the small sink under the skylight and the stove on which the kettle boiled at the far end, Lisbeth paddled to and fro, occasionally standing to chatter beside the hot plate, garlanded beneath the wreaths of washing and dried salt fish that hung from the eaves. The best cups were used, and the pair were plied with oatcakes and jam. This was the height of the salvage season and she had seen little of them over the previous weeks. Therefore, there was much on which to catch up, especially as they had just returned from making trips to the Shetland mainland and Fair Isle. She had a passion for gossip and thus with feigned casualness began to extract all their news.

Simon, who had been a journalist before he became a diver, was well aware of this trait and played her at her own game. After a while he announced, 'I have a piece of A1 Classified gossip for you, Lizzie.' She could not contain herself, 'Naar! What is it?' It was really very bad of him to tease her like that, but she was perfectly aware of what he was doing and they egged each other on, mercilessly.

Standing at the table, with my back to them, I concentrated on floating a newly found clutch of eggs in water to test for freshness, whilst listening just as avidly as the rest.

'Have you heard about Kenny at the Thule Bar in Lerwick.' This I knew was Jim's older even taller brother, who was very much a likeable rogue.

'Tell me' she demanded in evident anticipation.

'He'd been drinking, and slightly the worse for alcohol, struck up an argument with two large Norwegian fishermen, who just picked him up and threw him through the plate glass window.'

'Naar,' declared Lisbeth again, this time with a delightful mock incredulity.

Old Joanne's eyes were large and open with concern, 'Was he hurt?'

'No, he bounced, I think. Just two black eyes.'

Hearing that he was fine, Lisbeth's frame heaved with amusement and she was hardly able to get the words out for laughing. Only Tom was a little disappointed that there was no blood, as Kenny, true to form, had landed in the street almost completely unscathed.

'Two black eyes?' Lisbeth queried making sure that she had all the details right, 'and what happened to the Norwegians?'

'Apparently they were charged.'

The whole thing was a priceless communication and as soon as the Divers had left, she rang round the entire island like Reuters, in order to pass it on first.

This was my introduction to the ghastly men of my imagination. I was very quiet in those days, reserved more than shy. We had hardly spoken at all beyond a few pleasantries; making it even more surprising that Alec should always say that he fell for me at our first meeting at Ham, as I worked away self-containedly, in my flared jeans with pinned-up hair.

~~~~~

3

RMS OCEANIC

There are insignificant scenes from one's past which remain forever in the mind, because they capture the moment. It is how I come to remember so vividly building Lisbeth's peat stack behind her byre and seeing Simon amble along the edge of her meadow below, on his way to the Haa. He was silhouetted against the still Voe, with his hands in the pockets of his shapeless trousers and his red, stretched bobble-hat placed carelessly on the back of his head. I was aware of his progress across an otherwise static landscape without watching, and as he raised his hand in acknowledgement, across the long, whispering grass full of wild flowers, I paused briefly from my task and straightened to return the distant wave.

Since I had come, I had been so busy working for Lisbeth, tending sheep, mending fences and raising her peats, that I had hardly given the Divers a second thought. They were beyond me in many ways; theirs an alien world of salvage to which I found little to relate. In that instant, seeing Simon against the backdrop of the scenery, I saw him in a different context and realised how integral they were to island life. It was as if they had always been there. No gathering was complete without them.

Lisbeth had taken me to the end of term concert at the schoolhouse, when there had been genuine disappointment that they were on their wrecksite and unable to hear young Bobby Gear's rendition of *Da Divers*. This song had been written by the wonderfully titled Missionary Teacher, who had rather let his sense of humour and the fact that he was leaving the island for good on *Trygg* the following day get the better of him, by putting some pithy words in Shetland dialect to the tune of *The Weavers*.

How Lisbeth had laughed in her Sunday best, with her great belly shaking inside its corset. 'The mailboat he'd go out da Voe and never come back again! Naar, naar, naar! Yon's wicked,' she exclaimed, remembering how they had towed the *Westering Homewards* back with their rubber inflatable, after it had broken down.

~~

With very little television and a great tradition of story-telling, the Divers and their exploits were given wide coverage in every croft and in Ham we used to receive regular bulletins about their diving activities from Harry, the postmaster. Every one liked Harry. He was a shy, gentle man who after spending his life as a bachelor, had got the art of self neglect down to such perfection, that he had a coterie of motherly females who would press him with tea and 'a bite to eat', whenever he walked through their door. This, of course included Lisbeth.

'Ah, Harry! Sit deeself down and take a cup of tea. Tell me, what's the news?'

Harry spoke seldom, but he was so well respected, that when he did, everyone listened.

'Thank you. I'm just on my way up from the pier. I see that the Divers are preparing to lift the propeller bosses from the *Oceanic*. Great muckle bits of manganese bronze, they are. Alec reckons that each weighs about fourteen tons. They're fitting the new quadruple lifting blocks, now. Attaching them with wire to that baulk of iroko wood with the steel eye, that Jack Moore fitted in Scalloway. Alec said that without it to spread the load into the timber frames, they'd be sure to spring the deck.'

'Yon would never do,' agreed Lisbeth.

'No, golly gosh.' This was Harry's favourite phrase, which he used equally in both horror and wonderment. 'They've done well. Who'd have thought it. I remember when they arrived on the pier from Fair Isle, the year before last. The *Good Shepherd* brought them and all they had was that battered rubber boat and a few bits of diving gear. When I heard that they were going to try to find the *Oceanic*, I just shook my head. Some reckon that there's a nine knot current there, at times, but I doubt it. It can be bad, anyway. When Robbie Robertson tried to find the wreck in the early 1920s, he nearly drowned and declared afterwards that the wreck was so dangerous it was undiveable. I was so worried about them that I propped up my old army gunsights on the fence post outside the Post Office to make sure that they were all right … Still do, on occasion', he added unassumingly.

'How did the *Oceanic* sink?' I asked.

'Simon told me that she was taken off the Transatlantic route as soon as the First World War began, and requisitioned by the Admiralty as part of the Northern Patrol. They didn't look after her very well!' he cackled with his infectious laughter, shaking his head. 'Thirteen days they had her at sea, that's all and then they ran aground on the Shaalds. Golly gosh! Yon's devilish rocks. They come within a fathom of the surface, two and a half miles off the Voe, here. On a calm day, you wouldn't even know they were there.'

'Old Joanne and Tom remember seeing her – do you Harry?' Lisbeth guided him through the tale.

'Naar. I was just born. My mother always told me that I did, but I can't mind about it. Apparently, the great liner sat there, absolutely upright for a fortnight. My father was one of the men the Navy employed to take off what they could and when she disappeared one night in a storm, everyone thought she had been swept off into deeper water. What a surprise when Alec and Simon found her still on the reef. A seventeen thousand ton ship, just lying on the sea bed like a pack of cards.

'Jim was out with them, when they found her. They got nowhere the first day they looked and so he accompanied them with his own boat, the same one in which he brought you here.'

This was how I was gradually introduced to the ways of *Da Divers*. Harry knew everything there was to know about them, and through him I received an anthology of their most exciting tales.

The day they found the former *Queen of the Seas*, was only their second on the island. Simon was clad in his wetsuit, balanced in the bow of the rubber inflatable, poised to throw the grapple he held at the given word. Jim, bobbing around in the *Happy Voyager*, lined up the bearings his father had taught him. These were taken by sight. At the South End, the seaward slope of Da Noop had to disappear exactly between the chimneys on the Biggins' roof, and at the North End, a certain piece of cliff, a peat bank and the road had to be in line. This 'taking of medes' as it was known, was as reliable as it was ancient and mathematical.

The common belief was that the wreck was in more than sixty feet of water. 'Try here,' Jim had shouted. Alec cut back the throttle on the outboard and Simon jettisoned the tethered piece of metal, as far forward as possible, as this compensated for their drift in the tide. The rope was marked at fathom intervals by knots, and the depth was gauged by how many had disappeared. Murmuring, as if saying a wet, polypropylene rosary, he passed those that were left through his hands, adding them up, 'Five, six, seven...' If the sum was fewer than ten, he went in to investigate.

Having dived twice already that morning, he was beginning to tire. Both times he had had to haul himself down the rope, struggling against the force of the moving water to reach the bottom. Working with awkward gloved fingers, as soon the grapple was freed from its rocky hold, the adventure had begun. Instantly the prongs were released, he had been borne away like a piece of human jetsam. Kelp, boulders and sand had zoomed past his view as he had scanned for wreckage on both sides. Only minutes passed, but he had surfaced far away from where he had vanished, exhilarated and spluttering.

'Did you see anything?' Alec had shouted eagerly each time, cutting the outboard engine as he arrived to pick him up.

'No,' would come the reply through the wide gap in his front teeth, because he always left the plate sporting his incisors on the arm of the Haa sofa.

Now they were trying in a slightly different position.

'It's no good,' Simon had declared, 'it's only thirty feet. This can't be it. The *Oceanic*'s beam was twice this depth. If she had sunk here she'd still have been visible for months if not years afterwards.'

Jim and Alec agreed, and he had begun pulling on the grapple, only to find it was held solid. At first he was cross, because he would have to waste a dive retrieving it. Then a different thought went through his mind, 'Perhaps the grapple was fouled on the wreck?'

He had looked at Alec, who was obviously wondering the same thing. It seemed too incredible to be true. Rushing to beat the end of slack water Simon had quickly put on his fins and face mask. Alec held the aqualung raised for him to slip into. After a few hurried drags of the demand valve, to check that it was working, he had dropped backwards over the side of the rubber pontoon and with a brief flurry of feet was gone.

Pulling himself down the rope against the steadily increasing tide, he had to fight for every inch. It was like battling against a river in spate. The water pushed against his chest as if attempting to drag his body away, tugging at the muscles in his arms. The visibility was only moderate and the distance seemed never ending. As he struggled ever deeper, one moment he was peering into obscurity through an opaque marine soup, the next he was almost enveloped in the coarse fronds of brown weed, that lay bent and rippling in the flow. Pausing to orientate himself, he had been able to pick out one or two features. A number of large boulders lay strewn around. Then, gradually at first, in the gloom among the smooth shapes of nature, evidence of heavy industry became clear. First a jagged beam of rusted metal... next a plate of steel. Swiftly, as he began to explore, he came across the side of a ship, studded with portholes like huge pock marks. His heart beat faster. There could be no doubt of it from the sheer size of material that was lying around. He had discovered the *Oceanic*! The first man in over sixty years to see this ship, launched as one of the most palatial liners ever afloat. Here she lay invisible from the surface, having been devastated by the power of the waves.

Elation, however, had had to wait. There was a vital job to be done and moments were speeding away with the ever increasing current. Finning to the surface, with a spiral of copper wiring in his hand as proof, he had spat out his demand valve, panting and out of breath.

'I've found it Alec. She's there all broken up across the bottom. The current's hellish. I can buoy her, but I haven't much time.'

Alec's hands were already sorting out the buoy rope without him even looking. 'Here Sy! Now, try to get it on something where it won't chafe.' He and Jim watched the bubbles intently as Simon went down again, paying out the slack as required. When the sharp tug was felt, they knew it was secure, cut the end and tied on the marker buoy.

Another tug on the grapple line, which had been their anchor all this time, and they knew to haul it in. Heavy, and obviously weighted, it brought with it their first identifiable recovery, the brass casing of a deckhead light. 'We can hand this in to the Receiver of Wreck to become Salvor in Possession, that will stop anyone turning up.'

Simon emerged and was man-handled gasping from exertion into the boat. Slumping down, he half sat, half lay to regain his breath amid congratulations. 'Well done, Sy. Well done. It's just fantastic.' Such was the scale of his discovery, that it would never be paralleled in British waters, again.

From then on the Divers took every available opportunity to dive, repeatedly filling their rubber inflatable to sinking point with all the smaller pieces of non-ferrous metal. Valves by the score, copper piping, port holes, general brass fittings all lay scattered liberally around. Necessity spurred them on as the weather began to deteriorate with the coming of the new month. In the first fortnight of September alone there were eleven days when it was impossible to work on the wrecksite, due to fog or gales. Winter comes early in the far north.

The elements were not to be Alec and Simon's only trouble. Earlier the same summer, but unknown to them, a team of Aberdeen-based salvors had tried to locate the wreck but failed. These competitors were now furious because they had a salvage agreement with the owners of the *Oceanic*, Hay & Company in Lerwick. Within weeks of gaining their magnificent prize, the Divers found themselves being told to 'get off' in no uncertain terms, but knowing that they had much to gain, and little to lose, they chose to continue. Storm clouds began to brew and not just in the skies. The island was completely partisan in their favour, buzzing with anticipation of the impending fight.

The problems of running a salvage partnership on a remote island, from a house that has no electricity, telephone or running water, and a mail service that operates on anything from a weekly to a bi-monthly basis cannot be over stressed. Communications with the commercial world south were particularly difficult, and further complicated by such instructions as, 'If you want to contact me, please leave a message with Mrs

Holbourn on Foula 8 – but if it's raining the exchange doesn't work properly, and so you'll have to get her by phoning Foula 7.'

All confidential calls were made from the one and only telephone box. This was an old, red model, dated by its bakelite fittings and chromed 'A' and 'B' buttons. Little used, it doubled as a handy dry store for animal feed. Squashed together against sacks of Ewe & Lamb Nuts and Layers' Mash, Alec and Simon had held cramped, but animated conversations with all concerned; Andy Beattie, the joint managing director of Hay & Company; the oppositions's Glasgow-based agents; John Butler, the local Receiver of Wreck; and their own Edinburgh lawyer. As practically every phone call from Foula is long distance by virtue of its isolation, the regular interruption of pips for more money just had to be endured, the machine demanding more feeding than a fledgling cuckoo in spring.

Meetings, too, were awkward. At that stage, planes to the small island airstrip were few and far between. In order to get to the mainland and back in under a fortnight, the Divers' only real option was to go in the rubber inflatable, as hitching a lift on fishing boats could not be guaranteed. Putting their clothes in an old plastic fertiliser sack to keep them dry, they had donned their wetsuits and tied themselves in for safety, to make the rough weather journey to the Shetland mainland; looking more like extras from a James Bond film, than businessmen when they arrived.

By mid-October the atmosphere had become increasingly tense. Ten tons of non-ferrous metal had now been lifted from the *Oceanic*, and as the product of each new dive was declared to the Receiver of Wreck, the pressure mounted. The crunch came when the offer was made for Alec and Simon to work the wreck on the other salvors' behalf – this they neither accepted nor refused. Soon after two interdicts arrived. Their message was clear, a civil case had been brought before the local Sheriff in Lerwick and would be heard on the seventh of the next month. If either of them dived on the *Oceanic* in the interim, they would be in Contempt of Court.

By this point the battle had become front page, headline news in the local paper, involving as it did Hay & Company, Shetland's largest private concern. In a long article *The Shetland Times* outlined the case. No decision was made in the first hearing, as a month was allowed for the Pursuers to add to their original statement. It was an extremely anxious time. With no possibility of work being done, there was little point in both partners remaining on Foula and so only Alec had returned. In the cold and damp of the rundown Haa, he had tried to make the best of his time, writing, reading and learning to play the fiddle. At the beginning of December the case was delayed again, with the excuse that the Pursuers' documents had been stuck on the *St Clair* in Aberdeen, due to bad weather; the legal equivalent, perhaps, of the 'cheque being in the post'.

Eventually, four days before Christmas, Simon had got hold of Alec through Lisbeth to tell him the news. 'They could salvage the *Oceanic*, the case against them had been dropped!' and one very glad and dishevelled partner managed to catch a fishing boat, like hailing a taxi, in order to race home and celebrate.

Given the enforced halt, it was hardly surprising that they wanted to start the 1974 season as early as possible, and Alec was back the first week in February, partly in eagerness, but also to keep the wreck 'occupied'. Now the news was abroad that the *Oceanic* was located and workable, the last thing they wanted was to be ousted on a technicality.

With hundreds of tons of non-ferrous metal lying on the Shaalds, the initial progress was frustratingly slow, as the cargo carrying capacity of the rubber inflatable was limited by its buoyancy, and the day's haul was all too frequently curtailed by it threatening to sink. For a while this problem was solved by using a second, even tattier inflatable boat, which was towed in and out like a dumb barge. This arrangement was only considered as a stop gap measure, and ludicrously so ever since their third dive of the year. On this foray they had located not only the *Oceanic's* two massive propellers, each a staggering twenty-two feet in diameter, but five spare blades. From the instant he saw the hoard, Alec had been planning how to raise it and the hunt had been on for a proper boat.

Matters gradually began to fall into place, as soon as a salvage agreement was reached with Hay & Company. The Receiver of Wreck was then able to release their recoveries to be sold and their finances, which had been in cash ebb for nine long months, thus turned into cash flow. The *Fishing News* was scoured in earnest for a suitable vessel. Several offers were put in to no avail and it was not until the beginning of July that the ex-Norwegian fishing boat, *Trygg* was bought for the equivalent of six tons of gun metal scrap. She had been lying semi derelict in a Scottish port for several months and could be described as rudimentary, but sturdy and sound. Her length was forty-nine feet and her breadth over eighteen, which made her fat and dumpy. When she was built in 1939, she had had a tall mast which acted like a counter balance. This had long since been removed much to everyone's regret, for without it her motion was so quick that she bucked and tossed like a cork. In lumpy seas there were few who were not sick and for most it was just a matter of time.

This unusual almond shape and her immensely strong larch framing, however, made her ideal for lifting and with a few modifications she was put to the test. Using a combination of blocks of sheaves, shoring between the hatch and the gunwales, and a wire around her girth, Alec had devised a system based on his understanding of simple mechanics, which would enable her small one and a half ton winch to lift six tons, as if by magic.

One spare blade was recovered the first day out with this system. Two days passed with indifferent weather and they got the remaining four in a day, nipping out to remove them during the periodic intervals of slack water, as the tide turned. Twenty-four tons of manganese bronze, valued at around twenty thousand pounds, in just eighteen hours. It was an amazing achievement.

As if to emphasise just how quickly the pendulum of luck can swing in salvage, from bad-to good-to bad again, shortly afterwards, *Trygg* was nearly lost.

The Divers had set off with her to the safety of the Scottish mainland for the winter. One of the enormous, beautifully shaped propeller blades was gracing the pier at Scalloway, another was in the hold, along with much of the season's haul of scrap. It was so tall that the tip stuck above the hatch combing, and the deck boards had to be cut to fit round it and the tarpaulin nailed down. Sea conditions were rough and deteriorating. They were far to the north-east of Scotland, when the gale picked up. The night was wet and oily black. Alec, who was at the wheel, never saw the wave that hit them until it was half way along the deck. It was a freak, a giant, that appeared from nowhere. *Trygg* punched into it and came to a shuddering halt as if colliding with a brick wall. Such was the jolt that he was thrown across the wheel and hit his head against the wheelhouse windows. Simon, who had been resting aft in his sleeping bag, was catapulted from the ledge which served as a bunk, and landed on his feet on the floor.

There was so much commotion that there was no time for fear. The green water curled and rushed like a breaker, frothing and battering at the glass in front of them and at all sides. *Trygg* struggled to stay afloat under the weight. It was a moment in which their lives hung in the balance. If a second wave of equal size was to follow, she would founder and they would be lost without trace. For eternal seconds, she wallowed, more under the water than above. Thank God, that the hatch had been battened down securely or they literally would have been sunk; it was all too easy to overlook these precautions, as being time-consuming and unnecessary, before leaving the safety of port.

Bad enough, that the engine room skylight had been wrenched from its hinges and sea was pouring in below in a solid column. Rising within seconds to the level of the main engine, it covered the main air inlet and was sucked in. Ominously the main engine stopped ... which cut off the bilge pump and the lights. The only sounds that they could hear now were the groaning of the boat and the elements. Doors began to bang, books fell from the boxed shelves and items swept back and forth across the floor, as powerless, *Trygg* swung broadside on.

The immediate priority was to begin bailing out the water and their only salvation was the auxiliary hand pump that stood outside the wheelhouse door. Simon stumbled out into the lashing rain, exposed to the full force of the gale. The deck was completely awash as *Trygg* rolled from side to side, burying her gunwales underwater. Clutching on perilously, immersed at times to his waist, arms aching, heart thumping in his chest, he beat up and down, working the handle for all he was worth.

In the meantime, Alec had fallen as much as climbed down the ladder into the engine room, landing up to his thighs in the cold, inky brine that swept from wall to wall. The only light was from his torch as the emergency lighting had not come on. Flashing the beam rapidly around the small compartment the scene was dreadful. Wooden footboards and small oil drums tossed around, bobbing and semi-submerged. The flood was half way up the engine and the batteries that would restart it, had been burst from their box and lay strewn across the gearbox. 'Christ, what if they're broken?' he thought. Blotting out the worst of his fears, he lifted them to safety, before struggling back on deck to help Simon.

For that crucial period they took it in turns to man the pump. Minutes passed tortuously as each exerted his body to the point of exhaustion, to pause and then carry on. Gradually they began to gain. Alec returned to the engine room. Lashing the batteries back into position, he struggled holding the torch in one hand and the rope with the other. His fingers were so numb that they would not do as he wanted. With trembling spanner, he reconnected the terminals, and it was with utmost relief that the yellow glow of the emergency lighting flickered on, like the hope of a precious dawn.

He could now give his attention to the engine. The stench of diesel was nauseating. There was no surface that was not covered with bilge oil, making every piece of metal slippy to his insensitive touch. He knew that water had gone into the engine, but the question was how much damage had it done? Flicking up all four decompression levers, he pressed the button on the starter. It whirred reluctantly into action, in a low-pitched whine. The crankshaft began to turn. Rapidly, by closing each of the levers in turn, he found the cylinder that was damaged. Isolating it, by leaving the decompression open, he let the other three cylinders take over its work. Gradually they picked up speed. The flywheel began to gain momentum and suddenly the old Kelvin engine burst back into life. 'Thank God!' he breathed. At least now they had an even chance. Quickly he scrabbled to the wheel, putting her gently ahead, and easing her round to face the waves. The main bilge pump was working again. Drenched, finally Simon could come inside.

The rest of the night seemed endless. There was no sleep and they were worn out. Every revolution of the engine was monitored for signs of failing. Any cough or splutter might spell the return of imminent doom. Small pieces of debris that had collected in the water continually blocked the bilge pump, requiring one or other to go down and clear it. Somewhere in the early hours of the morning a fuel injection pipe burst, spewing diesel everywhere. Alec did not dare to stop the engine, for fear that it would not start again, and idled on two-cylinders while he made the repair.

It was twelve midday before *Trygg* limped into Fraserburgh on Scotland's east coast. The cylinder head gasket had been blowing badly ever since they had taken the wave. The head was removed to reveal a cracked liner. Spares were bought from a small engineering company and the problem was fixed by the next afternoon. Off they set immediately afterwards, just desperate to get back. Neither expected a welcome at Tayport in Fife as they tied up in the bleak, deserted harbour at 7.30 a.m. There was no one to greet them. Neither of them cared. They were just thankful to be there.

The entry in Alec's diary for that day was just one word, 'Dropping!'

4

PROPELLERS

That episode had long since been forgotten, by the time I had arrived the following summer. During the early salvage season, Alec and Simon had been concentrating on blasting the *Oceanic*'s two propellers. The work freeing them had been tremendous. Each weighed an impressive twenty-nine tons and was buried in the seabed amongst debris and rock.

Of the two, the port propeller was the most exposed and only three tides had to be spent digging beneath it to place the explosive charge. When it was detonated, the impact sheered the shaft, flung the boss clear and snapped off the two lower blades, which had been lodged in the seabed. Conversely, the starboard propeller proved stubborn. It was so deeply buried that seven tides had to be spent literally tunnelling beneath it. The sides of this hole were so unsafe, that they had to be shored like a mine to prevent them caving in and the sea did its best to fill up the diggings with sand, at every tide. Nevertheless, Alec had persevered; and with a combination of minute explosive charges, a chisel, a hammer, and a bucket and spade, he dug so far down, that at times all Simon could see as he dived close by, were the tips of his fins.

Fear of the roof collapsing whilst he was in there, had restrained him from excavating as much as he would have liked. Consequently the massive charge he placed, one hundred pounds in weight, was not as accurately positioned as he would have wished.

Connecting the two ends to the detonator, and backing out gently, so as not to disturb anything, he returned to the surface and clambered into the rubber inflatable. Simon paid out the mooring to let them sit at a safe distance, securing them some three hundred feet away whilst he kept the correct tension on the detonator wire. Sitting poised above the terminals, with the cable split, one wire in each hand, Simon held the squat, six-volt battery for him on the boards of the inflatable.

No bang of this size was set off without a tinge of apprehension. He touched the positive and negative, simultaneously ... The effect was instantaneous. A shockwave hit the bottom of the inflatable with such a kick that the battery leapt into the air and hit Simon in the face. In front of them, water erupted like a volcano forming a solid frothing mound, some seventy feet high. The whole of Foula was obliterated, reappearing moments later from the top downwards, as if rising out of a dense fog. It was all over in a trice. As the last droplets rained down on them, the surface returned to normal and it was as if nothing had ever happened.

Bright-eyed, exhilarated, the two divers sat overawed by the effect 'Cripes!' Simon mimicked in what-ho, school boy slang, summing up the mood, and they joked together all the way back to the Haa.

They had to wait until the following slack water for the visibility to clear. The result of their handiwork was disappointing, as the boss had fallen back into its hole and another thirty-five pounds was required to evict it, scattering the last of the blades around their respective boss, like discarded petals. Torn, and with chunks missing from when the *Oceanic* had hit the reef, they would be easier to lift than the spares, but the bosses posed a formidable problem and it was debatable whether or not *Trygg* would physically take the load.

There had been much preparation and when eventually the day came to raise the port boss there was an air of keen anticipation. It was an early start and few chimneys had started to reek, as the Divers headed for the Shaalds. A young islander, John Andrew Ratter, had recently joined their team. He had made his own wetsuit over the winter and taught himself to become confident with SCUBA gear in the Voe. Lean and fit, looking like a modern day Viking, with his crystal blue eyes and bushy beard, his sea-sense and nimble footedness on deck had quickly made him a valuable and trusted aid. On this job he was to assist Simon underwater, whilst his cousin, Davy, took the signals.

There had been problems getting the lower quadruple block to the bottom. The success of the enterprise depended on Alec's engineering and calculations, but leaning over the bow, holding himself from falling overboard with his heels under the opposite gunwale, he felt far from clever. The upper block was twisting and the wires were jamming.

'Right, John Andrew. We'll try again,' he commanded. 'There are so many falls of wire between the two blocks, that the lower one does not want go down under its own weight. Give me a moment to get aft and then we'll begin winching it down.'

They had only a hour in which the current would be slack enough to work. Precious seconds were flowing away. Strict orders were given.

'Keep well clear, Davy. Lowering, now!'

The wire vibrated and creaked as it disappeared over the side.

Suddenly, there was a pull for attention on the rope. Davy copied it, to show he understood the message and received a series of sharp yanks. 'Stop!' he cried and they waited, blind as to what was happening just a few feet below.

An age seemed to pass. Alec becoming agitated, momentarily quitting his post in front of the wheelhouse to watch where the bubbles of exhaled air were bursting on the surface. 'Come on Sy, what are you doing?' he urged with increasing frustration.

There was a long pause. Another pull on the rope. Davy gave the reply and they were followed by two more.

'Lift, Alec.'

The atmosphere was tense as he depressed the lever, concentration visible in every aspect of his face. His jaw was set and the veins stood out on his temples. His eyes never left the wire. Stealthily, it became taut. The bow dipped, as *Trygg* began to bury herself into the water. The Kelvin engine dropped an octave, roaring as it began to labour. Down she went, further and further. The timbers began to creak in protestation. Further . . . further . . . trickles of perspiration began to run down his face and neck.

A wisp of sediment, swept up from the bottom, hinted at imperceptible movement and he held his breath. Then, there was a backwards lurch, as the suction was broken and the boss came away. *Trygg* wobbled equivocally around her centre of balance, like a nodding donkey; her propeller as often out of the water as it was in.

Simon and John Andrew were now visible, bobbing at a safe distance like curious seals.

'Get well back, Davy, but keep that sharp axe handy – if this shifts, I'll have to sever the wires!'

They waited. 'She's settled down . . . it looks as if we're going to get away with it . . . Help Sy to get onboard and then I'll haul in, some more.'

For each twenty-four turns of the winch barrel, the boss was raised three feet off the sea floor.

The drum turned . . . John Andrew monitored the progress underwater, giving the final signal. 'How's it looking?' Alec demanded, as soon as he resurfaced beside the inflatable, which was tied alongside.

'That's about it. The boss is hanging about nine feet beneath the bow. Even with her head down, you should have plenty of water to get her into the Voe, beside the mooring.'

'Right. I'll secure the brake. Sy can release the bow mooring. I want you to follow close behind with the rubber inflatable – just in case . . .' he added surreptitiously, with a grin.

With the load secured and the Kelvin engine barely ticking over, the helm was turned and she was put gently ahead as they made slowly, but surely, for the Voe. Rapidly, there was a panic as Simon went to check the forward accommodation. No sooner had he gone down the ladder, than he reappeared in the hatch to sound the alert, 'We've sprung a leak at the bow – she's at such an angle. It's just under the deck, but it's coming in fast!'

'Hell! The bilge pump will be useless, it sucks at the stern and that's high in the air – all the water will be running forward! Quick get a bucket. Davy give a hand. You'll just have to do the best you can!'

With eighty feet of water beneath their keel at times, this was no place to sink. As they crept into the shadow of Foula and dumped their load beside the propeller blades there was a mixture of elation and relief. Just one more to get.

In retrospect, it was no wonder the Divers were local heroes, but I had been so busy working and exploring the island in those long northern days, with their almost seamless light that I was oblivious. I had seen the Divers at the nurse's party, were they were much feted and I had stood aloof. We exchanged but a few insignificant words.

The first time I remember taking undue notice of Alec was in the middle of July. He and Simon had just come back from spending several days in Scalloway with *Trygg*. They had ferried with them a group of students from the University of East Anglia, along with food and gear. I had some boxes from the butcher and baker to collect for Lisbeth and as I wandered down to the pier, the scene was rather like a small circus.

The main protagonists were partly driving, partly man-handling a car off the deck, which had been brought across for John Andrew. Two sturdy batons made a bridge to the concrete, but with a periodic swell sweeping in, *Trygg* was lively and timing was to be the crux. Far more men than were necessary had involved themselves, as the event was too unusual to miss and spectators, including the Divers' cooks and some of the students, watched from parapet close at hand.

In amongst all the activity and excited shouting, it soon became apparent to me that there was one person in charge. He was by no means the loudest, but he was without equal. With clear authority, that took no heed of the many contradictory opinions, he had the situation entirely under control; and with a minimum of fuss on his part, and a maximum of showman-like revving by John Andrew, the new acquisition shot ashore, to be admired by all.

Alec's quality of leadership impressed me for all my years, and as I picked up my parcels, I was not unaware of him as he chatted with Harry. It was obvious that they were having a post mortem about unloading the car, as the postmaster was shaking his head and sucking in his breath about one particularly sticky moment, 'O-o-o-sh. Golly gosh. Golly gosh,' he said with feeling and they both laughed, Alec relieved and carefree.

He stood at ease, agile and fit. Large areas of his face were covered with a thin film of grease, which made his teeth and the whites of his eyes shine unnaturally bright. He was virile and I found him attractive.

This glimpse into the realms of adulthood felt uncomfortable. He was ten years older than me, a breadth of time which at seventeen seemed unspannable, even frightening.

If an instinct whispered that my partiality was returned, I considered it to be mistaken.

5

MARRIAGE

We parted just over a week later, with a non-committal farewell and I assumed that I would never see Alec, again. *Trygg* was leaving for the south and I was going home to the Outer Hebrides. I do not believe in fate, yet we were engaged to be married within six months.

He proposed on a cold February evening in Tayport. I had been staying with his mother and father, who lived at Naughton in Fife and was shortly to depart. The wet had been relentless and we had just put a heater in *Trygg* to dry her out. The rain had stopped falling and the sky had become cloudless. Looking across the harbour, through the rounded windscreen of the Mini pick-up, the street lamps glowed orange and their reflection shimmered in the water. The vista was hardly charming, with the drab council tenement and modernist public lavatory to the fore. A timber ship had just unloaded its cargo on the broken tarmac and piles of new, clean wood dwarfed us all on all sides. The ambience was all neglect and industrial decline. If I had had any illusions about the glamour of salvage, they would have evaporated at this moment, but I was undeterred. It was a world that I was about to enter, irretrievably.

Alec had visited me on his BSA motor bike early in the New Year, soon after returning from a salvage contract in San Francisco. What my parents had thought of this roughie-toughie diver, in his leathers and helmet, they did not say, but my brother, Kit, had asked over dinner, 'So, what did you do in the War, Alec?'

'I wasn't in the War, actually,' came the polite, but stiff reply.

Far away from Lewis, we were alone now and I sat in the semi-gloom not in the role of a sister or a daughter, but as a prospective lover.

'I know that it would mean you giving up your agricultural course, but I was hoping that you'd come to Foula with us this summer.'

'But what would I do?'

'There's no shortage of work. You can run the Haa and come out to the wreck and when we're married ...'

'You haven't even asked me, yet.'

He grinned knowingly, as if it were all taken for granted and he had been caught out, 'Moya, I want you to be my wife … Will you marry me?'

'Of course I will.'

With this consent, I cast off my childhood, my family and home to make the single, most important decision of my life. We had only spent a few days together, all told, but I had no qualm. My knowledge of him from Foula had convinced me of that. Alec might test me, but he would never bore me. I had met my match.

Within weeks, I had retraced my steps to Shetland and was organising the Haa in preparation for Alec and Simon to arrive on *Trygg* and as soon as they did, I realised what is was to share a house with two bachelors. There were no concessions to my presence of any sort; diving and the *Oceanic* came first; the Crawford & Martin partnership came second; and I came third. I was included wholeheartedly, but nothing was going to change simply because I was there, least of all attitudes. These were simply awful. In fact, the feminine view on any matter was invariably a lost cause. Simon had a particularly quick wit and Alec would feed him lines, rather like the straight man in a comedy duo. They had their tongue-in-cheek phrases off pat. It was suggested not infrequently that girlie-wirlies could be placated with flowers, you just had to get the quota right – the bigger the misdemeanour, the bigger the bunch. Similarly, you could easily renew your flagging stock of goodwill with any woman, whatever the age, by noticing when she had been to the hairdressers.

The teasing was relentless. The knack, I knew from having a brother, was to ignore all provocation. It was a mistake to rise, but better to avoid all so-called women's topics of conversation in the first place. Dresses, hats, babies, children, make-up, underwear and recipes should not be mentioned, nor should one be tricked into venturing any opinion about them. As far as physical differences were concerned, to all intents and purposes, apart from shape and pleasure, the female body was considered the same as a man's. Its workings were never acknowledged to exist, so there was no fear of discussing them. Any sign of weakness was labelled 'typical' and tears were unthinkable.

If this was not bad enough, Simon could not resist stirring. One lunchtime in particular, I remember objecting mildly to something that Alec had done and his diving partner paused casually with his soup spoon in mid-air, 'Ah, ha! Are you a man or a mouse, Alec? Squeak up.'

'Oh, man of course,' came the happy reply. Fat chance I had of getting my way after that. For as long as we were a threesome, I was out-numbered, out-manoeuvred and out-gunned. In retrospect, there was probably no better apprenticeship for coping in an all male preserve. It was a case of either sink or swim.

The word Haa is Shetland dialect for Hall and conjures up a grandeur that was promised, but never fulfilled by the square, baronial porch tacked on to the seaward face. Fortunately, this was never completed and so the original, simple building was spared the incongruous turrets, that should have crowned its top, like a miniature Balmoral. The property had belonged to the lairds of the island for three generations, but after an early flush of enthusiasm, it had lain vacant apart from occasional summer use. This lack of attention had led to the roof leaking and flooding of the ground floor, but as far as the Divers were concerned, any shortcomings in the wind and waterproof department, were more than compensated by its position right next to the pier. They considered themselves lucky that their original temporary rent had spread into seasons, with care and maintenance being given in lieu of rent.

As a *des res*, it had no modern conveniences whatsoever. No loo or bath. What little water they had was collected off the roof in a tank and the supply was so short that all the clothes had to be taken to the burn to be washed. There was no electricity or central heating. The only light was natural and the windows were so small and deep-set, that even on the brightest days the interior was gloomy. The walls were damp and draughts blew everywhere, yet it was one of the happiest, friendliest houses in which I have ever lived. Many a visitor used to drop in for a cup of coffee on his way to or from his boat in the Voe. There would be a knock on the inner door and they would wander in. Frequently, John Andrew ate with us in order to catch the tides, and extras who were around at mealtime were welcome to stay. The chat was invariably about salvage and none of the utilitarian clutter seemed the slightest bit off-putting.

Downstairs there were just two rooms, both of which were multi-functional. We cooked in the kitchen, where there were two sinks, one for the dishes and the other for ablutions. This space was nominally mine and divided from the living room by the corridor that ran from the back porch. When everyone came back from diving, they would take their wetsuits off outside and if I were busy baking, Simon never lost the opportunity to entreat me, 'Don't peek Moya – I'm in the buff!' as he shot past to dry beside the open fire.

The only source of warmth, this was always burning and formed a constant lure. Coaxing the peats into flames was the first activity of every morning and similarly, banking them up was the last task of every night. On it we boiled all our water for tea and coffee in a blackened iron kettle and frequently this would erupt and overflow, filling the room with a sweet, musty aroma, quite unlike any other smell. Brewing up was by no means the only direct use of the heat. A length of net twine hung underneath the mantelpiece, and was always crammed full with thick, holey woollen socks and equally disgraceful underpants.

Alec's chair sat to the left of the fire and whatever chores he had to do in the evening were carried out on the hearth rug. The Tilley lamp would cast its theatrical shadows from its hook in the low, panelled ceiling, so that the large oil painting behind Simon's sofa and the carved oak cupboards took on sinister proportions. A stage director would have been proud of the shadows, cast large and distorted against the white painted hessian, whilst everything beneath waist height was a blur.

My first year, the prime task was removing the big end bearings. Blasting them from the two crankshafts was a time-consuming operation, but as the white-metal they contained was worth more than the propellers put together, it was a lucrative exercise. Success within the limited time available on the wreck depended on preparation. In the nightly gloom, the charges were prepared for the following day. This involved a white, plastic-coated primer called Cordtex. Combusting at a speed of two miles per second, it could be described as explosive washing line. Its job was to set off the more stable submarine blasting gelatine. Multiple lengths were used underwater and by varying how long they were, Alec could achieve split second timing. Sometimes he would use them as conduits to set off a number of small explosions, all at the same time. Alternatively, he would free buried items, by using one explosion to lift debris, whilst another would blow free whatever was underneath. Much of his success was due to detail; the Cordtex was measured and cut; all the ends were then picked out with the end of a spent match, filled with slow-setting epoxy resin, and left to cure. This prevented any water from being absorbed once it was submerged, which could cause a misfire.

His other forte was research. If the work was complex, he would resort to his copy of Sothern's, *Verbal Notes and Sketches for Marine Engineers*. This bible-like tome had been produced when steam engines were in their zenith, and explained the design of their every component and mechanism from boilers to valves. Studying it for hours, he used to puzzle out how to dismantle the valuable pieces he wanted by understanding how they were built.

The submarine blasting gelatine would be prepared just before they went out to dive. The sticks were sliced with a knife, or bound together using insulation tape, depending on how much was required. Sometimes, as little as a quarter of a pound was used. A complete record was kept in Alec's diary of the size of the bang, and its effect, with diagrams and remarks such as, 'Could have gotten away with 2lb' or 'not enough'. We got so used to having explosives around that, apart from some rudimentary safety precautions, we treated them as any other potentially dangerous tool. The petrol for the air compressor was undoubtedly more volatile, a fag would ignite that, so I never really bothered about having anything up to half a ton of what was effectively dynamite under the stairs, where it was legally stored. Even the arrangement of my bedside drawers did not perturb me, which was socks and knickers, shirts and jumpers, jeans and detonators. That was until we had a lightning storm ...

The night was foul and dark. Alec and Simon were sitting either side of the fire and I was working on the treadle beneath the north window, sewing my wedding dress. Suddenly, without warning, there came a searing flash out of the sky and a huge, blue bolt of electricity hit the rocks in front of my eyes.

'Good God!' I shouted, leaping to my feet, so horrified that I knocked over the chair, 'Did you see that!'

The men shrugged, indicating that they had.

'It's OK, we haven't been hit' Alec volunteered.

'It was so close ... what about all the bangs!'

'Even if it had hit the house, only the detonators would probably go off – you'd just need to buy some new clothes.' This was considered amusing.

To which Simon added, 'Besides, if the worst had happened, you wouldn't even have heard the bang'.

'That's absolutely no consolation at this particular moment. I'd rather be getting soaked by standing in the middle of one of Lizzie's fields!'

They gave each other a look which said, 'Women – they get like this at times,' and went on with what they were doing. Leaving me no real option but to go back to my bridal gown, even though I was not convinced that I was going to live to complete the seams, let alone see the day for which it was intended. With this and other adventures on the wrecksite, I became gradually steeled.

We had decided to get married on Foula and a date late in September had been chosen, as *Trygg* would be berthed in Tayport by then. Ours was to be the first wedding on the island since 1947, which made it special. There were no formal invitations. As was customary, a week before, Simon, as best man, walked to each croft in turn and bid them welcome. A few hardy relations, including my parents and Alec's mother made the trip and were billeted around. Seldom, even at funerals, had so many pristine, but aged suits, been taken out of mothballs at any one time. New dresses, too, were on show. Hair was curled and adorned, or damped and flattened, depending on gender. Lipsticks dug out from the back of drawers and applied, beards combed and stubble shorn. The effect was remarkable, and everyone laughed and joked at seeing each other so tidy and well turned out.

The tiny stone built kirk stands in no man's land between the settlements at Hametoon and Ham Voe. It is overshadowed by Hamnafield to the west and looks down across the moor, where the arctic terns have their territory beside the airstrip. So many people had wanted to fly in for the day, that the small Islander plane had to return to the Shetland mainland to make a second run. This scuppered what little timing there had been and I clearly remember waiting with my father behind the curtain at the back, whilst Bobby Isbister kept the minister and congregation entertained with his repertoire of tunes, including *You are my Sunshine*, executed with all the verve of a concert on the prom.

When everyone was eventually assembled, including the pilot, Ian Rae, who was a popular last-minute addition, the *Wedding March* sounded for Dad and me to step forward to be met by the reek of paraffin heaters and a sense of overwhelming goodwill.

The walls that contained us were bare. The only luxury was the pile of the deep blue carpet, which cushioned the fall of our feet between the hard, wooden pews. Even the flowers were simple, with only a couple of vases occupying the plain, arched windows which looked out to the Atlantic beyond. The view across the browning autumn heather was timeless. One of the three hymns we sang was, *For those in peril on the sea*. A poignant favourite, which seemed so applicable in that spartan, ocean-swept setting. We had been lucky it could be played, as the criteria on which the music had to be chosen, was in the order of notes left on the harmonium – as nesting mice had wreaked havoc with its range – scores Bobby could manage with his slightly arthritic fingers, and what we liked.

With little ceremony, and less preaching, our bargain was sealed. As we stepped outside, two shotguns were set off above our heads to ward away the devil. This was hardly Church of Scotland practice, but the more boisterous traditions of the Norsemen were beginning to show. Even the confetti was swept away on the breeze, more up in the air than on ground, as if it were out of place. Photographs were unposed snapshots, there was so much movement. Everyone was getting themselves ready for the procession to the school, where the reception was to be held. In this, at least there was a strict etiquette of sorts. Alec and I had to lead. Then came Simon with Francie, John Andrew's wife, who was matron of honour. They were followed by our relatives, all the other grown-ups and the children. The old and infirm, who were unable to walk or keep up the pace, piled onto the flat back of our battered Morris pick-up.

With my silk dress beating in the wind against Alec's legs, suit jackets flapping, hand bags swaying and hats being held on, it looked like a cross between a scene from the *Pied Piper of Hamelin* and an exodus of refugees. All the neatness, so painstakingly created in the forenoon was undone and everyone felt the better for it.

Once inside, as soon as the short speeches were over, the tables with food were put back against the walls and the serious business of dancing began. Ties were taken off, top buttons were undone and Harry and Jim took up their fiddles. Among the many reels, there was a special cheer for *Shaalds of Foula*, in which the rhythmic motion of hands, held above the heads of crouching partners, mimics the beating of waves upon the rocks. Alec and I left the party at midnight, leaving it to go on for hours. We walked down to the Haa to swap our finery for more normal clothes, before making our way to Loch Cottage, which Lisbeth had insisted we use for our honeymoon even though this was to last all of one night.

Our married occupancy of the island was similarly brief. Winter broke early that year as if to speed us on our way and easterly gales lashed the island. Within the space of ten days we had packed up all our belongings, caught a fishing boat to Scalloway and were on the steamer heading ultimately for Fife. One of the problems I had only vaguely considered over the summer, was having no home there. As an optimist, I had operated on the premise that 'something would turn up.' Thus when we had arrived and Alec had asked, 'Would you mind living on the *Trygg*?' I had replied, 'No,' thinking in all innocence that the question was hypothetical. A few hours later we were at Tayport transferring our bedding and pots and pans below.

The accommodation was forward, such as it was. The distance between the stempost and the hold bulkhead, being less than twelve feet. The angles were tightly curved on two planes, from the ceiling to the floor, and from the sides to the bow. There were no flat surfaces and no lining. All the heavy framing and planks was visible and with no natural daylight, I felt like Jonah inside the Whale. We had a small heater and a single gas ring for cooking. The top bunk was extended like a balcony to admit to married life. In many respects it was cosy, but depressing when midday coincided with low tide; as being moored against the south wall, we disappeared into the shadow and mud, only to emerge once darkness had come. The Haa, in comparison, was luxury and the thought of space and a busy season's schedule, wooed us back to Foula far earlier than we should have gone.

I had made my own way up to Fair Isle, as it was intended that we should meet up there. The entrance to the North Haven was difficult and the pier unlit, so that Alec had given me *Trygg's* estimated time of arrival to help guide them in. As heroic as being a modern day Grace Darling might sound – clad in oilskins, torch in hand, withstanding wind and horizontal rain for hours, to steer brave men to safety – the westerly gale was so bad, that I genuinely thought if they had any sense they would be sheltering in the lee of the Scotland mainland. I knew I was in bad odour, when there was a knock at the Bird Observatory door and a bedraggled Alec and Simon stepped in, to find me drinking hot chocolate by the fire.

Sea mood is so unpredictable. When the weather abated and we left for Foula, *Trygg* was cutting through a glassy surface and pilot whales were playing in the gentle wake. There was hardly a ripple in the water in the Voe when we tied up, lulling us into a sense of false security, thinking that spring had come early. Quite oblivious of the fate in store for us, we began preparing for the new salvage season. The five tonnes of food we had brought for ourselves and the island was unloaded and distributed. The explosives were taken out and stored. The mooring was dived upon and checked.

Trouble stalked us by stealth.

First the wind blew from the north-east bringing sleet and snow, which lay as a generous dusting of talc. For days the clouds hung low, laden and grey. The sea, sky and landscape merged into one bitterly cold mass. The swell was breaking, but conditions were not bad, as there was not the reach in between Foula and the Shetland mainland for any serious motion to set in.

Then, as the depression moved, the wind began to retreat round the compass, so that it came from the west. As the barometer dropped further, it picked up in strength. It blew and blew until we could see the Shaalds crash in dazzling fury on the horizon, like curls of decorative icing upon a heaving mass of grey. Still, *Trygg* was safe. She was protected by the island, but by now the storm was so severe, that the whole ocean was in violent motion, with crests metres high.

Wednesday 30th March, 1977, was to be the longest day imaginable. Alec got up at 2.00 a.m. in the morning to check the boat. She was coping with the surge that was powering around the headland into the Voe, but he was distressed by the situation. By first light conditions had worsened, as the wind shifted south.

I joined him just after the shipping forecast at 5.55 a.m. 'It's veering south-east – that means it's creeping round our side of the island.'

'What can you do?'

'Absolutely nothing ... We've missed our chance. The conditions have been so bad for the last twenty-four hours, that we could not make a run for Shetland without the risk of foundering ... Now it's doubtful if we could even make the stone's throw to the mooring, without the rubber inflatable being overturned. *Trygg's* on her own. There is nothing to do, but to sit it out.'

The wait was interminable. We all went through the motions of living, but hardly spoke and even the simplest tasks could not be concentrated upon. Every few minutes Alec, or Simon, or I would get up and go to the window to see if she was still there. The sky was so overcast that it was practically dark outside, all the colour and life seemed to have been taken away. There was the leaden monochrome sky, the foaming sea and the black menacing rocks. In this hellish natural torment, our valiant craft tossed and bucked. Three weeks previous, she had been our home.

As the hours wore on, the situation deteriorated further and by the afternoon the waves were cascading over the ridge of rock, to the south-east of *Trygg*. Her last defence was now breached and we could hardly watch as she rolled her gunwales under, broadside on. Even still, she would be all right if only the wind would back. Every forecast was monitored. We congregated around the old red portable, holding our breaths in case the crackling reception should fail just when it got to our sea area, 'Fair Isle. Southerly, Storm Force Ten, backing south-westerly and decreasing. Imminent.' Silently we all willed the predictions to have effect. 'Come on. Come on,' we each urged, 'Change!' If only the direction of the wind would alter, its strength would not matter.

The evening ticked away and still no improvement. The 12.35 a.m. forecast repeated its earlier message. The Norwegian forecast half an hour later, said much the same thing, but the elements were not paying any attention and the breakers had been rolling into the Voe for some while. Inanimate as they were, it was as if they smelt blood.

We were all exhausted. A vigil was useless. There was little to do, but to go to bed and hope for the best. Alec and I lay awake in the darkness. There was no light as the Tilley had been put out. Neither of us was sleeping. I found the strain of keeping calm so wearing, Anxiety, like an invisible hand clutched at my chest. Senses keen, eyes open and staring into oblivion, I listened to the wind buffeting around the Haa, hammering on the window panes as if to break in and get at us, there. The slates were rattling on the roof and above all this, roared the din of the sea. Suddenly, I heard another sound ... a different one; a clang, like a heavy sledge-hammer hitting a hollow steel pipe. I thought it might be nothing, but a few moments later, there it was, again. When I heard it a third time, I threw off the covers. Feeling my way, shivering and naked to the window, I feared the worst.

The author, aged 17, during her first summer on Foula, taking a rest from raising peats.

The late Lisbeth Holbourn, with one of her caddie lambs. (*Simon Martin*)

Britain's most remote inhabited island, Foula, with its five distinctive peaks. (*Jim Gear*)

'Da Divers' – Alec Crawford (*Simon Martin*)   Simon Martin

The voe at Foula – with Jim Gear's boat to the left and the *Haa* in the background.

RMS *Oceanic* being launched at Harland & Wolff, Belfast (*National Museums & Galleries of N. Ireland, Ulster Folk & Transport Museum*)

RMS *Oceanic's*, first-class Dining Room in which all 400 passengers could dine below allegorical figures painted by a member of the Royal Academy. (*National Museums & Galleries of N. Ireland, Ulster Folk & Transport Museum*)

One of the *Oceanic*'s vast crankshaft journals being ground on a lathe in the machinery shops of Harland & Wolff. (*National Museums & Galleries of N. Ireland, Ulster Folk & Transport Museum*)

A rare photograph of the *Oceanic* on the Shaalds – her steam is still up and her lifeboats are down. (*Illustrated London News*)

Harry Gear, the island's postmaster and most prolific peat cutter. (*Simon Martin*)

Crawford and Martin's first load from the *Oceanic* – scrap was lying everywhere.

Trygg practically sinking as she brings in one of the *Oceanic*'s two propeller bosses, weighing 14.5 tons.

Left The author, with her Matron of Honour, Francie Ratter, outside Foula Kirk on her wedding day.

Below The procession from the Kirk, keeping with tradition in Foula's first wedding for almost forty years.

Right Friends. (*left to right*) Best man, Simon Martin, Bride and Groom.

Above left Artefacts from RMS *Oceanic* with the famous White Star emblem. (*Simon Martin*)

Above right Telling its own story, one of the *Oceanic*'s six ton propeller blades is unloaded on the Shetland mainland. (*Simon Martin*)

Right John Andrew Ratter operates the *Valorous*'s winch. (*Colin Martin*)

Seventeen ton brass steam condenser with all its tubes removed, RMS *Oceanic*.

Trygg coming over Foula pier in pieces hours after she was lost.

The scene was spot-lit by a weak, three-quarter moon that had evaded the racing clouds. Its silver glow flashed in the ferment below. The movement was so intense, so confused that at first I could not focus on anything in particular. The rocks appeared and were immersed again in a writhing shroud.

The sound came again. I gasped as I realised what it was. It was *Trygg*. I could see her . . . she had dragged her anchor! She was right there in front of me in Batna Geo. Another wave seized her and tipped her right over onto her starboard side. Her mast hit the rocks.

Any emotion was useless. The end was inevitable. 'She's gone, Alec, I announced.'

Within an instant he was beside me. We both gazed, dumbly as the vessel that had given us our livelihood was tumbled over, failing in a mortal battle. Her mast hit the rocks again.

'Simon!' Alec shouted. '*Trygg*'s lost! Get up!'

Pulling on our clothes we clattered down the stairs and tumbled outside. Simon joined us to form a pathetic trio on the grass above the pier. The wind blasted our faces in triumph, as we stood mesmerised. An enormous wave had just rolled in. It picked *Trygg* up and cast her down on the barnacled foreshore as if she had been an eggshell . . . a gaping hole appeared. A second wave sucked her back, swept her up and did the same again . . . she was still intact. A third wave caught her in its grasp . . . flung her down . . . and devoured her. When it withdrew, seconds later, there was nothing but shattered timbers.

A stench of diesel filled the air.

I was shocked. I could not believe what had happened. My mouth dropped. 'I sailed on that boat,' I thought. 'I put my life in her trust and thought I'd been safe.' Now it had been made clear in the most vivid, dramatic way, she was nothing but a sham. I had been betrayed. She was matchsticks.

Alec shook his fallen head and turned away, beaten. 'I don't want to see anymore.'

6

ACCIDENTS

I watched for several minutes more, fascinated, horrified. Never had I seen the like before. Rent baulks of wood were being tossed around with abandon. The destructive power was remorseless.

It sickened me to imagine what might have happened if Alec and Simon had been onboard and jettisoned into the tumult. To think of them in the surf, tossed about like toys, battered, helpless ... drowning. My God, what could I have done ...? The answer was the same as for *Trygg* – nothing. I could have done absolutely nothing. I would have watched them die and it would have been the most awful thing possible.

Breaking the stare, I found Simon still beside me. I had not realised before how ludicrous he had looked. He had not had time to get properly dressed and stood in his old, woollen school dressing gown and wellington boots. What a sight, all white flesh, maroon checks and black rubber. Offbeat and anything but heroic, his appearance reinforced the human message. 'Come on,' he said, 'It's useless hanging around. Let's go in and put the kettle on. I'm freezing.'

Beside the newly revived fire we sat, shocked and despondent, each isolated by the experience. The conversation, when there was any, was pensive and disjointed.

'I don't know about you, Alec, but just at this moment I think I'd rather be a bus conductor.' Simon remarked.

'I wonder what went?' came the reply. 'I dived on the mooring only two days ago to check it. Even put new wire to secure the shackle pin. I'm sure it can't have come undone.' He shook his head.

'We'll have to phone Andy Beattie, tomorrow, about the insurance. I hope we're covered.'

'I'll dive and have a look as soon as it's weather.'

'Someone better go and tell Harry in case he goes down to the Voe, tonight,' I suggested. Harry the postmaster, never kept conventional hours and it was quite likely that he would wander down to look at *Trygg* and the mailboat, to make sure that they were both safe. The prospect of him seeing the debris coming over the pier and thinking that Alec and Simon had been lost was distressing and I volunteered to go. As macabre as it might sound, I wanted another look on the way. The event was so awesome, so immediate, that it drew me back.

Already shards were appearing in the Voe. An orange shape caught my eye. Strangely, the outline of the small life raft was comforting, bobbing and swirling in the surge in Lady Geo, the cove beside the mailboat crane. I asked myself whether anyone would have survived, had they been inside. Chillingly the answer was, no. It was only intact because it was light. Had it been burdened with the dead-weight of bodies, it would have been smashed against the far side of the pier. A horrible picture came into my head, so real and haunting that it had to be consciously suppressed. I made my way up the road.

The smell of the diesel was borne on the night air in a fine vapour, surrounding me like a mist for much of the half mile to Harry's door. Although it was after two o'clock in the morning, Harry was still up. As he opened the door, the light from the Tilley lamp on the table silhouetted him in the dark, so that I could hardly see his features. The ends of his tousled, grey hair and his stubbly chin caught the rays, creating a thin, golden aura like an eclipse. The tone of his voice expressed his surprise. 'Hello. What's happened to bring you up here at this hour?'

'Harry, we wanted you to know. *Trygg's* been lost, but Alec and Simon are safe. They weren't on her when she went.'

There was a pause while he took in the enormity of the news, and he looked away from me as if to think. 'I'm most terrible sorry', he replied shaking his head, 'terrible, terrible sorry.' He paused again, his tone genuinely upset, 'I looked at her earlier and just hoped she'd last out until the wind changed. The Voe will be at its worst now with low water.'

'It's dreadful.'

'But nobody's hurt?'

'No.'

'Then we can't really ask for any more,' he remarked with feeling, adding, 'tell them that I'll be down at first light, to help save whatever possible.'

We parted both knowing how insignificant we were in the face of such natural fury. I fought my way home against the gale. Just by Ham, there came a gust so strong that it stopped me in my paces, as if to prove the point.

Dawn was miserable and liquid. It turned up begrudgingly as if the effort was all too much. The immediate task was to save the rubber inflatable. This was still tied beneath the mailboat crane, barely afloat, punctured and filled with water. We had known it was in difficulties during the night, but the breakers had been so violent that we had not dared any rescue. News of *Trygg*'s fate had spread quickly around the island and there were plenty of hands to help lift it out. The iroko beam used for lifting the *Oceanic*'s bosses was also bobbing about and this was lassoed and secured to an eye in the rocks on the south side.

There was not much time to spare as high water was approaching. As the tide flooded and the sea level increased, chaos crept inland and breakers, once again, began to engulf the pier. Splintered pieces of *Trygg*, planks and framing three feet or so in length, were being spewed over the parapet, swilling where the rubber inflatable had been not long before. Mashed, they were only distinguishable by what was left of their paintwork. I noticed a piece of the accommodation, it was blue, and some of the varnished tongue and groove from around the front of the wheelhouse.

As the morning wore on, we began scouring the eastern coast for flotsam that might be a danger to other vessels, should it be washed out to sea. Lisbeth, too, made her way down, waterproofs on and scarf tied tightly around her head. She had tears in her eyes. 'When I saw the bits this morning being driven up the burn, Joanne and I feared the worst ... We thought Alec and Simon had been drowned, perhaps even John Andrew, too. Thank Heaven it's not true,' and she clasped my hands, with touching faith.

'Anyway,' she remarked, getting the better of herself, 'have you seen yon piece of your boat that's in my meadow, where the yellow flags grow?'

On inspection, we found what was about half of *Trygg*'s port side. Weighing over a ton, it lay beyond the footbridge well up the burn, about fifty yards above the high water line. Upturned, with all its frames showing, it looked like part of a skeleton and proved to be the largest fragment left. Tins of grease and cans of oil from the engine room came up over a long stretch of shoreline, stretching up to Veedal in the north, some quarter of a mile away. In Shutting Geo we retrieved some of our heavy rope.

Whilst Simon, John Andrew and I continued to work in the shore party, Alec went to Ham to phone. Just as with a death there were formalities to be completed with *Trygg* and he had to contact the insurers and the coastguard. We met over lunch, all except him tired and morose. 'While I was at Lizzie's, I began ringing around about a replacement boat,' he announced. 'There's one in Stornaway on Lewis that would do, but she's a bit big at ninety feet, so I called Tom Clark. He's south at the moment, but says that the *Valorous* could be available.' We were stunned, bereft. Not only had there been no decent period of mourning, but all the bits of *Trygg* had not been collected, yet.

'That was quick,' commented Simon.

'We've just got to press on,' came the rebuff. There was no point arguing with him, when he was in a determined phase.

An uncomfortable week was spent waiting for Tom to return to Lerwick. Alec was impossible to live with, as he could not relax. Forever, the question of 'How are we going to work this summer?' occupied his mind. 'What if we can't buy the *Valorous?*' 'What if she's too expensive?' He was distant and preoccupied during the day, and restless in bed at night. The tension was palpable and by the time he set off in the duly repaired rubber inflatable, I said 'good bye' with relief, as he opened the throttle and settled in position for the gruelling two hour run.

'You'll be sorry to see him go, Moya,' Simon ventured with heavy irony.

I sighed, worn out. 'I wouldn't give tuppence for him, now, but I suspect I'll be pleased to see him, when he gets back.'

'Oh ho! You just wait until I pass that one on', he declared, relishing the opportunity to make me squirm. Which he did, the rat.

Tom Clark was another diver of similar age. Alec and Simon had known him ever since their early Barra days, when they had simultaneously worked for competing outfits. Relationships between their respective bosses had been hostile, but as employees they used to bump into each other in the pub at Castlebay. Tom was a softly spoken Glaswegian, whose mildness of manner belied both his astuteness and his capacity for enjoying himself. He had grown up in an uncompromising part of the city, in which adolescent fights were the norm. He said at one period, he had been hit over the head with so many bottles that his scalp looked like crazy paving. It was a battle ground he had long since left behind, but surviving it had made him resilient. Setting up a small business of his own, about the same time that the Crawford & Martin partnership had been formed, he was now capturing the oil boom in Shetland, constructing new harbour facilities around the isles. It was a cut-throat industry, but his talent for civil engineering had made him prosper.

He had bought the *Valorous* to transport building materials to Bressay. That particular job was finished and currently she was lying idle. Generous to a fault – 'just take her' – he insisted, as they shared a pint in reunion. 'I haven't made my mind up whether or not I shall need her again. Just take her and give her back at the end of the season. No charge. That'll let you get on.'

Alec laughed in disbelief. Most people, even friends, would have taken advantage because he was desperate. Here was Tom, whom he had hardly seen for years, saying, just take the *Valorous* away. She was bigger, better and worth twice as much as the late *Trygg*.

'No, I don't want to borrow her – it's too much of a responsibility.'

'Nonsense, just take her. I know you'll look after her.'

Alec was adamant. 'I'd rather buy her and if you need her again, you can have her back for less.'

Finding that he could not be persuaded, the easy-going Tom gave in, 'O.K. O.K. Have it your own way,' he agreed and the deal was done.

Taking no chances with the weather a second time, it was late June before the *Valorous* was brought into Foula. The day was so calm and peaceful, that it seemed hard to recognise the Voe as the same spot in which we had lost *Trygg*. Tied at the end of the pier, a stream of sightseers came to survey the new acquisition. Sleek, with proper accommodation aft, a steel-lined hold amidships and a Department of Trade Load Line certificate to carry twenty-five tons of cargo, she was more than fit for recovering the remaining non-ferrous metal from the *Oceanic*, and yet I confess she never gained my affection in quite the same way.

With her arrival, my summer settled into as much of a routine as any which is dictated by wind and tide. There were always chores – cooking, house-keeping, fighting a rear guard action against complete disorder and washing all the clothes in the burn. I also kept a vegetable garden, landscaped the yard and put a new roof on the front porch as part of the rent, but it was not enough. I bored easily and needed a challenge, too, and so began to spend an increasing amount of time on the wreck.

This made the days very long. I had to be the first up in the morning to make the porridge. Two hours had to elapse between eating and diving, and so if we had to be out especially early and I was less than enthusiastic, I was simply pushed out of bed. Simon used to say he could hear the thud, followed by a sharp complaint. Once breakfast was over and all the equipment was ready, we would head out to the Shaalds with the *Valorous*. Depending on whether it was spring or neap tides, we would spend anything up to several hours lifting. On our return I would make lunch. The aqualungs would be charged and then just before the following slack water, it was out to the sea, again. In the evening, however late we had finished, there was supper to prepare. Visitors were always welcome to join us. The water was heated on the fire for the washing up and when this was eventually finished by the light of the Tilley, I could sit down.

Like any apprentice, I was a goffer, especially on deck. Everyone, Alec in particular, told me what to do, but I worked hard . If I went out, both John Andrew and Simon could dive and this doubled the lifting rate.

Alec would work the winch and orders would fly, 'Quick as you like, Moya, get a strop ...! Release that rope ...! Get out of the way ...!' I used to leap around, trying hard both to keep my wits about me and not do anything wrong.

Taking signals on the rope. One pull for attention. Repeat. Two pulls for lift. Repeat and sign 'Up' to Alec, by twirling an upturned forefinger in the air.

Valorous's derrick was forward and she lifted over the side. First the slack would be taken up and the hoist rope would crack like a whip without warning, as it came under tension. Then the deck would begin to list. Five degrees ... ten degrees ... twenty degrees ... further ... a little further until we would be heeling far over. The engine would be labouring and the pulleys complaining.

'It could be the impeller,' Alec would shout. 'It's caught. I'm just going to sit on it a minute, to see if it pulls free.' Alert, the adrenaline would be shooting up and down my spine. Just a little further in our arc and we would capsize.

There would be a sharp lurch to port. It was all over. We would return to a more even keel, as the object came away and the sweat was over. Until the next time.

For me, the recovery would be an unknown quantity until it broke the surface. I would hang over the side, expectantly, waiting for a glimpse.

'Stand back. It will swing.'

I would do as I was told. Every piece of metal was dangerous and would career to and fro at body height, given the slightest leeway. Alec would hold the irregular shape against the side of the hull, awaiting a moment when there was little or no roll and like landing a fish, he would skilfully tweak it over the gunwale, depositing it in the bottom of the hold with a resounding clang.

When I first began as a *deckie*, the broken shapes that came onboard, seemed so divorced from the *Oceanic* as a great ship, that I got no clue to her grace or character. Many of them came up attached to lumps of rusted cast iron, disembowelled. An enthusiast of steam, Alec, would explain what their task had been, like a pathologist. 'That big brass cog, with the deep set teeth, is from the steering gear, aft. There were two of them, one on each steering engine. They ran against the rudder quadrant.' A fabulous copper monster appeared, all curls of tubes and jangling like a metallic hydra, 'this is one of the salt water distillation plants for making fresh water'. The four, seventeen ton condensers were blown apart, the tubes that were their innards coming up, like bundles of brass spaghetti and this led to a scratchy drawing on the principles of triple expansion engines, with their high, intermediate and low pressure cylinders, all of varying sizes. From being something obsolete and long forgotten on the seabed, unlike her stable mate, the *Titanic*, this little known ocean liner began to take form in my mind.

Alone in the Haa one wet afternoon, curiosity got the better of me and I raked around for what information we had. There was a blueprint, I knew, somewhere in the back of the oak cupboard in the corner behind Alec's chair. Pinkish and fading, this line drawing looked like the end of a roll of wallpaper. When laid flat, it extended to more than both of my arms outstretched and I had to pin it down with books, on the floor in front of the fire. The broadside view in neat, intricate pen work was so pleasing to the eye, that it captured her elegance as no photograph I had seen. Slim and streamlined, it was obvious from her classic proportions why the *Oceanic* had been dubbed the White Star Yacht. The stem slanted slightly forward, the stern was countered and the low superstructure was crowned by two tall, raked funnels.

With the copy of the *Marine Engineer* from 1899, I began to place the black and white stills we had chosen from the collection at the Liverpool Maritime Museum in their relative positions, beginning with the machinery and engines.

Caught for posterity in the engineering workshop of Harland and Wolff in Belfast, a group of overalled men posed in front of the two of the boilers they had constructed. The boilers dwarfed them, eighteen feet in diameter, gleaming and complete with their furnace doors. In the machine shop, a toolmaker placed his hand against the enormous, one hundred ton crankshaft journal, as if even he was awe-inspired by precision on such a vast scale.

The propellers were captured on her launch, rotating as they were forced into the water. and this moment was described, in the eye witness account in the *Marine Engineer*. Labelling it the shipbuilding function of the century:

Long before the appointed hour of eleven o'clock, Irish time on Saturday, 14th January, 1899, guests and spectators could be seen at every vantage point from the appointed seats, to the rigging of the ships in the docks to vessels under construction. The crowd was at least 50,000 strong. The yard was closed to all but the workmen immediately concerned. All was quiet and not a shout or sound was heard save the clang of hammers and battering rams relieving the wooden shores. Punctually, the firing of the signal rockets began. Soon, a red flag with the word, 'Launch' upon it was unfurled from the taffrail. Then came the cry, 'she's moving'. Slowly and imperceptibly she started. Steadily she gained speed amid a grand volume of cheering, which even the discordant shrieks of thirty to forty sirens failed to drown. Soon the water covered the lower blades of her propellers and these began to turn with the pressure. A heavy wave suddenly swept the quay, and as suddenly retired. A great sound of breaking ropes was heard as the restraining cables tore from their hemp bindings, and the vast ship was stopped within the length of the ways, and floated before the grandstand for all to admire – the largest ship in the world.

A mere box at this point, no expense had been spared in fitting her out. The *Marine Engineer*, again put words to the images before me, *a ship instinct with life, beautiful in her appearance and filled with every luxury!* The first class Dining Room was remarkable. Its oak panelling was washed with gold. Daylight was admitted through a huge glass dome, the base of which was dominated by four allegorical figures, representing Great Britain, the United States, Liverpool and New York, painted by a member of the Royal Academy. The main staircase, hung with panels of Turkey red silk, led to the first class Drawing Room on the deck above. Carved mahogany doors opened onto a bright room, crowned by an upper dome of stained glass and scattered with Louis XIV furniture. This was the ladies' domain. The men could gather in the club-like ambience of the Smoking Room aft, with its murals of Columbus discovering America, embossed leather chairs, Italian figurines and sea-nymphs.

The most palatial vessel ever afloat, she struck out for New York on 6th September 1899, the vision of Thomas Ismay, the President of the White Star Line. Sadly, he had become seriously ill and could not make the journey. She was to be his epitaph. His monument to a marine world that had witnessed the most tremendous revolution ever, the change from sail to steam. Her five decks were described as *an ocean city, more like a modern sky-scraper than any craft of earlier days.* On the upper levels, the boat and promenade decks, the life of the rich was one of idle amusement. In the 'basement' the stripped and toiling stokers, fuelled fires in conditions that would scorch the hide off lesser men. Tiers, just a few feet high, separated the relaxed from the perspiring, with a hierarchy of chefs, valets, maids, stewards and engineers filling the real, as well as the social gaps, in between.

Imagining the two thousand souls who regularly sailed with the *Oceanic*, over four hundred of whom were crew, I could understand how she had captured their affection. She was a *Greyhound* of the Atlantic, the favourite of men like the banker, J.P. Morgan and the millionaire, Cornelius Vanderbilt. Charles Lightoller, the only officer to survive the sinking of the *Titanic*, described her as his great love. He left her to join the other's ill-fated maiden voyage and returned once the inquiries into that catastrophe had ceased. Separated by only a couple of years, two losses could not have been more dissimilar, either in loss of life or how they captured the popular imagination. The *Oceanic* took nobody with her, and faded from popular memory. Yet, Lightoller wrote that he had never been so fond of any ship, either before or since, and her loss was like the snapping of all links with his past. Macabre interest persists in the other to this day.

On 1st August, 1914, the *Oceanic* left New York for the last time. For some months she had been bringing home hundreds of American citizens fleeing the imminent hostilities in Europe. She slipped home in darkness with her lights blacked out, gone for ever was the era of affluence and Empire she had embodied. Three days out, the radio brought the message that war with Germany had been declared.

Like a number of great liners before her, she had been designed to Admiralty specification, in order that she could be quickly converted to a fighting ship. Within twenty-four hours of her arrival in Southampton, she had been stripped of all movable fittings and surplus lifeboats and eight, six inch guns had been installed on her upper decks. Bunkering, and loading stores and ammunition had taken a total of two weeks . With a supplement of Naval officers and crew, she sailed on 25th August to police foreign shipping movements as an armed merchant cruiser. A fortnight later, almost fifteen years to the day of her much feted maiden voyage, she hit the reef of the Shaalds and came to an everlasting halt.

The Ship's Log reports the incident in stark prose:

8.45 a.m. Vessel touched lightly. Stopped both engines. Full astern both. Soundings forward give five fathoms each side. Lowered the boats to sound around the ship.
    Engines worked as required to get ship off.

At first everyone believed that it was just a minor bump. The silent jolt, felt at the moment of impact, had not seemed particularly bad. Well schooled procedures were put into action. Orders were barked out and the situation was assessed. This disciplined activity came as a welcome diversion until the telling moment when the order to 'Go Astern!' was rung on the ship's telegraph. As the two vast triple expansion engines began to rotate the twin screws, every man on board paused with bated breath, waiting for that slight, almost negligible movement that would tell him that the *Oceanic* was free ... it never came. All attempts to reverse her off proved futile and ominously, the worsening swell began to grind her up and down against the unyielding rock. At 5.00 p.m., the tired and dejected Naval Captain, William Slayter made his final entry in the Log:

Thought inadvisable to tow ship off, even if possible.

A sad recognition that even in the unlikely event that they managed to get her free, she was so badly damaged that she would probably sink. Shortly afterwards, he bowed to the inevitable and abandoned ship. There she remained for the next two weeks, sitting majestically upright with only a slight list to port. The stores and as much equipment as possible were recovered with the help of the islanders, who were more than delighted at such an unusual opportunity of work. Then in the space of one night, the *Oceanic* disappeared in a storm, leading all to suspect that she had been washed from the Shaalds and had sunk in deeper water. What really happened was a salutary reminder of the power of the sea. For the ship that had taken twenty months, fifteen hundred skilled men, and seventeen thousand tons of steel to build, was demolished overnight by the pounding of the waves.

I caught my own glimpse of her fate early in our last season, 1979. As ever, we had been occupied with blasting, waiting for the weather to improve and it was *Valorous*'s first day out lifting. I happened to gaze over the side. The sea was so calm and the water so clear, that the high afternoon sun penetrated the depths. I suddenly realised that through the liquid haze, I could discern metal columns on the bottom. They lay scattered, topsy-turvy, like the supports of a broken bridge.

I was fascinated. 'Alec, I can see the wreck!'

'It's because we've blown away all the kelp.' We leant over the gunwale together to get a better view and he pointed below. 'They're the pillars which supported the cylinders and look ... There are the ends of the cranks. You can see the con rod running off into the weed over there. We're just to east of the reef. This is about the highest part of the engines left.'

Visually, it was like catching sight of the lost city of Atlantis. A chance event which took the story of the *Oceanic* to its final conclusion – scrap. A sad end, but not one to get maudlin about. Nobody was lost and just raising one's eyes to the lonely memorial on the cliffs at Durga Ness, brought home the real tragedy of the Great War.

Marine salvage has its values in order because it places life before property. Ships and cargo can always be replaced, especially if they are insured, not so people. Shortly afterwards, I had this priority strongly reinforced. Alec had three potentially fatal accidents in the space of eleven weeks. These had a lasting impact, in that I understood how important he was to me and I should take the opportunity to say and show it, for tomorrow he might not be around.

On a pleasant, but breezy Monday, towards the end of May, the *Valorous* was on her mooring, and Alec, Simon and John Andrew were on board cleaning and stowing scrap. I was enjoying the lull and was just about to step into the Haa after returning from a short walk, when Simon rushed round the corner. 'Quick, Alec's been hurt! He's been hit by the steel beam. We've managed to get him to the pier. John Andrew's gone to get the nurse and I'm off to call the air ambulance!'

Up until that moment, I had not a care in the world. Careering blindly past the *Westering Homewards* and down the slip, I could not see Alec at all. I shouted out his name wildly and a groan, mixed with a muffled laugh like a cough, translating as 'I'm down here, you silly woman,' alerted me that he was lying at my feet. Semi-conscious, lying face down and slumped on the concrete beside the steps, he had been camouflaged. I knelt to tend to him. There was no sign of blood, but it was obvious he was in great pain.

'Hold on. It's going to be all right. Help is on its way.' Apart from touch and reassurance, there was little to offer. Time dragged pitilessly. John Andrew was the first to return. Screeching to a halt in his battered old car, he was accompanied by Maggie, the nurse. She hurried, beginning her examination without a moment's hesitation.

'How heavy was the beam that hit him?' she quizzed John Andrew.

'It must have been about half a ton.'

'And you say that it caught Alec across the back?'

'Yes. We were shifting scrap in the hold. The wire went tight under the beam and lifted it out of its sockets. Alec saw it coming and tried to get out of the way, but it pinned him against the steel lining.'

'And he didn't lose consciousness right away?'

'No, he shouted to us to help him out. He knew he was hurt badly, but he managed to get himself here before he collapsed.'

'Right,' she said. 'Well, his blood pressure is O.K., which means that there is no serious internal bleeding. I'm going to sedate him now and we'll just have to get him to hospital as quickly as possible.'

Within an hour and a half, Alec was in the casualty department of the Gilbert Bain Hospital in Lerwick. Dirty from breaking up cast steel, he was a startling contrast to the crisp white linen and pristine surroundings. The nurses looked horrified as his face, forearms and hands were covered with a paste of orange rust. Desperate to insert an intravenous drip, none of their swabs would reveal his skin, until in a moment of inspiration one of them tried some floor cleaner.

I was ushered away to wait in reception. Sitting quietly, looking out through the panoramic window across the sweep of Lerwick Sound, I must have cut a distant figure. Eventually, a young house doctor came. He told me that Alec's kidneys have been severely crushed and might have to be removed. They would run more tests and he'd be operated on in the morning.

John Andrew's aunt and uncle lived in Scalloway, I knew they would give me a bed. On the short bus journey across the spine of Shetland, all the possible consequences churned in my mind, 'What if he couldn't ever dive again ...?' 'What if he had to go on dialysis? That would be the end of salvage.' 'If I gave him one of my kidneys, would it mean giving up having children?' I was composed until Peter Ratter opened the door. In his slippers, with his pipe in one hand and his newspaper in the other, he could not have been more surprised. 'My, my, lass, what are you doing here?'

'I'm sorry to bother you ... I didn't think you'd mind, but ...' tears prevented further explanation.

A kind hand was put on my shoulder. 'Come in ... Come in ... You'd better speak to Bessie.'

Simon had always joked that Alec had cast iron guts because of his appetite. I thought there could be some truth to the witticism, when the junior doctor gave me the good news the following day. Alec was passing a lot of blood, but neither of his kidneys had been ruptured. They would have to monitor him carefully, but given time he should mend on his own. I was allowed to sit by his bedside. Dwarfing the mattress, he was ashen with a rusty tinge. The hollows of his eyes were dark and his cheeks drawn.

It took ten days for him to be released. When we flew back to Foula, he was still very feeble and it took another six weeks before he was given the all clear to go back to salvage. At the beginning of July, there was enough scrap to make a trip south to Scrabster on the Scottish mainland. Alec stated that he felt fit enough to skipper the *Valorous*, but did not want to go home, because everyone would make a fuss. Knowing him to be stubborn about receiving such attention, the unloading was completed and he was left behind with John Andrew for company.

Simon accompanied the lorry to Glasgow, and having business to attend about our new farm, I met up with him at Naughton. The house and grounds were in full swing in preparation for a garden party in aid of King George's Fund for Sailors. It was like walking into the pages of *Country Life*, with all the marquees and the Band of the Royal Marines parading on the lawn. Alec's father in particular was in his element, entertaining the Flag Officer Scotland and various other Naval VIPs. The leafy surroundings were full of pomp and circumstance, and we enjoyed the break.

What a contrast awaited us in the cool of the following evening, when we stepped off the train at Thurso. Stiff from sitting for six hours and weighed down with an assortment of spares, we were decanting ourselves along with a collection of special treats, when Simon was pounced on by a middle-aged man in half uniform.

'I'm the Harbour Master from Scrabster,' he announced bluntly, 'and I've got the lifeboat out looking for your partner.'

Ignored, I stood behind holding some trays of strawberries. Shocked and hurt, I wanted to interpose, 'Never mind Crawford & Martin. Alec's my partner. Surely, if he's lost at sea, it matters most to me!'

Mac, as we soon found out he was called, did not mean to be unkind, he was just remarkably tactless. Ordering us into his car, he drove us the few miles to the port and told us what he knew. 'Your partner went out mid-morning in that rubber boat of yours to investigate wrecks on Stroma and Swona, at the east end of the Pentland Firth. He told the Foula man that he'd be back at 6 p.m. and when there was no sign of him, two hours later, the alarm was raised. Enquiries were made on the islands. He was seen on both, but has gone. The lifeboat's carrying out a sweep. The Foula man's gone with it.'

'It sounds as if Alec's broken down,' Simon suggested.

'He could have.'

With darkness beginning to fall, things did not sound good. Mac did not say, but I knew the Pentland Firth to be one of the most dangerous stretches of water in the British Isles. Ten miles wide in places, it was the channel between Orkney and the mainland of Scotland, in which the Atlantic and North Sea met. The currents that swept through it reached speeds of up to seventeen knots. Large ships were sometimes swept backwards. The area was hazardous enough in daytime, let alone at night.

We were left to our own devices, only to come across Mac again just before midnight. Sitting on the wooden bench in front of the harbour office, in case there was any news, he noticed us as he tried to unlock his front door. 'Come on inside,' he gestured gruffly. On hearing that we had not eaten since lunch, he produced two doorsteps of corned beef sandwiches and a couple of mugs of hot tea. We sat on the faded crimson chairs and warmed ourselves on the bar of the electric fire. As if clearing his throat, he rumbled, 'You're welcome to stay.'

The radio set in the corner was switched on and throughout the early hours of the morning we listened to the 'PAN' warnings on Channel 16. They were broadcast every half hour to alert shipping to Alec's plight, 'PAN.PAN..PAN... PAN.PAN..PAN... PAN.PAN..PAN... ALL SHIPS. ALL SHIPS. ALL SHIPS...ALL SHIPS. ALL SHIPS. ALL SHIPS...' The dispassionate voice then went on to describe the situation in graphic terms, 'Keep a look out for a single man adrift in a rubber inflatable boat ... was due to return to Scrabster at 1800 hours and has not returned ... could have been swept out into the Atlantic.' The bleakness of it all seemed to be reinforced with every repeat and I found it impossible not to fear the worst.

For Alec, broken down and at the mercy of the wind and tide, his predicament was a cause for concern. He was chilled and cold with damp and the sea conditions were deteriorating, but all this did not matter as he huddled on wet floorboards. He would be safe as long as he was in open water. What he feared most was being cast up at the bottom of cliffs. He listened intently for the tell tale 'hush' of breaking waves and saved his anchor for such an emergency.

More than once, as he shifted uncomfortably, he cursed his luck. Up until the point that the outboard engine had ground to a halt, he had been enjoying the day. He had visited the wrecksites he had wanted to see on the islands. Both Stroma and Swona had been evacuated about fifteen years before and were uninhabited apart from a few visitors in the summer months. The neat, single storey houses with their heavy flagstone roofs, were beguiling despite their closed doors and smokeless chimneys. Some were beginning to fall derelict, others remained with their tables set as if the occupants had simply got up and left. Discarded agricultural equipment lay rusting in the dockens around the byres.

He was well on his way home, with time to spare, when the high revving whirr of the engine was interrupted by the most awful grating sound and it promptly cut out. Opening it up, he tried to effect repairs with the tools he had brought, but a stray bolt had rattled loose and whipped round the magneto, chewing through the wire and he could get no spark. Still undeterred at this point, he had taken the flywheel off, when a Soviet factory ship hoved into view. Initial relief turned sour, when it seemed they were intent on running him down and he put his life jacket on, quite prepared to jump over the side. At the last moment, as the hull loomed high above him, it veered away. He stood waving his oar from side to side, in the sign of distress, to the crew who were looking down over the rail, but to no avail. One of them took a photograph and waved back with his hand in salute.

Hope began to fade, as it became apparent that he could not fix the engine without several new parts. A ferry on its way to Orkney passed in the distance ... he set off a couple of flares ... but they were not seen. He was drifting ever westwards and as darkness fell the lights of settlements on the Scottish mainland were passed. He set off four more flares, but no response. As the night air cooled, a heavy mist began to form. 'If this doesn't clear,' he thought, 'I could be lost for days!' and he rigged a sea anchor to slow his inexorable progress. There was renewed prospect of rescue around four in the morning, when he could hear the distant chugging of a boat engine, muffled in the fog. It was Mac, with Simon and me in the harbour launch. Looking at the chart and his tide tables, and doing some calculations, he had reckoned that the lifeboat, which was doing a thorough sweep, was still too far to the east. Travelling at two knots an hour, this would put Alec already into the Atlantic, and so he decided to chance a look. Our world was a pocket of moist grey vapour, like the inside of a cloud. Within it, the clatter of the engine sounded harsh, its rhythm interrupted at regular intervals by the blast of the foghorn at Dunnet Head. The effect was disorientating to say the least, but Mac was not perturbed and steered by aid of the compass. After about half an hour he cut the engine. 'We should be in the right area now,' he confided, and we shouted in every direction for all we were worth, straining to hear any reply ... There was none and after a fruitless hour we returned to port, more concerned than ever.

As the sun rose and gained warmth, the visibility began to improve making the lifeboat's task easier. Having cut backwards and forwards across the Pentland Firth through the entire night, they eventually came across Alec twelve miles off the mainland of Scotland and eight miles off Orkney. John Andrew had not left the deck all that time and was rewarded by spotting his friend first. Many of the men onboard knew Alec and there was much leg-pulling, as well as relief, when he was hauled onboard. 'We were beginning to think that you were like the Vikings, on your way to America,' someone quipped.

The third incident happened not three weeks later. It was the most undramatic and yet, the most sinister of all. Alec had been diving in the Voe for much of the morning. He was rigging a lift on each of the propeller bosses, to transport them beneath the *Valorous* across the twenty-five miles of open sea to Scalloway. As they lay in just five metres of water and there was no limit to bottom time at this depth on the decompression tables, he was unconcerned how long he had spent. It was a lengthy job and he had to swim up and down at various intervals to collect tools and shackles and so forth.

All was fine when he first came back to the Haa, but sitting in front of the fire to get warm, he complained of a headache. Soon afterwards he began to feel so unwell that Simon and I had to help him upstairs to bed. There he lay, unable to raise his head from the pillow. He could not focus, nor bear any light and was soon physically sick. The onset of these symptoms was so rapid, that I feared he had suffered a stroke. When Maggie, the nurse, arrived, she was tight-lipped. From what little she did say, I knew it was serious. The air ambulance was called and once more Alec was stretchered into it with all haste. I distinctly felt it an event that was getting far too regular.

At the Gilbert Bain the doctors were perplexed. There was no evidence of an actual stroke, and yet many of the indications were there. All they could do was keep him under observation. Within a couple of days Alec got better and was discharged and it was only later that we were told by a specialist in diving medicine, that he had had a cerebral bend. Research had only just been revealed that you could get 'bent', by repetitive diving in shallow water. He had been exceptionally lucky that the gas bubble had lodged behind his eye, where it could swell without doing any permanent damage, or else it could have meant death or paralysis.

The incident marked my end on the *Oceanic*. Being on the Shetland mainland, I took the opportunity to catch the ferry south, and was never on Foula with either Alec or Simon, again. Alec flew back to the island with the doctor's instruction, 'Don't go back into the water this year!' ringing in his ears, but it was wasted breath. The bosses in the Voe beckoned and if I could not stop him, I would rather not watch.

Lifting these awesome lumps of cast bronze onto the Blacksness Pier was Crawford & Martin's final flourish. Over two hundred and fifty tons of non-ferrous metal had been recovered in 192 days – some of those days being as short as twenty minutes, due to the tide – and there was little now to do on the *Oceanic*, but some tidying up. Soon came the day when the buoy marking the wreck had to be cut and the act seemed rather symbolic, like lowering the flag on a far flung dominion. It marked the end of a unique chapter in our lives, meeting, marrying, our first years together – with Simon thrown in for good measure.

I was a girl of seventeen when I arrived on Foula and a woman of twenty, who had nearly been widowed at least three times, when I had left. Never have I faced a more concentrated period of all round learning in my life. Seamanship, salvage, engineering, men, all were part of the course and in myself I had had to learn to conquer fear and find courage.

Memories of the White Star Liner, *Oceanic*, a wreck which is now known as *The Other Titanic*, shall remain forever, along with those of the island and its folk. Fond recollections of Lisbeth and Harry and visitors to the Haa; easy, carefree walks around the cliffs on blustery days, when it was too rough to dive; skinny-dipping in the rockpools at the Taing, where no one could see. Shared people and events, which became our touchstones many years later, when Alec and I were struggling, lonely and separated, thousands of miles apart. These all represented a happy past in which we were ever united, giving us the strength to carry on.

7

HMS ARGYLL

Kilburns is a narrow farm which runs along the ancient raised beaches of the River Tay. Without exception, all its thirteen fields face north, and each bears a name from the past: Jock's Hole Northside: Fountainhead: Cottar's House: Five Acre and Ten Acre, sit around the house and steading. Scroggieside, Scurr Whins and the Kirkton fields are to the west. There is not one, whether now in crop or ley, that I have not ploughed. Their every contour, hollow and outcrop is familiar to me, and similarly I can remember the texture of the soil as it changes from shiny clay in one area through to loam in another, sometimes within just a few paces. The views across the estuary to the Angus and the Sidlaw Hills are spectacular and often, right to the end of May or beginning of June, we can see snow on the distant heights. Quiet, secluded and slightly overrun, they form one of my favourite places in the world.

Walking down the track from Naughton on that summer's day early in August, I was unperturbed about leaving Alec and all his accidents behind. The last two and a half months had been like being tied to the back of an emotional roller-coaster and I needed to get off for a short while – the ride would go on without me, I knew. What a contrast the fertile land with its mature trees to the windswept tundra of Foula, how relaxed and tame. The pleasant breeze, rich with pollen, whispered through the growing crops. The wild cherries bore small, hard ripening fruit. It was with a sense of pleasure that I thought they were ours. A little past the bottom of the shelter belt, mid slope lay the small, brick cottage which we would shortly share alone – no Simon, no John Andrew – just us, and after a trying season, I was looking forward to being by ourselves.

Alec had been brought up on Kilburns and lived in the farmhouse until the age of sixteen when his parents moved into Naughton, the 'big house', just over the hill, inland. His was without doubt a privileged upbringing and our lives were quite different in this respect. My own childhood had been unusual, but by no means affluent and whereas his father was a retired, archetypal brigadier, with a clipped moustache, who was an indirect descendant of Admiral Duncan; my mother is a very private, serene woman, who was put in an orphanage and later adopted after all her immediate family died of T.B. when she was two. These disparate histories affected us both in positive ways. Alec had that ease which sometimes accompanies Old Money and was fortunate enough to inherit one hundred and eighty acres and a fishing station. I had the no nonsense views of a science-based education, mixed with the enthusiasm of an inventor father, and fifteen pounds in the bank – and so our legacies were shared.

Being the second son in any landed family is never an easy position. The historical choice of career has always been the Army or the 'cloth' and for a short period of time it looked very likely that Alec would enter the first. He won a scholarship to Sandhurst at the age of sixteen, and everyone was immensely proud. Brows furrowed, however, when he announced that he had decided it was not what he wanted. His every spare moment away from boarding school was spent on the river. When he was barely in double figures he had owned a salmon cobble for net fishing. Before he was old enough to drive, he had bought a thirty-four foot sprat boat. His father would not lend him the money for the purchase and so he went to Douglas Young, Chairman of Young's Seafoods and organised a loan – his father was furious. By the time he was in the Upper Sixth at Trinity College Glenalmond, he was employing three men and had a small scrap business going on the side. He kept control of this empire, with the aid of a 1936 O.K. Supreme motor bike, which an old blacksmith in Harrietfield colluded to hide round the back of his shed for a small rent. At 'Coll' it became apparent that he was not always where he was supposed to be.

There is a marvellous story, told by his father, of the Warden, as the headmaster is called, who was not a popular incumbent, ringing up to complain, 'We're having great problems with your son. We just can't keep him in – he's always going off'. To which the reply was, 'Good God man! What do I pay you three hundred of pounds a term for? If you can't keep him in – lock him up!' As he delivered the punch line the old fellow's shoulders would heave with mirth.

Alec's dual life as school boy entrepreneur fell apart just before his 'A' levels. He had done the run to Newburgh one evening, to check the catch, when his thirty year old transport broke down on the way back and he was missed at roll call after Chapel. This misdemeanour could not be overlooked. It was obvious to many of the masters that he ignored their authority, and even more clear to the boys, who were really rather impressed by his exploits. Under these circumstances there was simply no argument about it, Alec was deemed subversive and had to go. It is a reflection of the attitudes at the time, when all schools were far more dictatorial, that he was treated with more austerity than if he had committed a petty crime.

The establishment was to inform Alec's parents that he could not sit his exams, even at any other school, unless he was examined by a psychiatrist first – there clearly must be something mentally abnormal about him because he did not conform to any of its values. This might have been well meaning, but it smacks of cruelty. The beatings and strictest of orders had not curbed Alec, so they chose to punish him in some other way. Whatever the motive, his parents should have raised two fingers and fought the suggestion tooth and nail, but shamed by their son's expulsion and concerned that he would get no qualifications, they dragged him off to the 'shrink'. This poor man declared that Pupil No. 168 was perfectly normal and wondered what all the fuss was about, but the system was upheld and what's more, was seen to be upheld – Crawford got the lesson he richly deserved.

He was in deep disgrace. Unceremoniously collected with his trunk and all his belongings, rugger boots and creations he had made in 'Tech', he was an outcast. 'What's Granny Sprot going to say about this?' he was chided on the way home and this concerned him more than anything because he was so fond of her. The entire family talked about him, to say nothing of all their friends. Many thought his escapades amusing, but few broke ranks and the 'worry he caused' hung over his head like a cloud. It was purposefully dissipated, however, by his favourite grandparent, who announced to all and sundry that she thought, 'it was the best thing that ever happened!' God rest Ethel Sprot. She had been a handful, too, in her day and obviously remembered what it was like to be in the dog-house.

This is the episode which labelled Alec with the epithet, 'difficult'; although now, with hindsight, I think all who cared for him would say that 'independent' would have been a better word. Feeling alone and a misfit, the experience cut hard. He never stopped seeing his parents in the following years, but their relationship became increasingly strained. In many respects, he was growing too like his father for them to get on, both had conviction and qualities of leadership, which of course made them singularly bad at accepting each other's views. I believe what infuriated the Brigadier most was that he could see Alec's potential, and yet the career which had given him, personally, the reputation he most valued, the latter had openly eschewed.

Alec was steered towards university at Aberdeen to study agriculture. The idea was that when he left, he should help run part of the estate, as his older brother, James, had recently gained a commission into the Queen's Dragoon Guards. The study kept him more or less out of trouble for three years and enabled him to get a pilot's licence and spend time with Ross's deep sea fleet, fishing off the coast of Norway. On returning to Fife, however, he soon realised that it was not what he wanted. Amidst complete exasperation, he gave up the life of a young country gentleman to train as a hard hat diver with Siebe Gorman Ltd. Competent in underwater cutting and welding, and proficient with explosives from an earlier summer job with Nuttall's, he soon managed to get his first job in marine salvage.

Enter the Newlands family. They were characterful scrap merchants who lived at Pittenweem on the East Neuk of Fife. Joseph was the father, who used to cut the top of his boots to make them more comfortable, so that they flared out like the paper garnishes that sometimes cover the ends of lamb chops. Daniel, Isaac and Michael were the sons. They came from very religious Closed Brethren stock that still flourished in the tight-knit fishing communities and were as decent and hard working folk as one could find. Recently, under the auspices of Danny, as he was called, they had ventured out onto the water and were using a small, old fishing boat, the *Vesper*, to take non ferrous metal off wrecks in the Firth of Forth. The foray into wrecking was not a long term success, but I am sure it still pleases him that he gave Alec a start.

It was not the sort of profession his parents had ever envisaged. Life was austere, he lived from hand to mouth. The diving might be fun, but it was not a 'proper job'. Alec made his way up to Barra in the Outer Hebrides with one of Danny's other divers, Peter Grosch, where they had hoped to start up a small salvage business of their own. Winter seas had called operations to a close and Peter had returned to the bright lights of the mainland to spend his share of the earnings from gathering clams, which had been their salvation, when Simon Martin turned up from Tiree. They had met only once, a couple of months before, when Simon had given Alec a lift back from Oban as they both went home for Christmas. His finances were pretty ropey too, at the time, but he remembered seeing this hitch-hiker in an old army great coat, walking along in the pouring rain and thinking he might be poor, but this guy was going to spend the night under a hedge. In fact Alec was in such dire straits that he had resorted to penning an article about his exploits for the *Dundee Evening Telegraph*, in order to raise a few pounds, memorably entitled, 'For Four Days our only Food was Porridge!'

Simon was on Barra with some cohorts to dive on the Dutch East Indiaman, the *Adelaar*. He, like Alec, had been temporarily abandoned, both having been left with the instruction to keep an eye out, in case the temptation of their respective booty being nicked by the other, or Tommy Clark's set, became too much. They were both hacked off, and getting to know each other over a pint of beer in the island pub, decided to dump their absent friends and venture off together.

They got on well right from the very start and had much in common. Simon was a son of the manse and ex-headboy of Glenalmond's arch Scottish rival, Loretto; he had been two years ahead of Alec, but they knew many of the same people and their sense of humour was equally disrespectful. Urbane, easy-going and communicative, Alec's parents became very fond of him. I think it was to their inordinate relief, that even though their son was not doing what they had wanted, at least he was in partnership with someone of whom they approved, and as the months passed they became closer to both.

Time does temper emotion. It was many years after we had been married, that I was chatting to Alec's father, and he confessed, 'Do you know, the Army said that Alec was one of the best candidates that they had ever had? They kept his scholarship open for two years after he had given it up, in case he changed his mind?' There was a pause, in which he reflected on the occasion, adding, 'and then they asked for all the money they had paid in school fees back!' and with this awful thought, he roared with laughter.

If it can ever be said that Alec settled down, it would be during that autumn of 1978, following his accidents. Having prepared and sown the arable land in the spring, leaving it to be sprayed by contractors while we were away, we came back straight into the harvest. During those first few days I was alone, I cleaned out the granary, emptying the silo bins of the previous year's remains and sweeping away the chaff. Foul water collected in some of the pits and at the bottom of the elevator, this had to be baled out. The dresser, dryers and all the grain moving equipment had to work. The day after Alec returned south, the combine began cutting and we threw ourselves body and soul into gathering our first crop. After the severity of the Shetland climate, it was a wonderfully satisfying experience to grow such produce. Load after load of plump malting barley was run back from the field in the high-sided trailers and dumped in the back pit. From here it was shifted using augers and a system of moving slatted chains. When all the machinery was going full pelt, the noise was amazing, like the rumbling of a watermill, and the air in the loft was filled with billows of dust.

We worked in our shirt sleeves, from early in the morning to late every night, cutting, carting, baling and drying. On the evening that the maltster's buyer came to inspect our product, he found us beavering away in the dim of the ground floor, our faces covered in a pale powder except where our dust masks had been. He complimented us on the quality and offered us a good price. At that point, a tired, gritty pair, we could not have been more content.

So, for a short period, the land interested Alec, wooing him back like an old flame and during those weeks, when the leaves fell and the days shortened, he recalled his past knowledge. He showed a curiosity about fertiliser rates, field drains, chemical sprays, drainage and grass seed, and became active in buying farm machinery. Then in November, there was a relapse. He went out for a couple of days diving on HMS *Argyll*, a Devonshire Class Cruiser, which lay on the Bell Rock, twelve miles off the coast. The weather conditions were not good enough to go into the water, but his mind began mulling over the possibilities.

On Christmas Eve a coaster, the three hundred and sixty ton *Fendyke*, went aground at the mouth of the Tay and that was it. When everyone else was sitting down to their Christmas lunch, Alec was organising a contract with United Towing Ltd to provide services with the *Valorous*. That was the last of him I saw until 11th January. More and more of his time was spent on the boat, until one day in spring, he announced that they were off to the *Argyll* and with a wave of the hand, said 'Goodbye, just in case I'm not back, ten tonnes of seed potatoes are arriving tomorrow'. Energetic and restored to health, the sea called him back and raising a cloud in the wake of his transit truck, he disappeared – an incurable salvor. Before the week was out he had negotiated an agreement in the name of Kilburns Salvage Company Ltd.

We were both directors of this new concern, but the sea was his main responsibility and the land, mine. I continued to work hard physically, despite expecting a baby. The pregnancy did not affect me much and was largely ignored, apart from having to zip my boilersuit over an increasingly noticeable bulge, before clambering into the cab of the crawler tractor. I had recently spread my wings into livestock by buying thirty tupped ewes, and with the aid of a one day course, neighbourly advice and a veterinary book in my hand, I had proceeded to lamb them myself. On my twenty-first birthday, I was eight months with child, managing the farm and the salmon fishing business, and had not seen my husband for over three weeks. None of it bothered me at the time. The fact was, I was so disgustingly fit that I could touch my toes right up to the day our son was born.

It would be fair to speculate that Robert might not have appeared on American Independence Day, had I not run round the Scurr Whins with my young sheep dog, Flossy, in the early morning, rounding up the lambs. Delivering several fishboxes of salmon and seatrout to a wholesaler around lunchtime, I had felt uncomfortable, but there was getting less and less clearance behind the steering wheel and I thought it just the squash. It was only on the way back that I realised my labour had begun. This was remarkably inconvenient. I had planned to get the fishermen's wages at the bank and if I did not, there would be grumbling and teasing in equal amounts. The matter was so personal, I could not face the humiliation and decided to press on.

As I got out of the van, there was an unmistakable sensation, which warned me that the birth was far nearer than I had supposed. 'What am I going to do now?'

I had a choice. I could panic and drive myself directly to hospital in Dundee, or keep my composure and pray that I would not make an exhibition of myself.

Standing at the counter, the queue seemed to go on forever and I shuffled from foot to foot, anxious. Eventually came my turn. My mouth said, 'May I cash this cheque?' but my mind demanded with the gruffness of a robber with a shorn-off shotgun, 'Hand over the money, quick!'

The methodical pleasantries seemed to take an age.

'How would you like it?'

'It's written on the back.'

'Thank you very much, Mrs Crawford.'

'Thank you,' and I grabbed the £1000 and made my getaway out of the doors of the Bank of Scotland in Cupar, as promptly as any felon.

I was relieved to find Alec still at home, because it was windy. He had been hay making in the Cottar's House field and accompanied me to the maternity unit, where a large, healthy boy was delivered with a brief, but respectable interval to spare.

The funniest part was the next morning when he came back to see me. All the other husbands bore small gifts or flowers, but mine had all the catch receipts, with the red book for making out the fishermen's wages slips in his hand.

'Why have you brought those?'

'You're so much quicker at doing them than me, I thought that you could work them out.'

With Robert only hours old in the plastic 'goldfish bowl' beside me, my female view was simple, I had done more than my bit and retorted peevishly. 'Alec, I've just had a baby . I really don't want to know.'

To which he looked at me in amazement, clearly wondering how I could be so irrational.

'But you're just lying on the bed doing nothing, much of the time. It will only take you a few minutes to do the calculations, but it will take me hours.'

I was unmoved.

Alec, ever industrious, was nonetheless very proud of his son, who, within days, was strapped to my chest and out and about in the fields.

For those summer months our lives went on helter skelter, but under ever more incompatible regimes. Alec was subordinate to the moon and wind, I was controlled by the sun, and rain. His day had to be flexible, based on the tide times which altered each day, so that he could be away before dawn one day and back after midnight the next. There was no knowing where he would be, or when he would arrive. Neither was there any demarcation for weekends. My programme on the other hand, had to be more or less regular, revolving as it did around Robert and the Agricultural Wages Board, Hours and Schedules of Pay, and his old, sit-up-and-beg pram, was parked on many a grassy knoll as I wandered off for a few minutes to check the sheep. We had virtually no social life and the odd dinner party I threw was the cue for some unforeseen incident. Alec would arrive back, just as our guests were about to go, and enthral them with his tale of what had happened, while I was like a limp rag from having not only delayed the meal, but entertaining on my own for hours.

It is probably because of the daily strains she brought and the fact that I was never actively involved in the lifting work, that I began to dislike the wreck of *Argyll*. For Alec, on the other hand, she was a turning point. Facing the problem of carrying out regular heavy lifts, he considered the methods he had developed over the years and found them wanting. Accordingly, he began to experiment and challenge his technical approach. Making this the point at which he graduated from being a salvage diver into becoming a salvage engineer.

HMS *Argyll* was built by Scotts of Greenock and completed in 1906 as one of six sisters, the most famous being the *Hampshire* on which Lord Kitchener and over six hundred men were lost. Each was built in a yard around the country at the cost of £850,000, as part of the response to the German Navy Laws of 1898 and 1900, which aimed to construct a great battle fleet. The First Lord had warned the Cabinet in October of 1902 that, 'the German navy is being built up from the point of view of a war with us' and the same year, all their keels were laid. The writing for the 1914–18 conflict was on the wall.

The vessels had a maximum speed of twenty-two knots and *Jane's Fighting Ships* of the period rated their importance just a little less than the battleships *Royal Oak* and *Hood*. Each of the Devonshire Class Cruisers was armed with an array of guns, ranging from three to twelve inches in diameter and two submerged torpedo tubes graced the bow.

For defence, there was a belt of armoured steel amidships. This nickel chrome alloy came in moulded slabs just over ten feet wide. These were staggered in position like bricks in a wall and protected three-quarters of the waterline, being bolted to the hull with a layer of teak wood in between, which acted as both sandwich and cushion. The thickness of the plate varied according to its purpose, increasing from two inches at the bow to six inches amidships, where it shielded the vitals. The decks also had a two-inch reinforcing belt and the guns were encased in six-inch housing. The conning tower with all its important communications was fortified like a bastion at the fore end, with metal twice as thick. The total weight of all this material was a phenomenal 6665 tons. In the event of the *Argyll's* loss it proved worse than useless. For instead of being attacked and sunk by the enemy, she met her end by steaming directly into a charted reef, on which her added protection held her firmly down – not very dissimilar to the *Oceanic*.

Steaming south from Scapa Flow to Rosyth in the Firth of Forth, on 27th October 1915, she had had to bypass a suspected minefield, seventy-five miles east of Kinnaird's Head. There was bright moonlight and she had been zigzagging two degrees either side of her course and travelling at a speed of twelve knots. This was calculated to take her seven miles east of the Bell Rock, which though marked with a lighthouse was unlit because of the war. Captain James Tancred's report to his superiors of what happened next, lays out the sequence of events and is all the more believable because he sounds so very fed up:

> At 8.00 p.m. the moon being obscured, ship was steadied on her middle course, speed reduced to 15 knots, speed was again increased to 16 knots at 1.09 a.m. 28th October.
>
> There were rain squalls during the middle watch, but visibility between squalls was good. At 3.00 a.m. I came on deck out of my Deck Cabin, where I had been sitting in my chair, and found it raining heavily with a rising wind and visibility appeared to me about one mile.
>
> At 3.40 a.m. Lieutenant Commander Glen ordered sounding party which did not get to their stations till the morning watch. At about 4.25 a.m. I heard the hail, 'Sailing ship right ahead'. At the same time, the Officer of the Watch gave the order, 'Port 20. Hard a Port. Full Speed Ahead Port. Stop Starboard', and reported a lighthouse right ahead.
>
> Lieutenant Commander Page, who was Officer in Charge of Deck, and who was on the Lower Bridge, ran to the Upper Bridge and gave the

order, 'Full Speed Astern Starboard'. I followed him onto the Upper Bridge, and gave the order, 'Full Speed Astern Both'. The ship struck forward and the following signal was made 'Argyll' to All Ships:-
'Argyll' ashore on the Bell Rock.

Perhaps I ought not to feel sorry for this man, especially as Jellicoe recommended a court martial for both him and Glen, but I always imagine him as a decent officer, who trusted his men. Sitting in his duffel coat, with his feet wedged against the desk, and a mug of something hot in his hand, he would be relieved that they had skirted the minefield. There was perhaps some comfort in the fact that the moon had gone and they were less visible, after all the *Pathfinder* had been torpedoed off Dunbar and that was not at all far away. He was probably pondering their entrance to Rosyth and hoping that the channel had been properly swept. After Orkney he was looking forward to getting ashore at this base and having a drink with friends he had not seen for a while. Maybe he was contemplating his leave to visit loved ones … then all hell broke loose and crunch!

Owing to the speed at which she struck, there was a considerable impact, but none of the sailors was seriously hurt. The lighthouse keepers, too, would have got a bit of a surprise at their large and unexpected intruder. Within half an hour it became evident that the *Argyll* was badly damaged; she would rip her bottom as the tide fell and there was not a chance of saving her. Four hundred of the men were taken off by the destroyer, *Hornet*, which bravely came alongside and the rest were ferried in the ship's boats to the *Jackal* and a trawler which lay astern. All secret books and documents were saved and the fires were extinguished in the stokeholds. As many of the guns, and their mountings were saved as possible, along with ammunition and personal effects, but any attempt to salvage her was postponed to the spring in the hope that she would last the winter. It proved vain. The seas claimed and broke her, and due to her accessibility, she became well picked over the years by piecemeal salvors.

Before he even surveyed the wreck, Alec knew that the propellers, condensers and torpedo tubes and all the most obvious fittings were long since gone. 'You're wasting your time. There's nothing worth having left, ' he was told knowingly by local fishermen, but he was not so sure.

When he arrived on the site with the *Valorous* that first morning in mid-April, there was a heavy swell running. This necessitated a swim to the lighthouse in order to consult the three keepers, there. Few knew the habits of the reef better, as they spent months overlooking it at a time. Simon, who had come along for the excitement, decided to kit up, too, leaving Bill White, a new employee, at anchor, The men were pleased to be consulted and over a cup of tea, they spoke of their observations. 'There's always less motion on the ebb tide. The bow of the *Argyll* lies about fifty yards off,' and one of them pointed out the small, west facing window. 'It's stern lies almost directly towards the mouth of the Tay and one of the big forward guns shows at low water. It always looks quite sinister pointing its barrel out to sea, as if it were still ready for the enemy.'

'Are you going to use explosives?' another asked, rhetorically. 'Well, if you are, just make sure that you don't use too much, because some of the lads before you used to make our tea cups rattle up here!'

Taking the hint and promising to bring some newspapers and fresh milk on their next trip, the ex-partners made their descent and set off to explore the shallow waters of the wreck for themselves.

A dappled light filtered down from the surface, bathing the scene in tones of green. On the bottom, the shingly sand was littered with chunks of rusting steel, like pieces of bold, abstract sculpture. They came across the boilers and the triple expansion engines. In order to obtain a closer inspection, Alec cut at the roots of the brown, glaucous weed that clung to the main bearings. Clearing it out of the way with a sweep of his arm, he could see that they were covered in concretion. There was no doubt to their integrity. None of the brass bearings, with their valuable white-metal liners had been removed. Grinning, with teeth clenched around his demand valve, Alec gave Simon the thumbs up sign and signalled to the starboard side amidships, where he would examine the armoured steel.

Here, the plates were eleven feet long, by four-and-a-half feet deep, and six inches thick. They had fallen outwards and lay hidden and partially buried in their natural surrounds. On the port side, it was the other way round. The metal had collapsed inward and the two-inch armoured deck had caved into it, lying higgledy-piggledy. It seemed rather incredible, looking at the corroded jumble to think that it would soon be purposeful, again. Some would go for sensitive scanning equipment, as it had been smelted prior to the atmosphere being contaminated with nuclear fallout. The rest would go to make stainless steel in all sorts of forms; valves, wire, tools and possibly even knives and forks. Whichever the product, it would leave a good profit and when they returned to the surface, and clambered into the inflatable, Simon gave his congratulations. 'Not bad for a wreck that's been completely looted,' and with this they both had a quiet laugh.

Before July was out and Robert not four weeks old, Alec had all sixteen main bearings, worth £40,000. Following his experience on the *Oceanic*, his blasting had become so skilful, that all but one could have been put back into service again. His charges were so small and precise that the lighthouse keepers never felt a thing, and as the summer progressed he had pipes, fittings, generators and all the thrusts and eccentrics. Days were spent in preparation work, 'banging' the armour plates. Soon they were recovered and began to be amassed.

He was not content though. As heavy lifts, the plates were still being slung under the *Valorous*, exactly the same way as they had retrieved the bosses from the *Oceanic*, except that a set of four chains and clamp took the load instead of a wire strop. The method worked, but it was far too slow for hundreds of tons and on the odd occasion that one of the clamps slipped, or the load became unevenly balanced, there were problems. If Alec was going to make big money on the *Argyll*, he would have to improve the recovery rate and this meant change. Fortuitously for him, it was just as we were beginning dressing our disastrous potato crop – the one he had suggested we should plant before disappearing off on the *Valorous* – that he began the next phase of his plans, as this meant collecting *Dunoon Boat* from the west coast.

To accomplish technical goals, a man like Alec dreams and sometimes his mind thinks far ahead. He had known for years that he wanted a steel-hulled boat, because they were so much more robust and had religiously scanned the *Fishing News* for candidates, just in case. As far back as the first winter we were married, I can remember going with him to see a small trawler, owned by a thin, pale undertaker in Barrow-in-Furness. Heaven knows how it came to be his property, but we never found out as he had wanted too much money, and so the search carried on.

Just before we returned to Shetland, the spring *Trygg* was lost, the opportunity arose to purchase a bath-like torpedo recovery boat. She was ugly to look at, but being deep drafted and dumpy, this ex-US Navy Box 'L' hull had a good grip on the water for lifting over the side. Alec concluded the deal for £2500 and drew up rough plans for her, but little else. She sat on the stocks at the back of a boatyard in Dunoon, seemingly forgotten with grass growing out of her wheelhouse, for the next three and a half years, and so it was that she became known as the *Dunoon Boat*, because she and this town on the River Clyde became synonymous.

Towing her back through the Caledonian Canal was a long, wet and miserable haul during its short operational day of 9 a.m. to 4 p.m., which corresponded exactly with the hours of light. A bridge would not open here, a lock gate stuck there. The whole scene was saturated with water, clouds wreathed the desolate brown hillside and there was a constant squally rain. It took five days in all to make the sixty mile journey from Corpach to Inverness. Venturing out into the North Sea, matters got no better, a winter sea and bad easterly forecast made them take refuge in Buckie. Consequently, it was not until the 20th December that the new addition arrived off Tayport, but Alec was not deterred in any way. In fact, he was just getting into his stride. The very next day he bought what was left of HMS *Argyll*, so that we had two thirds of our fleet on the surface and the remainder beneath the water.

Work on converting the *Dunoon Boat* began whilst most other people still had their hangovers from Hogmanay. The steel deck housing, which took up about half of the aft deck smacked of too many crew with too little to do and was unceremoniously removed with a burning torch. The engine had been taken out by its previous owner for overhaul and would have to be put back. Drawing the tailshaft to see if it was scored, gave considerable difficulty as the propeller had been damaged and had to be machined.

Towards the end of January, enough preparation work, cutting and welding had been completed to launch the 'blob'. This was an ex-Admiralty buoy, the shape and colour of a thick, black 'Licorice Allsorts'. It was fitted like an outrigger on the starboard side and would be attached to the boat through the hull using two 'I' beams. Its function was to give extra buoyancy when lifting over the side. The forces it produced were colossal and so the body of an old crane, minus its tracks was placed amidships and bolted into 'I' beams to help hold them down. A small wheelhouse, taken off an old trawler, the *Lincoln Castle*, was placed aft and work began on fitting the engine. As the days began to lengthen the intensity of work reached fever pitch, as if it was spurred on by some primeval urge. All hands were diverted to salvage, including Charlie Barron who was an excellent mechanic, even though he was supposed to be working for me on the farm.

The winter for me had been hard. Day after day had been spent in the draughty, unheated tattie shed and yet we had had ware potatoes sent back from almost every wholesale outlet in the north of Britain, because they had been damaged by slugs. Practically every tuber had a neat, drill-like hole in it and the bagged heap for selling was being rapidly dwarfed by the pile that had been rejected and would have to be fed to cattle. Every time the phone rang, it was the merchant saying that another load was coming back from Gateshead or Glasgow, and we would have to pay for the transport and all the cost and labour of grading them again. I had also bought more sheep and built the flock up to seventy-five ewes. What's more, as crazy as it sounds, I was pregnant again.

Everything was so busy. In the week there were people everywhere, orders being given, bits being made, the lambing had started, so that there was not enough time to question the way we were carrying on, working flat out from morning to night. I realised that there was something amiss the night Alec arrived home at nine o'clock, having driven the enormous thirty-two ton Coles crane he had just bought all the way from Peterhead. It was a Saturday, everyone else was off. He had been away for three days, much longer than expected because these second hand purchases are never without their problems. The brakes had seized and the master cylinder had to be freed. The engine had missed going up hills and the fastest he had been able to go was twenty miles an hour. It had been frigid inside the cab.

Arriving home cold and tired, but justifiably pleased with himself, he was quite put out to find the cottage in total darkness. The door was shut, the stove was out and there was no meal waiting – the place was empty and soulless. I was up in the Flagstaff field on the hill, where I had been for the past three hours, struggling in the lights of the Land Rover to deliver a pair of mispresented twins – one of which had died. Robert was being looked after by a cousin. When eventually we got him home, there was hardly time to kindle an uncharitable fire and produce something to eat from the dwindling stock in the cupboard, because I had not had time to shop in days, before it was time to go to bed.

'It's been a hell of a journey and I was looking forward to you being home,' Alec informed me as we both shivered for warmth beneath the covers.

'What am I supposed to do?' I replied. 'I did not know when you were arriving. Besides, I can't be everywhere – I've already asked Charlie to do the midnight to six a.m. shift!'

About a fortnight later I fell ill. The weather had turned bitterly cold with sleet and snow making the lambing miserable and the initial response from all the men was that I was skiving and just could not take the pace. I was made to feel pathetic. Lying in my bed, a pool of sweat on my chest and hardly able to lift my head off the pillow, work proceeded on the derrick for the *Dunoon Boat* in the yard and I was left alone. I could not eat and could hardly drink. Having cut myself off completely by both living and working entirely in a male world, I had no close female friends. Alec's parents were away. There was no neighbour to bump into, who might notice I was not around. No old schoolfriend who might just call in or phone out of the blue. I was isolated in my rural cottage far from any observant or sympathetic eye. No one to suggest that my temperature ought to be taken – if I had been an engine I would never have been allowed to get into such a state.

On the fourth day, well over half way through my term I went into spontaneous labour. The doctor was called. I was packed off immediately to hospital, but it was all too late and our son was stillborn. The whole experience was painful and bloody, and the midwife took him immediately away. I needed a transfusion and was given morphine, but that was only the start. My condition steadily worsened until I was delirious and that night I nearly died.

As a child, I had always been terrified by death and yet when I knew it could be waiting for me, it was not fear I felt, but profound disappointment. I remember dimly, through a haze, recognising Alec standing beside my bed and knowing that I might never see him again. Barely conscious, I struggled to make sense of the notion; part of me felt complete for having known his love and reciprocated it; part of me felt sad that it would not continue; but what upset me most was not being able to see Robert grow up, he was only nine months old and there was so much I would miss. Yet I trusted that Alec would bring him up properly.

Apart from thinking the registrar was loopy because, at some stage he asked me, 'Were you at the theatre last night?' and I could not conceive how a doctor would expect someone, prostrate and in a surgical gown, could possibly be out on the town enjoying themselves. I do not remember anything else for quite some while. I had caught something awful and unsuspected from the sheep. It was little known at the time that I was running such dangers, or I certainly would never have taken the risk. An infection invaded my whole body, attacking kidneys and liver, and killing my blood cells. It was not until my face, lips and hands began visibly swelling that alarm bells began to ring for the medical staff and I was given massive doses of penicillin. During those three days and two nights, when my life hung in the balance, a battle went on that devastated me physically and seared away almost every ounce of spare flesh.

When they let me out of hospital a week later, it was Simon who came to pick me up, as Alec was out on the wreck. It was the start of the season, he had been out the day before, but this was his first opportunity to dive. I did not mind at the time, because I was just so relieved to get home. The next day was a Friday and he went out again ... and the next day ... and the next. I remember stopping him once, as he was about to go out the door and asking him if he would stay. I just wanted to be with him for a short while, alone. I had lost our baby. And there was so much hurt inside me, I needed so much to tell him how desperately sorry I was, but I just could not get the words out.

He was not harsh, or unkind in his words, but he refused. 'The weather is good and the men depend on me. I have to get on. Anyway, what can I do? Your mother is here to look after you.'

I wept. I had never put many demands on him. Never asked him to choose between salvage and me before. How could he do this to me? Ambition and responsibility versus biology and emotion. It was an age-old clash.

Alec's going cut me deeply, however, events pass and priorities change. The intervening years have taken their toll. He has mellowed and become more thoughtful, and I am the one who is hardened and less sympathetic.

Nevertheless, at the time, the schism made me accept that there is a fundamental breach of understanding about the most important things in life, that can separate even the closest of men and women.

8

SUB-ZERO

The sheets of armour plate began to multiply at the pier at Tayport and on the farm, like piles of neatly sliced brown bread with the crusts cut off. Replacing the *Dunoon Boat* engine proved more troublesome than had been foreseen, as its bed had gone out of alignment when it was on the stocks. Alec, pragmatic as ever, decided just to forget about propulsion, towing his new lifting vessel out with the *Valorous*, like a dumb barge.

This determination to make things work, with its courage to sweep aside aspirations as well as time and money spent, has always been one of his outstanding qualities as an engineer. Too many people strive for absolute perfection and never get their designs through the prototype stage. How many times had I heard him tell me, 'I don't care what it looks like, just as long as it works.' Results were his only goal and often, he would get them by sheer cussedness alone.

Simon, who was so easy-going that he could not have been more different, had recently married the writer and broadcaster, Alison Macleay, and was enjoying domesticity. He still came out to the wreck, but not as frequently as before, although he could always be relied upon to give a hand if Alec was stuck. There were other changes, as Bill White had moved onto another job, and we were joined by a contemporary who had married into the family.

Charlie Butterworth was tall and wiry with tousled golden hair, and a beard bleached white at the extremities by the salt and sun. His skin, which was weather-beaten, completed a picture of health. With such colouring, complexion and an affinity for the sea, it was hardly surprising that he was often mistaken for a Norwegian. Norse-like he might have been in looks, but not in behaviour, for he was immensely polite to the point that it was painful. In intellect, university don was more his style. This was clearly emphasised when he put on his round, steel-rimmed glasses. He was the only chap we ever employed who used to read Latin prose while we were steaming out to the wreck, screwing up his eyes every now and again to change his focus to the horizon. This love of books was no show, for he had an insatiable desire for them and digested even the driest material. 'What's that about Charlie?' someone would ask. Putting it down courteously, he would begin, 'It's very interesting ...' and go on to explain without a hint of sarcasm, as if addressing an equal. One of his mannerisms used to be to twist the corner of his moustache when speaking seriously and so on occasions like this, it would end up with a curl fit for the wickedest of 'penny dreadful' villains.

He was not only clever, he was fun. His broad smile was his most disarming feature and this combination of brains and non-conformism made him as much a misfit as the rest of us. A good degree in botany had lead to teaching in Shetland for a while. This he hated, soon giving it up for running a small fishing boat with his wife, Daphne, who was one of Alec's numerous cousins. He revelled in this, but his real passion was mountaineering. Awkward at chit-chat and a disaster at parties, he would shift in embarrassment from foot to foot, on the cliff face however he was so self-assured, there was hardly a moment's hesitation. We all had a soft spot for him and it was shocking when, in 1988, he died potholing. He had been around at all the major events of our lives, such as our marriage on Foula, the children's births and subsequent christenings, and had always been so fit, that I would have put a bet on him sharing old age. Like many of his friends, we felt robbed when he was gone.

Soon after he began work on the *Argyll*, it became the norm for just the two of them to work the wreck together, Alec would dive and Charlie would operate the crane. Like the *Oceanic*, the blasting work was done beforehand over a number of tides, so that a considerable number of plates were freed. In this way often five or six of them could be loaded in one tide.

The hook would be secured underwater and the instruction to lift given. The crane engine would hum away as the slack was taken up. Suddenly water droplets would spring from the lifting wire as it was pulled tight, and simultaneously the machine would toil under its load, growling deeply and belching out black smoke. Within moments, the Admiralty buoy, which was positioned aft on the starboard side, would be partially forced into the water as the plate came off the seabed and it absorbed the *Dunoon Boat's* list. The whole hull would tremble perceptibly under the strain, just as one's hand shudders trying to push an inflated ball beneath the surface.

At such a shallow depth, it would be only moments before the steel shape was revealed in the daylight, glistening and sharp edged. As it was raised above the height of the gunwale, it would rotate gently, free from restraint. There was always a delicate moment, a split second, when the fourteen ton weight was extended and high up. Judgement at this point was extremely fine. If the derrick was too far out, then stability would be rapidly compromised. If it was too close in, the plate could swing against the hull and perforate it. Charlie, biting his lip in concentration, would use his innate sense of balance to measure the situation, gauging the slightly jerky motion before committing himself. Once he began to slew the weight into the hold, there could be no hesitation, or else the momentum would swing the plate to port like a pendulum, and they would conceivably capsize. There was always an involuntary pause in breath as the load shot diagonally downwards, to clang against the far hatch combing, before coming to rest in the bottom of the hold. Then came the inevitable sigh of relief.

There was only one really frightening moment. This was when the brake failed one day when a sheet was suspended high in the air and Charlie had no option but to drop it back into the sea. The rigging blocks, which had a reduction of five to one for lifting, now acted in reverse. For every foot the plate descended, they had to pay out five feet of wire. The result was spectacular. The winch barrel in front of his cab paid out at an alarming rate, rattling menacingly and accelerating with every split second. Impotent to stop it, he did the only sensible thing and dived for cover behind the wheelhouse. Not an instant too soon, as the momentum tore the end of the hoist wire out of the cast steel winch barrel, shattering it in the process.

Alec, who was finning in the water, was lucky not to be in the line of fire as pieces of shrapnel, spinning like medieval weapons, traced a graceful arc in the air and landed further than the forward gun, a considerable distance away. It could have been a nasty accident, but it was not, and in the lapse of time it took to tow the *Dunoon Boat* back to Tayport, they both agreed with a laugh that the event had been really rather impressive.

By the beginning of November 1981, we had exported over 1000 tons of armour to West Germany, and sold over 500 tons of scrap steel and fifty tons of non-ferrous on the home market. Financially, the operation had been incredibly successful, but for many months Alec had been worried about where to go next. Even with our running costs, the *Argyll* was the last viable commercial wreck within diving depth around the British Isles. There were another two armoured cruisers, the *Monmouth* on Lundy in the Bristol Channel, and the *Drake* off Northern Ireland; but we were not permitted to recover either, as the former was in a newly designated marine conservation area and the latter was under the control of the Ministry of Defence, which was concerned about the security implications of us using explosives.

Faced with such an unpromising future, we discussed giving up salvage altogether and considered the alternatives. There were few indeed. Alec had always said he would never be satisfied with farming. It was not just that our acreage was small and could only provide a subsistence living, the work failed to give him a challenge. I knew this to be true. I had never seen him so *piano*, as the time he ploughed the Flagstaff field with the old red David Brown tractor. It had no cab and he huddled, pinched and cold, inside his buff coloured duffel coat, like a sack of potatoes that has sagged. To insist that this lifestyle would be his only future would have been short-sighted. It would not have destroyed him, because one day he would simply announce he had had enough and search for something else. Similarly, although he had recently qualified as a time-served British Deck Officer, he had no desire to work for a large established company, be it in marine salvage or anything else. 'I want to go on,' he told me. Besides, for four years, ever since he had visited Risdon Beazley's vessel, the *Droxford*, during the winter break on the *Oceanic*, his imagination had been fired by other dreams.

This large, purpose-built ship had just returned to Southampton from her first season off the coast of Tunisia, lifting tin. Alec had been given an introduction to her master, Bill Ross, a courteous, dark-haired Scot, who had been happy to give a young, aspiring salvor a guided tour. The exact date was 8th December 1977. At this point, Risdon Beazley Ltd were without doubt the world leaders in cargo recovery. They had dominated this specialist field, unswervingly, some might say, ruthlessly, ever since the Second World War. There were tales of them intimidating would-be competitors who tried to muscle into the lucrative waters off the Scillies and south-west Peninsula. Rumour had it also that Risdon Beazley, the founder, had never bothered about confidentiality agreements with his crews in the early days, but would inform them darkly, 'breathe a word of this to anybody and I'll break both your legs.' Whether this grape-vine gossip was true or false, really did not matter; the effect of the company's success was to raise it to the status of a living legend. Since 1947 they had salvaged over sixty wrecks, lifting metals that ranged from gold and nickel to wolfram and bismuth. The *Glenartney*, to which they were to return in the spring, lay at the unprecedented depth of 300 metres.

Accordingly, it was an honour for Alec to look over the *Droxford* and it was with keen expectation that he stepped down from the train, on that grey winter day, feeling the raw blast of the wind off the Solent. In the event, he could not have been more surprised as the flagship of his imagination, turned out to be obsolete.

She was around 1300 tons gross and very old fashioned in her lines, much resembling the Aberdeen-built side trawlers that used to fish for cod off Iceland. This did not matter, but the fact that she was steam-powered did.

She burnt nine tonnes of heavy oil per day, just lifting onsite. Additionally, her crew was enormous, being at minimum thirty-five. In a period of spiralling fuel and wage bills, there was no doubt that she was uneconomic, as vast quantities of metal would have to be salved simply to cover her running costs. Her technology, too, was outdated; there was no remote control; all the underwater work was directed using a telephone by a man sealed inside a one atmosphere observation chamber; and on the surface, each of the six mooring winches had to have its own dedicated operator.

At first, Alec could barely conceal his disappointment, and it was only as he stood on deck at the end of his tour, thanking his host, that his vision cleared. With good design and modern equipment, the *Droxford* could be replaced by a much smaller vessel, one that could operate at a fraction of the expense. This inspiration was to alter the rest of our lives.

It lay subdued all through the *Oceanic*, because Simon was never as keen. It was only after we had founded Kilburns Salvage Company together, that he began to get free rein. It took our final year on the *Argyll* to accumulate sufficient money, after taking over all the assets in Crawford & Martin, to begin experimenting. We bought a cargo of pig iron which lay in a sunken steamer, the *Malin Head*, in the shallow of Gill's Bay. This wide, crescent shaped indent is in an exposed position, just west of John o' Groats. The metal on the wreck was not particularly valuable, but it was easily accessible. With an ill-suppressed excitement that was undiminished by hours of work, a grab and hydraulic power pack was rigged up on the *Dunoon Boat* and she was towed north for her new task.

The trials were an absolute disaster. The bars of iron lay in neat rows in the hold. Any cathodic protection on the hull, which might have helped preserve them, had disappeared long ago. Consequently, everything that was ferrous was degenerating electrolytically and the metal we were after had long since fused together into a solid mass. The grab simply would not bite into it. Explosive charges made little difference, blocks of only four or five bars would come up and sometimes small broken bits. Welding sharper points into the grab improved the recovery rate, but even still the result was lamentable and the total result for a week's effort was only twenty tonnes.

Alec, however, was not daunted. He returned to finish the *Argyll* over the summer, but all the time his mind was elsewhere and as he brought in the armour plate, he wrangled with the problem of making cargo recovery economic. Books, like *Seventy Fathoms Down* and *The Egypt's Gold*, by David Scott, were read again and again. These human accounts chronicled the painful development of remote lifting by the Italian company, SORIMA, in the late 1920s. In fact, it was they who had pioneered the

'Eye and Tool', the system of observation chamber and two-wire grab, which had only just pensioned off with the demise of Risdon Beazley Ltd. Technology had literally stood still for sixty years. Here we were, knowing that there was tremendous scope for development, but having to catch up on half a century of stagnation. No wonder we had such a learning curve, as there had been no improvement from which we could benefit.

By this time we had been moved into the farmhouse for about six months. The upheaval had not been great, as we had only transplanted ourselves to the other side of the steading and our possessions were few. Even after five years of marriage, we owned more spares and repairs than chattels and furniture, as they were so much more useful. The battered refectory table, which I had never liked, was set down in the kitchen. It has stayed ever since. Now it has been the focus of so much family life, from breakfast to birthday parties; the setting for so much momentous business discussion; the place where Alec has rested his drawing board for so many winters; that even though I could afford to replace it, I choose not to. It represents so much that is simple and good.

The joins in our interests were so seamless, especially in those early days when the children were all small, that we never saw any paradox of having such a domestic 'board room', Its benefit was a solid fuel range. Its downside an obstacle course of toys spread across the floor. Besides, it was the more conventional of our venues. We often held directors' meetings in the bath, on the condition that Alec despite being chairman put up with the taps. This sort of intimacy was not just physical. We used to talk and talk, invariably about salvage. I would be instructed about engineering design and the finer technicalities of some piece of equipment or other. We used to spend so long, that the water would repeatedly chill and have to be topped up with warm.

One evening, amidst the stirrings of winter, there was a familiar scene that could have been mirrored by any young household. I put a mug of coffee for us both down on the table and collapsed on to one of the hard, wooden chairs beside Alec in a state of maternal exhaustion. One blond infant was tucked up in his cot upstairs and a new, down-haired baby, slept in his Moses basket on the sofa. The chores had been done, and for a few brief moments our lives were our own. Despite the dark and cold, the curtains were open, as we had a wonderful view across the wide river, and it was always spectacular to glimpse the iridescent lights of suburbia, far removed, as they winked through the lanky geraniums on the window ledge.

Alec looked tired. He was no busier than usual, but had been preoccupied in thought for weeks.

'Made any progress?' I asked.

'No. I've got to get something sorted out for next season. We could try and get some more armour from the *Argyll*, I suppose, but there's not much left and it's all difficult. The *Dunoon Boat* has served its purpose, but towing it around is hopeless. There's no future in that, we've got to work deeper and go further offshore if we're going to go into cargo recovery. It's our only avenue, but we need a proper vessel.'

'Seen anything you have liked?'

'No. Not really and there's absolutely no question of affording a new one. The plans we had drawn up by the naval architect had a cost estimate of one million pounds – and that's without any lifting gear. We're going to have to get a second-hand one somewhere, but I can't find anything suitable on the market, as yet.'

I slipped my slim fingers into his strong hand and pressed gently in reassurance, smooth against rough. Like the diving signal for attention, the message was echoed and he smiled slightly, but appreciatively.

He continued, affirming his thoughts as much to himself as me, as if it helped to hear them spoken. 'There are still a number of deeper wrecks around the British Isles that have considerable quantities of non-ferrous cargo on them. I've got their positions and know they're a commercial proposition given the right technology.'

This hastily noted information he had scrawled in green ink across pieces of lined foolscap, and were hidden tantalisingly in a file. But we both knew their forfeit. We would have to spend all the money we had accrued. It would be the classic gamble of quitting whilst we were ahead, or betting on an even bigger jackpot – stick or twist?

During the next hour or so, we went through his rough sketches and drawings again. Days, weeks and months of thought had gone into his plans for updating SORIMA's working methods, using equipment developed for the North Sea oil industry. The investment would be enormous. His ideas were unproven. No one else used an electro-mechanical grab and it would be a tremendous risk. We could lose everything, the *Valorous* the *Dunoon Boat*, the house, the farm.

Nursing mothers are not deemed to be adventurous, but I had no doubt where the future lay. It was for our new son, Drew, as much as Robert, that we had to take the chance of creating a unique business. The farm would never support us. What is more, I did not even enjoy my work on it anymore. Livestock husbandry, especially the lambing, had been the only real skill I had and since losing the previous baby, my only dealings with the ewes had been on sufferance.

My life had got worse, not better. Simon used to administer Crawford & Martin, and now I dealt with the salvage company on top of all the farm paperwork. Plus there was the salmon business from May to August. Recently, it had seemed that I had all the boring things to do.

'I'm just responsible for all the things you've no interest in,' I had told Alec flatly some weeks before, when I was particularly fed up. He denied this, of course, despite it being absolutely true.

Heartbreak and drudgery left me to hate our time on the *Argyll*. For me, the wreck had become a curse and would always be synonymous with personal loss. It had trapped me in a way of life I would never have chosen. From being a free spirit in Shetland, I had been confined to Kilburns and a rigid social structure in Fife. I hardly went to sea anymore and as much as I was attached to the property, and wanted to bring up my family securely there, I could not contemplate either me or them being hemmed in by the boundaries of county life for ever. Salvage might spell 'danger', but it also offered 'opportunity'. The latter secured my support for Alec's new venture. I, too, wanted a share in something challenging, despite the uncertainty it would bring. We agreed fully on the course to take.

'If only I could find the right boat!' Alec exclaimed in frustration.

'Oh, something will turn up,' I reminded him.

People talk about predestination, but I do not believe in it. To my mind fate is a flow of consequences that can be diverted by one's own actions and what happened next convinces me of this.

When Alec went up to the *Malin Head*, it cost us time and money for little return. His base, albeit briefly, was Lyness, on Orkney. In the near deserted harbour lay a burnt-out fishing boat with its wheelhouse cut off. It was built of steel, measured about twenty-six metres in length, with a generous beam and an attractive transom stern. Despite fire damage and neglect, it looked structurally sound. Curious, and with little to do one afternoon, he and Charlie slipped aboard and had a scout round. There was no major damage to the hull or the machinery in the engine room and Charlie remarked, casually, but in all seriousness, the way that friends do who really know you well, 'Here's your recovery ship, Alec.'

'Yes,' he agreed, already seeing her take shape in his mind's eye, 'she'd be ideal.'

They began making enquiries about K 508, the *Responsive*, immediately. Orcadians, like all islanders store information about boats as a matter of course, and so it needed only a couple of conversations to establish the vessel's history. She had been launched as the *Claben* in 1968, as Scotland's first purpose-built purse seine netter for Jim Lovey of Peterhead, and after changing hands several times and names once, she had caught fire off Shetland, where she was declared a write-off. The insurers paid out £270,000 on the loss and she remained tied up in Lerwick until Angus

Sinclair, a previous owner, bought her back for a much lesser sum. It was he who was keeping her in Lyness. He had cut off the wheelhouse to refit her for 'the mackerel' off the West Coast. Alec contacted him, but he had no wish to sell and this came as a setback.

Alec forgot about her for a long while and pursued other avenues somewhat in vain. Most of the steel boats available were much smaller, at about twenty-one metres in length and were going for anything up to £75,000. By early December, when he had searched hard and not found another hull he liked so much, he contacted the owner again, just to see how he was faring. There was always the chance that he might have lost the impetus for putting her back to sea and if this was the case Alec was going to offer £45,000. The greeting he got on the telephone was an astonished one.

'News travels fast,' said Angus Sinclair, 'who told you that the *Responsive* just sank?'

'Nobody,' came the reply, equally intrigued, 'what happened to her?'

The explanation was a tale of further misfortune. Only two days before, during a very low tide, she had caught a trawl gallow under the open structure of the concrete pier. All too soon, water found its way through the scuppers. With the wheelhouse removed flush to the deck, it was not long before it poured down into the engine room exhaust, which was just a hole. How rapidly she filled up no one knew, but by the time she was spotted it was too late. As she disappeared beneath the water, she broke her ropes and had just sufficient buoyancy to drift off a little and sink. Her bow was visible at low water, but her stern was much deeper. She lay at a steep angle, had a forty-five degree list to starboard and was blocking both piers..

Indeed, she was nothing but a liability. Too far off for a crane to reach her and too deep to be pumped out at low tide, she presented the worst of possible combinations. The harbour authorities were agitating to get her moved and with no insurance, shifting her would cost Angus a fortune. Naturally he assumed that this salvor had heard of his predicament and was after a bargain.

Alec came off the telephone and explained the situation. 'What do you think?' he enquired.

He was so bright-eyed at the prospect. 'Why not?' I replied with a laugh, knowing it was not the most prudent decision I had ever made.

Preparations began immediately and Alec flew to Orkney the next day. One of the few things I have kept for posterity is Angus Sinclair's receipt, made out in neat handwriting on personal stationery, acknowledging the sale of the *Responsive*, 'as she lies submerged at Lyness,' to Kilburns Salvage Company Ltd, for the sum of £3000.

With the deal complete, Alec lost no time at all in mobilising to win his prize. There was too much equipment to take in the transit truck, and so Charlie Barron was despatched to Aberdeen to put one load on the Orkney ferry, *St Magnus*. The following night, heavily laden once more, the two of them traced the long, winding road north. The snow, which had begun as a light dusting, turned into a blizzard. Frequently it was a 'whiteout' and there was nothing to guide them, but the tall black and white poles which marked the verge, like a slalom. Tired and thankful, they eased to a halt beside the drifts that were beginning to accumulate against the Scrabster Hotel.

Early next morning, the shoremen stamped their feet and beat their arms for warmth under the street lamps at the pier. It was so raw and dark as the truck was loaded onto the Stromness ferry, that when dawn came, it was a study in pewter. The wind agitated the Firth and produced stark, crested waves. Understandably, it was with a hope that the weather would improve, that they transferred all their belongings, truck and all, onto a small fishing boat for the last leg of the journey. Lyness is situated on the south-east of Hoy, where it is protected from the worst excesses that sweep across Scapa Flow. Once an important base in the Wars, it had boasted little in more recent years than a few windswept houses and a derelict naval camp. On such a bitterly cold day, it looked just about the most uninviting place on earth – and was set to remain so for quite some while.

Scotland, had fallen under the grip of gales and sub-zero temperatures that were to last for six weeks. It was to become the coldest period in forty years and as the solstice drew near in Orkney, the daylight became depressingly scarce. It did not appear until ten in the morning, only to disappear at three in the afternoon. For much of the time the two salvors persevered with their mammoth task in darkness, like a couple of troglodytes.

Diving began right away, as Alec wanted to inspect the hull for damage. The conditions were rigorous, but he was staggered the next morning to find the wetsuit he had hung to dry in the 'portakabin', frozen as stiff as a board and had to thaw it out in front of the gas heater. This became a regular routine. He told me later that he had never been so perished. He had to steel himself to get into the sea, and thought he was becoming an old woman, until one afternoon it snowed heavily and he realised just how arctic it was – the flakes were building up on the surface around him, like a crust.

The air temperature plummeted. Soon, every time he surfaced, his demand valve would ice up and cut off his air supply. He had a brief respite waiting for a special adapter to be sent from Aberdeen, but there was plenty of other labour to do. Charlie was a stalwart. Whether onshore, welding up fittings, or in the rubber inflatable, wearing so much insulation to keep himself warm that he looked twice his weight, he matched Alec hour for hour. In such awful circumstances, many employees would have given up and gone home.

At first the progress was constant, but slow. A firm of construction engineers, Lilleys, were working close by and must have felt sorry for the pair, as their crane driver brought his machine along to clear debris from the *Responsive*, free of charge. They also loaned an additional compressor.

By sheer doggedness, alone, Alec sealed off the section forward of the engine room, containing the fish hold and the forward store. The fo'c'sle door had been relatively easy to seal, but the hold had been a curse. The heavy steel hatch cover had to be removed and fitted with pipes; a short length was required for pumping in air; and a much longer one, reaching the bottom of the hold, to let the water out. Before it could be put back, several loose pond boards and five hefty trawlboards had to be manhandled out the way, using lifting bags. Precautions also had to be taken, to prevent the air pressure from buckling the hatch cover. To prevent this, two railway sleepers had to be clamped on top of it lengthways, by wires spanning the gunwales. These were winched bar tight, by hand, using a Tirfor. All of this preparation was made more awkward and time-consuming because of the list. Once the missing herring scuttles in the deck had been blanked off, they were ready for a trial run. It was with expectancy that the compressors were fired up to pin-point the leaks.

Air blasted out at the bow, through some bolt holes for a winch that had long since disappeared. They were in an awkward spot and had to be sealed using plates. No sooner had this repair been effected, than water was found welling up from the sonar pod, below. Air was also escaping beneath the concrete under the whaleback forward, and one of the scuttles was not tight. All these escape routes had to be blocked, if there was the remotest chance of forcing the sea out.

There was a second, more serious attempt. Just when they thought they were getting somewhere and had the *Responsive* nearly two metres out of the water at the bow and supported by lifting bags at her stern, a scuttle gave way, shooting into the air with the report of a small cannon. There was an exhalation of pent up air, rapidly followed by a furious rush of bubbles as the hull settled to the bottom, again.

What a setback. Alec and Charlie were devastated. All that effort for nothing. In fact, they were worse off. It had become obvious that they were not going to accomplish the job with the equipment they had, especially as they needed more lifting bags. There was no other option, but to make the long journey back to Fife, where they could gather what they required, warm up and generally recover. Understandably, they departed with mixed feelings. At least it was Christmas.

In the short time they were away, they tried to convince themselves that matters would be much better on their return, as tiredness had exaggerated their discomfort. Standing on the harbour edge, one glance over the glacial landscape proved this thinking wishful. Yet, the bottom line was that the forty tons of metal beneath the surface was now our responsibility and there was no other alternative but to carry on.

With great determination, using compressed air and hand winches forward, and lifting bags aft, they moved the *Responsive* forward a metre or so each high tide, until at last the stern was uncovered at low water. They were getting somewhere. At least now she was between the piers and they had the chance of dragging her closer to one side, where they could get the crane in to help with the lift.

At this stage, her bow was facing north and a pulley block with seven to one reduction was rigged to pull it around and closer in. The enormous length of wire that ran back and forth through the sheaves was attached to the gunwales amidships. It was shackled to a chain which had been fed across the harbour in the form a 'V', the far ends of which had been secured, by digging in two widely-spaced anchors behind the east pier. All the airbags that Alec could muster were tied aft, until he was running out of places to attach them. These were inflated and hand winching with the Tirfor began …

Charlie, using a metre length of thick galvanised pipe as a lever, racked the mechanism back and forth to pull her forward on the wire. Alec manned the pumps, but even with the forward section airtight and eighty tonnes of lift at the stern, the hull hardly moved. Hell's teeth!

Back to the drawing board. There was a watertight door between the hold and forward store, but they had treated the two compartments as one, because it was distorted and did not fit any more. Gaining access at low water, and balancing precariously on a floor that sloped steeply to starboard, they shovelled away a load of rotting, fishy skeletons. The stench was indescribable. It was with an effort not to retch, that they installed hydraulic jacks against heavy battens and forced the steel shut against new neoprene seals.

Two more compressors were borrowed from Lilleys and air was pumped into the forward section once again. The store was clear, but the hold was still about a quarter full of water, as the hull was at such an angle that it was out of the reach of the long pipe. Alec was worried that he now pumping so much pressure into this section, that the deck around the hatch combing was going to buckle and still the stern would not shift!

Changing tactics at the next high tide, he placed all the lift on the starboard side, and winched her bow across the rocky bottom, clockwise, towards the east pier. Miraculously, she righted herself. Now wires could be laid under her transom stern and lifting bags attached. Soon, these were in place, but time marched on. They would have to wait six hours for low water, in order to plug the hole for the exhaust with chicken mesh and quick-setting cement. The aft hatch was also sealed. It took another tide before a platform could be built to take the water pumps. This was to be placed on the deck where the wheelhouse had been, so that the inlet and outlet hoses could be fed through the conduits for taking the controls into the engine room. Everything was in place. 'If this plan does not work,' Alec thought, 'we'll be facing a bill to cut her up.'

The scene was lit by a diesel generator from lights high on top of a tripod mast. Stage-like, they cast their warm ethereal glow on the activity of the two lone, possessed, characters below. Their backdrop of pier, quay and sea was dismal. They did not have to act to imitate the conditions. Their backs were hunched, their face, feet and hands numb, their fingers fat and swollen. As the tide turned and began to rise, the low 'thrum' of one engine was joined by the higher pitch of the water pumps, as they were set to work. Their capacity was adequate, but for some time it seemed as if they were not having any effect. The waiting was endless. Flashing a torch round the shadowy recesses, each seal was rechecked. Imperceptibly at first, there was a slight motion ... a swaying, like an attack of dizziness ... there it was, again!

'She's moving!' Alec whispered, hardly believing himself.

'Come on you bitch!' Charlie urged.

'We're doing it ...!' Alec announced, clenching his fist is a gesture of spontaneous relief. 'At last!'

After twenty-nine days of awful conditions, neither wanted to face anymore. Yet they both knew that there was some way to go. As the water was steadily removed and she became increasingly buoyant, her motion became pronounced, due to the free surface effect of the remaining liquid inside. They were on the alert until it had stopped sloshing around the engine room and accommodation, aft. Similarly, every so often, there was a brief moment of panic when one of the pumps choked with dirt. It was not until eight o'clock, long into the dark, that they knew they had won. Pumping for another two hours, just to make sure, they collapsed into bed at midnight in their digs at Rinigil. One phase of their mission had ended and they arose the next morning tired and stiff to begin the next. The main engine had to be stripped immediately, if there was any chance of it running again.

The *Responsive*'s interior was not an encouraging sight. A thick film of bilge oil covered every surface from the fish hold bulkhead to the fresh water tanks at the very stern. All the ceiling, walls, floor, steps, every vertical, horizontal and diagonal face had a covering of black, gelatinous slime. Nowhere could a hand be put that was not revolting. The air was foetid and chilled, every breath condensed and hung like a cloud. Drips of greasy water plopped down the back of collars, into hair and upturned eyes; and as if to show that they were not entirely governed by gravity, dribbles also ran up sleeves.

The main engine was an impressive, six cylinder Lister Blackstone, bolted amidships. Glinting in the rays of the inspection lamp, showing all the scars of the fire that had written the boat off, with blistered paint and scorched metal, it looked as if it was seized.

'Quite some mess, eh Alec?' Charlie asked rhetorically, 'we'd better get to work.'

The first task was to wash the main body down with degreasant and then strip off the manifolds, panels and turbo in order to get at the insides and spray the moving parts with diesel. The cylinder head studs were locked solid and Charlie spent one whole day, with uncooperative fingers and a slippery spanner, trying to free them. Alec could monitor his progress from the amount of cursing he heard, as he repacked the leaking stern gland and eased off the steering gear. Struggling with heavy chain and tackle, they worked together to remove the heads and paraffin was poured into the cylinders. Getting the crankshaft to move took the force of both a hand winch on the flywheel and a hydraulic jack. Once it began to move the whole mechanism soon became looser, enabling each of the bores to be rubbed down with emery paper as it was patiently turned. The gearbox and drive were then drained and filled with oil The auxiliary engines got similar treatment and it took five days of filthy toil to get the equipment into a condition in which it would cease to deteriorate.

The *Responsive* was then moved to the concrete pier which had been the cause of her second demise. There she was secured with heavy ropes and fenders and left until July. At this point both Alec and Charlie felt that they would not care if they ever saw her again, even though she was ours and afloat for the total cost of £8000.

The first chance I had to have a look at this new possession was in the summer, when she was towed to Victoria Dock, in Dundee, and tied up in the corner beneath the Clock Warehouse. She was rusty, with the odd patch of navy blue paint. The only superstructure was a small whaleback forward, which Alec promptly informed me was about to be cut off. Her deck was covered in a brilliant orange dust, the colour of sienna and there were ripples in the steel above the engine room, caused by her fire.

'What do you think of her?' he asked eagerly, his enthusiasm being renewed by an ultrasonic survey that had proved her structural integrity to be remarkably sound. 'Do you know her plate is ten millimetres thick at the bow. That's amazing. I've found out that she was built to Lloyd's 100A plus ten per cent.'

I would never have believed it, if he had not told me. 'Superficially, she looks awful,' I admitted, 'but her shape looks good.' He flashed me a winning smile, it reinforced why I was such a good wife, I could be depended on to say the right thing.

We were viewing her amidships, and walking along the cobbled quay to the bow, he drew an outline in the air of where the new forward wheelhouse was going to be. It would be set low to reduce wind resistance and the aft end would be abutted by the new hatch. This would be spacious and would open into the compartment that was currently the fish hold. The decks directly aft of this would have to be cut out and replaced, and there would be a large 'A' frame at the stern. He could see it all in his mind's eye. I was impressed.

Emboldened by my response, he stood closer and lowered his voice in confidence, 'Don't tell anyone or they'll think I'm crazy ... but, I am going to fit her out to work the *Glenartney*.'

'You're joking,' I hissed. 'The *Glenartney* is in over three hundred metres of water. It is the deepest cargo recovery operation in the world!'

'I know, but all the equipment aboard this ship will be designed to three hundred and sixty metres.'

'No?'

'Yes,' he replied and gave me one of his unwavering stares, which I met. After scrutinising him for a moment, I gazed at the *Responsive* again and impossible as it seemed, there was no doubt he was serious.

'Well, if anyone else finds out, it'll be the funny farm for you,' I warned mockingly, and we both shared the joke, even though it was too near the bone to be comfortable. His target wreck in the Mediterranean could not have seemed further away. We both knew it would be difficult, but neither of us foresaw just how hard. The next few years were to bring each of us to our knees in exhaustion and despair at times.

THE *RESPONSIVE*

Resuming work on the hull was rather like coming downstairs the morning after a party thinking that one had tidied up the worst the night before, only, with refreshed eyes, to realise the full extent of the mess. What had seemed acceptable following all the rush of salvage in the bleakness of Orkney in January, now seemed unimaginably sordid in the brighter, calmer environs of Dundee in July. Just freeing off the wires that battened down the hatch cover and looking into the hold made one's heart sink. It was full of sodden debris and the smell was rank. Several tonnes of heavy purse-seine net lay in a complete jumble, its coarse flat mesh glossed and slippery with oil. Entangled in it were scores of plastic fishboxes, the majority of which were broken and smashed. Rubber baskets, ice shovels, ropes and soft orange buoys, became apparent as the larger items were removed, all filthy and ruined.

As unpleasant as the exhumation process was, it was just a preliminary. The engine room was a priority as the treatment the main engine had received in Lyness was only a temporary measure and now it had to be dismantled again. Before this could happen, however, a certain amount of preparation work had to be done. The thick, reticent oil that had settled back in the bilges like molasses had to be pumped out into barrels by hand; all the draping of twisted electric cables, fuel pipes and hydraulic hoses had to be stripped out; and the whole place pressure washed.

This unenviable array of labouring jobs fell to Roy Malcolm from Tayport. A tall, wild man of ancient Scottish stock, he was temporarily off the road as a long distance lorry driver and had arrived on the quay on the off chance of employment, keen to turn his hand to anything. No one could have worked harder in such unpleasant conditions.

He used to arrive at 7.45 a.m. clean, with flowing red hair and beard, put on his waterproofs and disappear below deck. That would be the last anyone saw of him until teabreak, when, blinking in the sun, he would clamber back on deck, sleek with oil in the guise of one of those Texans who cap gushers. Even when it was time to go home and he got the worst off, returning as we all thought to a quite an acceptable state, it soon became apparent that our standards were suspect, for the conductress on his bus route gave him an ultimatum on the third night that she would not let him on board again, unless he brought his own newspaper to sit upon.

'Well, it's one way of making sure that you get the seat to yourself,' he dryly observed.

Invariably, Roy's job was solitary, there not being any room for a mate, and so as he persevered out of sight whilst Charlie Barron tackled the burning work on deck. Using the oxy-acetylene torch, all the steelwork that was either redundant or fire-damaged was systematically removed, and the small mast and much of the whaleback forward; the hatch combing and plates amidships, along with the last traces of the wheelhouse; and the entire gunwale aft and round the stern, all went. Then, as soon as the engine room was ready, they swapped locations and he proceeded with the operation to save the Lister Blackstone ERS 6M.

This time it had to be completely dissembled – pistons, liners, crank-shaft, tapits, turbo-charger – they all had to be taken out and by the time he had finished there was nothing left but the casing, manifolds and cylinder heads. It was the biggest such undertaking he had tackled, but despite this, Alec was quite content to leave him to it as he had such a gift. Setting Roy the task of needle-gunning the hull to remove the rust, he preoccupied himself with design.

There was not an inch of his new acquisition which had not been scrutinised several times. His tape measure had been extended in every permutation of length, height and breadth. As he splayed himself across a void, the reading would be mulled over. 'Seven foot six to play with.' He would visualise the possibilities in his mind and letting the end of the metal tape rewind with a snap, his grey-green eyes would fix on something quite invisible which only he could see. 'Yes. That's fine,' he would announce, making a quick sketch in his notepad, never explaining quite what 'that' was.

Conversely, there were other measurements that were not to his liking and he would look severe, frowning as he sought to alter his cerebral plan.

All the information would be assimilated and particularly in the quiet of home, he would spend hours in thought. Within moments of sitting in his battered old leather arm chair by the stove, he would become distant. A mention of a meal would bring him back momentarily and he would shift to the table, but after a few brief words with Robert about nursery school or friends, he would slip away again. His emerging designs possessed him so wholly, that he would only come back to us once they had been committed to paper. This process was rather like an exorcism, and accordingly there was a certain amount of ritual about it.

First, he would pull out the small drawer from the cabinet in the office that contained all his drawing instruments, and place it on the far end of the kitchen table, in front of the dresser, where he normally sat for meals. Then he would bring out his large, heavy drawing board, which had been removed from its cast iron stand. After checking the white parchment top sheet, to make sure it was still blemish free, he would cut a length of opaque draught paper from its roll and secure it squarely, using masking tape. A cup of coffee was essential. Placed at a safe distance, where it had no risk of spilling onto any of his much cherished textbooks, he would pull up his carver chair. After a brief pause, the concepts which were still as ethereal as the clouds to everyone else, would begin to emerge.

Scale was crucial. As a gauge, he would use the battered nail on one of his powerful thumbs to mark the length of a specific item on his ruler and then make several light outlines on the draught paper, using a pencil. These were mere shadows of the positive swirls and marks in his notes, each page untidily filled with rapid diagrams and accompanied by a mass of formulae. Only when he was content with the size and layout, would he proceed. From this point on, the lines were quite different in style. Whether they were curved, straight or angular, they were meticulous and I believe that this change marked the boundary between art and applied science.

Watching Alec distil his ideas until they were clear as spirit, made me aware that great engineers are on a par with composers. The only difference in that one 'sees' in his conscious and the other 'hears'. Both decipher their imaginings using symbols, translating them into a medium in which they can be read by others, to re-emerge as a dynamic and three-dimensional whole.

Alec would persevere with hardly a respite, sometimes for days at a time, until all the perspectives he required were complete. The muscles in his neck and back would be cramped, as much with tension, as from sitting bent over his board for so long. Only when he had systematically inked over the pencil lines, could he relax; for a careless slip of the ruler, or a moment's forgetfulness with a sleeve could ruin the output. He proceeded from top to bottom, and then turned the board at right angles to complete what had been the vertical lines. Once the precious results were finished and rolled in their protective tube ready for the printshop in Dundee, he would come back to us.

Tired, with dark shadows beneath his eyes, he would search me out wherever I happened to be, and putting his arms round my waist he would kiss me on the lips and greet me as if he had just awoken from oblivion, 'And how are you?' even though I had been around all the time.

A good sleep usually restored him to his normal self and post-breakfast, by the time he had rather reluctantly got into boilersuit after his more comfortable cords, and begun to tie up his steel-toe-capped boots, the ages he had spent preoccupied would be quite forgotten, and a note of enthusiasm would creep back into his voice as his mind began racing onto other things. 'I'm just going to check how they're progressing on the boat and then I'm going to go up to Peterhead to look at a second-hand Gardner engine that sounds as if it would make a good auxiliary. I'll call into Mills of Montrose on the way back, just to see what they've got. I'm going to need a lot of steel, even just for general work, and it will cost an awful price if we have to buy it new ... See you when I get back ... Bye.' He would smile engagingly, as if to say, 'I know I've been a drag, but you know you wouldn't have me any other way.' The door would be shut with vigour and he would be gone, off on the trail of suitable machinery and materials and I would let out a pent up breath, thankful it was all over until the next time.

Without doubt, it was Alec's ability to forward plan and his pleasure in a bargain that saved us a fortune in refitting the *Responsive*. In those early months, when she was being prepared for conversion, he astutely divided his time between taking on small specialist salvage jobs to keep the money flowing in, and scouring industrial and maritime Scotland for the fantastic array of equipment and parts he required.

With regard to the credit side, much of the work came from friends, who knowing that Alec had no income, decided to harness his talents. Tommy Clark, who sold us the *Valorous* when we were on Foula, had just bought much of the scuttled German Fleet lying in Scapa Flow, and said he wanted a salvage survey done. These wrecks are famous throughout the world, and their names: *Kron Prinz Wilhelm*, *Karlsrhue*, *Markgraf* and *Dresden*, among others are evocative reminders of the Battle of Jutland. They all lay around the forty to fifty metre mark, showing various degrees of damage, some on their sides, the others upside down. Swimming over them in a professional capacity, was what many sports divers did for pleasure.

Literally, while Alec was still submerged on the *Koln*, I got a call from Murray Fenton, the founder of a company of ship surveyors, who lived in a village just up the river. He telephoned to ask if Alec would go to Tripoli in Libya, to represent the interests of hull insurers by examining a cargo ship, the *Parga Star*, which had sunk in the harbour. Opportunities like this did not come up very often, so with Tommy's report hardly off the typewriter, the cold waters around Orkney were rapidly exchanged for the heat and hassle of North Africa.

Ironically, Smit Tak, the Dutch salvors, who had taken over and subsequently shut down Risdon Beazley Ltd, were working close by. Alec met their salvage officers with respect, curiosity and a certain wry amusement, thinking how heartily these hard-nosed businessmen would have laughed, if he had told them his plans for his hull in Dundee and the *Glenartney*. Still, nobody but he and I knew the secret. Murray Fenton and his managing director, John Noble, were both very kind to us and further engagements followed in Sicily and Algeria, which all helped to pay the bills.

Such was the breadth of our interests, that sometimes we managed to combine income and expenditure on the same contract. Roger Miles, whom Alec had known since his days with the Newlands in the Firth of Forth, had recently taken over the breaking of the aircraft carrier, HMS *Ark Royal* at Cairnryan, near Stranraer where the Northern Irish ferries dock. This vast ship had been partly demolished, but needed to be pulled further up the beach, for the pier cranes to reach aft. To achieve this, what was left of her had to be trimmed and it was Alec's job to remove the rudder and both propellers using explosives, before cutting off the last eight metres of her stern.

With all his blasting experience and a ship to kit-out, the contract was tailor-made. He would set off for Ayrshire with his team, the transit truck relatively empty apart from diving gear and tools, to return a few days later with it groaning, and piled high with innards from the once-illustrious ship. Hydraulic motors with air brakes and reduction gear heat exchangers, brass deckhead lamps, copper cable, mahogany duckboards would be heaped in the back, all built to the highest specification and in tip-top condition. 'Come and look at this,' he would demand with glee and never one to miss a bargain, the sheds at Kilburns began to fill up, soon looking more like Devonport Dockyard than a farm.

His penchant for a good deal and haggling, coupled with his preparedness to tackle even the most colossal structures, was aptly caught in a pair of cartoons, sketched by Alison Macleay, Simon's wife. Both show me looking somewhat shell-shocked on finding the oil platform *Beryl Alpha* in the farmyard. In the first Alec is earnestly explaining, 'But Moya, Roger had three of them ...' and in the second, I stare open-mouthed as he changes his tack by encouraging, 'But Moya, think what it would cost new ...' I have had them framed, since neither caption was very far away from the truth.

By late October, with the foundation work completed, and the hull clean and without a superfluous piece of steel, we put together a team to begin what was officially deemed to be a 'refit', but which was tantamount to a new build. We were lucky in that a large ship repair yard in Dundee had just laid off its workforce, and there were some extremely good engineers available. Many of them were in their forties and fifties and had served their apprenticeships in the Caledon Shipyard. The site was now rubble, and the slips were gone, bulldozed away, but what a legacy it had bequeathed to the community. From the consultant naval architects to the steel fabricators, we soon found that they all knew each other, having learnt their trades and skills in 'The Caledon'.

Up until this juncture, things had run pretty much as we had envisaged and so I suppose it was inevitable that we should begin hitting unforeseen obstacles, sooner or later. The legislation governing the building and standard of British Registered ships is laid down in numerous statutory instruments. For example, No. 1089. The Merchant Shipping (Load Lines) (Deck Cargo) Regulations 1978, No. 795, Merchant Shipping (Crew Accommodation) Regulations 1978, No. 544, The Merchant Shipping (Fire Appliances) Regulations 1980, and so on. These are augmented by Merchant Shipping Notices, known as 'M' notices, which were advisory, not mandatory. Their titles are even longer, M. 984, Use of Liquefied Petroleum Gas (LPG) in Domestic Installations and Appliances on Ships, Fishing Vessels, Barges, Launches and Pleasure Craft – this notice supersedes Notice No. M.603. Having worked on and around fishing vessels almost all his life, Alec knew full well the standards to which they were built. Consequently, as the *Responsive* had complied to Lloyds 100A1, plus ten per cent – far exceeding the Department of Trade's requirements for vessels of her size – he had had no doubt that she would pass her Load Line Certificate with flying colours.

It was not so. As the naval architect began to fine tune the plans for the layout and superstructure, he was coming up against increasing difficulty with large swathes of the rules. The problem, it seemed, was completely bureaucratic. By virtue of the fact that we were salvors, the hull's classification had changed and the new specifications and stability conditions which it had to meet were completely different. It did not matter that the *Responsive* had fulfilled the highest standards, nor that she had proven herself by fishing to the north and west of Scotland throughout the worst of fourteen winters, thereby gaining an enviable reputation for sea-keeping, she was not the same. Her shape and displacement might well be unaltered, but she was not a seventy-six ton fishing boat any longer, she was a one hundred and sixteen ton cargo ship and would therefore have to comply with Class VIII Load Line requirements.

At first we laughed, 'No, no. She's not a cargo ship. Cargo ships are enormous. They're shaped like baths and load in the calm of port, and steam from place to place. We're still going to behave exactly like a fishing boat – that's why we chose this hull. We'll go out empty, to load at sea in varying weather conditions and come into port to discharge.'

How could we be so foolish to think such heresy, when faced with an uncompromising diktat … didn't we know that the Department of Trade did not have a category for salvage vessels, therefore they did not exist!

What the situation boiled down to was Lobby. The fishing industry had considerable political influence and could sway the law-making process. The commercial shipping fleet, however, held no such favour. What is more, it was deemed a relict of the Empire by Whitehall and the bottom line was, if those in power could hardly be bothered with the needs of the great Lines from the past, why should they care two jots about minnows like us? The consequence was ill-thought legislation and the decline in the numbers sailing under the Red Ensign spoke for itself. It had plummeted to around eight hundred and this was no doubt the administrative rationale for lumping weenie ships like ours, with rather more substantial craft of up to 8000 tons. The absurdities this generated were manifest, but the one we remembered with most delight was the positioning of the explosive store. We wanted to put it in one of the ballast tanks aft, but according to printed instruction, it would have to be placed so far forward of the accommodation and engine room, that it would be a hundred metres beyond the bow.

The implications in terms of time and money soon became apparent and matters, which had not boded well, soon became rapidly worse. The senior surveyor from the Department of Trade in Leith, drove all the way to Dundee to clarify some issues and on seeing the *Responsive*, refused point blank to come aboard.

'You'll be wasting your money,' he told Alec in his bluff Newcastle accent.

His advice, well meant though it might have been, fell on stonier ground than the shores of Loch Eriboll. Anyone who knows Alec, appreciates that he rarely loses sight of his objective and can be at his most charming, when he is most cross. Thus the retort, 'I don't think so,' sounded pleasant enough to someone unaware of the warning signs. 'While you're here, I was wondering if we could just look at something forward …?'

The three new engineers, plus Charlie Barron, Roy and the naval architect stood on deck, like an assorted and extremely partisan welcoming party. One or two had their hands in the pockets of their dark boilersuits to keep them warm, the others nonchalantly wiped their fingers with bits of rag in preparation for teabreak, as if unconcerned. All waited avidly to see who was going to win the battle of wills. A few more protests were made from the quay, but went unheeded and so, outnumbered and outgunned, the surveyor was forced into his white overalls by sheer stubbornness on Alec's part, and donned them begrudgingly, beside the boot of his car. Not a word was said. Each employee knew better than to gloat, but a few raised eyebrows flashed silent messages, recognisable as 'Well done, Alec … He didn't want to – but you made him,' and 'Lucky he didn't come a few months ago.'

The surveyor's examination was not only reluctant, it was cursory and made all the worse because as soon as he reached the forepeak he asked, 'Do you have anywhere warm to sit?' Poor man, had he known then the conditions in which the *Responsive* had been brought to the surface, I doubt if he would have made such a seemingly innocent request. As it was, this unwitting plea for comfort ignited Alec's fuse far more than the inability to answer any direct question, despite having been sent the plans two weeks before. Livid, his self-control was maintained until he came home in the evening and vaunted his wrath on crossing the threshold.

'Politicians – they make me so cross!' I heard a minister from the Department of Trade and Industry on the radio, banging on about the usual line for businessmen, "What's needed in Britain is entrepreneurs with incentive, who will invest money and take risk," and what does his bloody department do, demands £500 up front before sending me a surveyor, who drives all the way from Leith at my expense to tell me I'm wasting my time, when I've lifted a perfectly good hull from the seabed.

'The individual who came today could hardly tell us a single thing. He kept on saying that he would "have to go and look it up," when we asked him where we could put things … but the forward water tank, which we want to keep where it is, where it has always been since the boat was built, "might have to be moved!"

'It's ludicrous!'

'Six pieces of government legislation have affected us in the last two years: Diving Regulations: Certification of Deck Officers: the Carrying of Certified Engineers: New Tonnage Measurement Regulations: the Scrap Dealing Act: Merchant Shipping Load Line Regulations. For crying out loud, it would not only be illegal to carry out our operations now with vessels like *Trygg* or the *Valorous*, but there would have to be so many people on board that there would be standing room only!

'Do you know that we would need two certificated deck officers just to get to the Bell Rock because of its latitude. It's only twelve miles offshore. On a fine day you can see the lighthouse from the top of the hill, behind the house!

'I've had absolutely enough. How on earth is anybody supposed to create anything new in this country with all this red tape? It's gone berserk!

There's nothing for it – we're never going to sort the matter out by ourselves. I'm going to write to Barry Henderson!'

Shortly afterwards a letter, toned down in its language, but containing much of the sentiment, was sent off to our Conservative Member of Parliament. The missive stressed our inability as a small company to pay the costs of complying with inapplicable legislation and what we needed from the Department of Trade was not proscription, if we were going to succeed, but help, this element was underlined.

Our elected representative took the matter up with his colleague, the Parliamentary Under Secretary of State, whose reply was a gem of doublespeak. He began by saying that he could not believe that the difficulties that we had been facing stemmed from a lack of co-operation or help from his Department's surveyor. 'Converting a fourteen-year-old fishing vessel for salvage work inevitably poses problems for the owner and surveyor alike. Whereas Mr Crawford can rightly point out the similarities between the two types of vessel, the fact is that their construction and arrangement are governed by quite separate pieces of legislation.'

The lunatics had obviously taken over the asylum – this was our very dilemma in a nutshell. He then went on to give chapter and verse on some of the particular points we had raised, and ended with the sentence, 'I hope I have been as helpful as possible to Mr Crawford'.

We were incensed – of course, he had not! He had taken three pages of embossed paper to put up two fingers and say 'tough luck, chum'. Presumably, he thought we were just the sort of smelly, tiresome hoi-polloi who cluttered up his Honourable Friend's constituency office. This notion caused us great mirth, as we rather liked Barry and he was married to Alec's first cousin.

CHAPTER

~~~~

10

THE *REDEEMER*

It is impossible to identify when the *Responsive* became the *Redeemer*, as there was no discernible point where the cross-over became evident. In fact, the transition was so subtle and over such a long period of time, that it was more of a metamorphosis than any clear change.

There were certain quintessential events that stand out, but on the whole, the eighteen months that it took to convert the vessel seem to have merged into a blur – a monotonous and prolonged diet of engineering and all its associated complications and expense.

For several months we kept the *Valorous*. She was tied alongside and we used her as a convenient store, shelter and brew-up facility. Very early on, I do remember standing on her aged wooden deck and looking up at the massive steel hull of the *Responsive*, wondering how we could own something quite so vast and substantial. Then as work progressed on this replacement, I found my allegiance had been diverted without me even noticing; and in an idle moment caught myself standing on the steel deck of the *Responsive*, looking down at the *Valorous* and wondering, 'How on earth did we ever manage to salvage so much with something so inadequate and small?'

She had done such sterling work on the *Oceanic* and *Argyll*, that I had been oblivious of her short-comings and had never noticed how cracked and battered her gunwales were before. The sight of it led me to gaze at the wheelhouse, which, even though it was newly painted in preparation for sale, looked well past its best and more suited as a garden shed, with its crude windows and quaint, brass-ringed doors, than any real form of protection from storms. The winch and derrick seemed remarkably lightweight, too, and yet all had performed so well.

Initially, that such thoughts should even emerge seemed disloyal, but on mature reflection, I had to accept that they were inevitable. Our ambition had embarked us on a journey and these new opinions were simply evidence of just how far we had moved on, in a relatively short period of time.

~~~~

The *Valorous* disappeared under its new command in early July and with her went the remnants of our carefree past. We resigned ourselves to a laborious future. In the lee of the clock warehouse in our quiet corner of the dock, only the view across to the static frigate *Unicorn* and the cold draught that seemed to vent directly onto us through the gap in the buildings, remained the same.

Apart from his trips abroad for Murray Fenton Associates, Alec was now working on the *Responsive* more than full-time. There were no weekends off, no outings, no fun and the grind was relentless. It seemed that no sooner had one task been completed, than another two appeared in its place, both bigger and more difficult than the last. There was rather a hint of 'Alice in Wonderland' about it. One could imagine her opening a wooden Russian Babushka and finding against all rational expectation, that each subsequent doll was larger and not smaller than the last. Similarly, the enormity of our project seemed to grow with each achievement, rather than diminish in size.

Consequently, the strain of organising such exacting and wide-ranging tasks began to mount on Alec. It reached such a pitch, that it nearly broke him. 'Do you know,' he confided wistfully, during one of our quiet moments together at night, 'if I allow myself to think about all the jobs that have to be done at once, it makes me feel physically sick? The only way I can cope with it mentally is to break everything into stages and only when we get to the end of one, begin contemplating another.'

'I'm so sorry, Alec,' I soothed lamely. We both knew that we had committed ourselves so irrevocably, that there was no solution but to press on.

There was progress. Events occurred that brought hope and satisfaction, but their enjoyment was all too brief. It was the repetitive need to draw on one's reserves in order to just 'get over the next hump' and the constant fear that one day, either or both of us would crack, worn out and emotionally bankrupt.

For example, when the pre-fabricated wheelhouse had arrived on its articulated lorry, there was tremendous elation. It was a thrill for everyone when the crane lowered it into position. Thin air was replaced by form, and we no longer had to use our imaginations to visualise the new salvage ship.

This positive impact, however, was short-lived. Within days we saw that we had been duped by a cruel illusion. The new superstructure was nothing but an empty shell. The very presence of which broadcast the fact that the whole forward section would have to be fitted out. For a start, the armoured glass windows and watertight doors would have to be fitted, but they were just a minor part. It was all the remote hydraulic and electric controls that would have to be delivered to the bridge; the speed controls for the main engine and the Morse links for steering; to say nothing of the loo, the galley and the accommodation below. Insulation, panelling and plumbing, the list of tasks went on and seemed endless.

One of the most exciting moments came when Jim Anderson and Brian Houghton, the two most experienced engineers, got the main engine running, again. It was rather like raising a body from the dead, it had been inert for such a long time. Over the past few months, a total overhaul had been undertaken and all the ruined parts, pistons, liners, bearings, turbocharger and so on, meticulously replaced. Alec was with them and pressed the starter button. There was a brief pause and then a click.

These sounds were imperceptible on deck. The first thing we knew of their success, was when a puff of dark black exhaust belched from the funnel, hovering like a ring blown by a practised smoker, before being dissipated by a clearer, greyer trail. This was quickly followed by a tremor, as vibrant as a pulse, which throbbed through the ship. She was alive. Everyone felt the transformation and brightened as they sensed the prospect, however distant, of casting off the mooring ropes; cheered by the sense of freedom that comes from severing the physical links to the shore.

Below decks, the scene was far from Utopian. The noise was deafening. Working in ear defenders, the animated men shouted to each other above the din. The array of temperature and pressure gauges were checked with all the anxiety of monitors in the intensive care ward. Hands were placed like surgeons' to feel for vibration and detect problems. The exposed valves were scrutinised as they hammered away for all they were worth. As the heat in the compartment built up, the oily rags that had been used to detect leaks by wiping the numerous joints, were absentmindedly mopped over faces, minds transported far away in mechanical glory.

The hatch combing, the tripod mast, the forward and aft mooring winches, at the time each was an addition that brought our end goal one step nearer, now they just seem to merge into a haze of men, tools and toil.

It is curious the things that one does remember; the bacon rolls for lunch that were bought from the shack that passed as the harbour cafe, and contained such charred and shrivelled rashers that they looked as if they had been fried in sump oil; the engineer who had fallen out with his wife, and slept in his car at night beside the quay for four weeks; the casual hand who, showing off, threw his brush on top of the funnel which he was just about to paint, only for it to disappear straight down the six-inch exhaust pipe, and Alec looking thunder as it all had to be dismantled below in order to get it back again; and always, always, there was more cost. The ship just seemed to swallow fittings and invariably the big items like the main winches were the cheapest. It was the fistfuls of hydraulic parts, the pipes and connections, which cost the most.

We had deliberated for quite some while what to call our new salvage vessel. We had wanted something apt and unusual, but as no two craft can be registered under the British Flag in the same name, we had to wait to hear about our choice. When it was confirmed, it took a bit of getting used to, as we had called this hole in the water into which we had poured money, 'The Boat', for so long that it seemed a little pompous to make a change. There was no going back. Officially sized steel letters were cut; two Rs, four Es, one D and one M, and welded in their order on the port and starboard bow, and similarly the legend, 'Redeemer, Dundee' was emblazoned on the stern.

A day had been set for a commissioning service, Thursday 20th June. Even in the depths of penury, we knew that we must celebrate the collective achievement. All the full-time men had worked hard, and so many people with whom we had dealt had been both generous and supportive, that a party seemed to be the least we could do to mark the event.

New tarpaulins were laid on the hatch the night before and she was moved to the south wall beside HMS *Unicorn*, our companion in Victoria Dock for longer than we cared to remember. She was the oldest British vessel afloat, and had been mothballed shortly after the end of the Napoleonic Wars. Seeing that we had gazed at her black and white hull in all weathers, it now seemed quite appropriate that we should celebrate our imminent departure in the space and comfort of her roofed-over main deck. In the morning, *Redeemer*'s mast and derrick were dressed with signal flags and number pennants, and the final preparations completed. Beds were made with sheets and blankets, cutlery, pots and pans installed and the inevitable bottle of champagne rigged, ready for the ceremony at 2.00 p.m.

As a gathering, we came from all walks of society, from engineers, welders and contractors and their wives, to the youngest, our children Robert and Drew, and the oldest family and friends. If the event was exclusive, it was not in position or title, but in diligence and heart for life. Everyone who had contributed to *Redeemer*, even the surveyor, was there and rightly so. Suits and hats predominated, there was not an overall in sight.

A smooth, upturned box served as a makeshift dais on the quayside. Alec gave a few brief words of welcome and it fell to me to proclaim the immortal phrase, surprisingly chokey words when you really care. I composed myself to stop any waver in my voice, 'I name this ship *Redeemer*. God bless her and all who sail in her!'

The champagne bottle smashed on the second, slightly more vigorous attempt and there was applause and a cheer. Father McBride, whom we considered to be the unofficial harbour padre, gave a short blessing, which was particularly special as he was the current owner of the *Vesper* of Danny Newlands fame, on which Alec had begun his diving career.

Once the formal proceedings were over and we had moved aboard the *Unicorn*, John Noble of Murray Fenton Associates, who had come up from London especially, delivered an excellent speech. In all it was a great success. A few brief hours of gaiety snatched in the eye of the storm.

Four weeks later our salvage vessel quit the dock gate en route for her first job. Her finish was immaculate – I cannot say she has looked quite so tidy ever again. In her were transplants taken from the range of the entire Fleet – Naval, Merchant and Fishing – from the most prestigious, like the aircraft carrier, HMS *Ark Royal*, to the humblest fishing boat, such as the *Sanboanne*. Even down to the cotton mattresses, and the vitreous china which bore the 'ESSO' logo, so much had a pedigree. We could not have done without them. These cast-offs had enabled us to create what was effectively a purpose-built ship at twenty per cent of new cost.

The Department of Trade kept up the extension of its powers right to the very last. Finally realising the ramification of making us comply to Class VIII for cargo ships, they demanded we carry out lifting at sea calculations as supposedly a statutory requirement. It was only with one last thrust, that Barry, our MP, got the Secretary of State to acknowledge that it did not form part of our Load Line certificate and we were legally allowed to sail as a British Registered Ship.

With the children I watched *Redeemer* sail out of the River, following her in the car to Broughty Ferry Castle at the mouth. Patrick on my hip, the other two running around, we stayed until she was almost indistinguishable and then, with a final unseen wave directed towards Alec, turned our backs, heading for the pressing business of the nearby swings in the park.

As we played, and I pushed the children higher and higher to their glee, I thought of the different, but equally liberating pleasure their father would feel as they reached the open sea. The kettle would probably have been already boiled, and intent on the voyage ahead to Fraserburgh, he would have put us all to the back of his mind long ago.

'How peculiar,' I thought, 'to work so hard to get rid of the man you love ... how lonely it will be without him.'

11

CARGO
RECOVERY

The light on Orkney that late summer day, was as rich and exotic in quality as a Gaugin painting giving bold dimension and unfathomable shade. *Redeemer* was reflected in the limpid water in a perfect image, reproduced with such symmetry that she gave the impression of being a huge and angular butterfly; the red of the hull vibrant against the blues and greens of nature.

This was our first contract, and as irony would have it we were tied against the pier at Lyness on Hoy. The beautiful weather was playing tricks on us, so that not only did we find it difficult to believe this was the same vessel Alec and Charlie Barron had wrested submerged, but that we were even in the same place.

Magical the scene may have been, but the purpose of our call could not have been more prosaic. The fuel storage tanks at the derelict Naval base just along the road were being cut up, and we had been hired to run supplies for the main contractor. At that moment we were waiting to be unloaded by crane, and the aft deck was filled by a large saloon car and scores of gas bottles, transported in steel crates like fourpacks, known as quads. We would be 'turned around' and gone by dawn.

Those trips up and down the east coast of Scotland, Lyness-Fraserburgh, Fraserburgh-Lyness, twice a week, continued throughout the winter like a haulage route and could not have been more welcome for paying the bills, not even as the nights lengthened and gales took their grip. Our vessel had always had a good sea-keeping reputation as a fishing boat, now we had the chance to prove her after her conversion by putting her to our own test.

All too frequently for our own comfort, we were chased down the coast of Scotland with a north-easterly on her port quarter, but she showed no vice. Similarly, going the other way through head-on storms, when towering waves would be shipped as solid lumps of swirling green water, that would crash against the armoured glass of the wheelhouse with such force that it made even the bravest heart pause, she would raise her bow on cue and cast them aside. In this way, she soon earned our respect and we were reassured that we had made the right choice.

After the Orkney run ended in the late spring, we were quickly offered other jobs. *Redeemer* was recognised as being a flexible and useful craft and we found her much in demand. She ran to Norway with specialist equipment for the oil industry. Days later, a rescue boat was taken to the far away Brent Field. On another occasion goods were delivered to the supply vessel, *Northern Fortress* and no sooner than that was done, a small fishing boat was lifted off Jura.

The income from this outside work was good and it had turned the quality of our life around. For too long we had had high capital expenditure and no real funds coming in. The whole process of operating a family business had been fraught and mean, and this had impinged on our home. Now that the monetary pressure had eased off slightly, the relief was so overwhelming that it was like removing a physical burden.

There were other complications, however. I was expecting our fourth child and was at a low ebb, as yet another pregnancy coupled with so much hassle over the years, began to take its toll. It was not that I was unhappy, just weary. Alec had been based at Dundee for a short while, testing *Redeemer*'s hydraulics on the *Argyll*. He had been steadily upgrading them, in preparation for lifting operations, ever since she had been commissioned and they had become most sophisticated.

Much of his time was spent on the Bell Rock, but in the periods in between he had been at Kilburns and it had been good to have him around. It would have been easy at this point, perhaps even financially advisable, to ask him to give up his dreams of the ss *Glenartney*, lying off Tunisia, and stay closer to home. He could have made a living plying round Britain and the near continent like a latter day Para Handy, or by undertaking small civil engineering contracts. Many would have considered such an existence to be idyllic.

The notion, as simple and alluring as it might seem, was never serious. We discussed its possibility once in our usual 'board room', me pottering at the sink and Alec in his battered leather chair by the stove, the boys occupied with a scatter of toys at his feet. Neither of us were fools. We both knew the implications of returning to salvage with all the arduousness of 'No Cure/No Pay'. The possibility that things could get grimmer, again, had been at the back of both our minds. It was he who had broached the subject. 'Do you think we're doing the right thing with *Redeemer* pressing on like this? Ought we stick with commercial work – it would be much easier?'

Above Devonshire Class Cruiser, HMS *Argyll*.

Right A sheet of armour plate slung beneath the bow of the *Valorous*, before it was steamed the twelve miles to Tayport.

Above The *Dunoon Boat* with a 12 ton inboard lift of armour plate from HMS *Argyll*, on the Bell Rock. Charlie Butterworth is at the controls, Alec in the water. (*Richard Preston*)

Left A rare day together at Kilburns. Robert centre.

Right One of HMS *Argyll's* massive guns being lifted out at Tayport. (*Alison Macleay*)

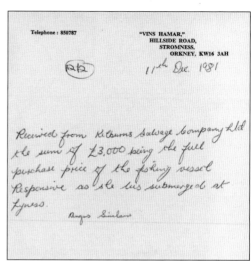

Telephone : 850787

"VINS HAMAR,"
HILLSIDE ROAD,
STROMNESS,
ORKNEY, KW16 3AH

212

11th Dec. 1981

Received from Kilburns Salvage Company Ltd the sum of £3,000 being the full purchase price of the fishing vessel Responsive as she lies submerged at Lyness.

Angus Sinclair

Above Copy of the receipt for the *Responsive*, as she lies submerged at Lyness, Orkney.

Left The *Redeemer* as the *Responsive* before she had a fire, and sank.

Below Alison Macleay's cartoon captures Alec's inability to resist a bargain. *Beryl Alpha* is a North Sea oil platform.

"But Moye — think what it would cost new!"

Left The *Responsive* finally breaks the surface, during Arctic conditions, the winter of 1981–82.

Below Alec and Charlie Barron with the newly raised *Responsive* at Tayport. (*The Evening Telegraph*)

Above Giffy Sutherland.

Left Redeemer's main engine, refurbished after being submerged.

The *Responsive* half-way in her metamorphosis into the *Redeemer*.

'Salvage is so glamorous ...' The author anti-fouls the *Redeemer* in dry dock.

Above *Redeemer*'s commissioning at Victoria
Dock, Dundee.

Tony Long.

Below *Redeemer* back at Lyness, Orkney, on her first job.

Above The engine room skylight is lifted off the
ss *Buitenzorg*, Sound of Mull.

Left Brian Houghton – 'Electric Legs' – with one of the
first pigs lifted from the bowels of the *Buitenzorg*.

Below The electro-hydraulic grab on the ss *Manipur*, off
Cape Wrath.

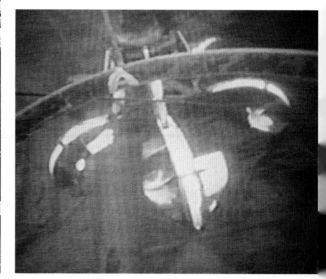

'It has its attractions,' I replied with candour, 'and we really know so little about cargo recovery – it's going to be an uphill struggle. But what about you?'

He gave the matter deep thought, eyes wide, as if focused on a future that only he could see, which played before him like a film. The vision of endless crossings between small island ports, mixed with short bursts of marine labouring for the construction industry, did not appeal to him at all. It was not for such employ that he had put himself through the hell of lifting and fitting out a burnt-out hull. Looking up at me in earnest, he sadly confessed, 'The trouble is, I just don't want to do it.'

'The soul is dead that slumbers?'

We both knew the poem.

'Precisely.'

The matter was settled.

Our first target with the *Redeemer* was the *Guido*, a 2000 ton steamship that lay in seventy metres of water, thirty miles off Rattray Head, a bleak, comfortless headland, which juts far east into the North Sea above Aberdeen. It was a tactic of 'U' Boats to loiter off such landfalls, to claim their victims as traffic either picked up or left the coast. This unsuspecting prey had been on her way from Hull to Archangel on the 8th July 1915, when her voyage was abruptly curtailed by a torpedo.

Alec had been given reliable details of her whereabouts by Captain Ross, who had told us that Risdon Beazley Ltd had partially worked her in 1962, when they recovered one hundred and fifty tons of lead and sixty-seven tons of tin. He had also added that this latter figure was most intriguing, as the manifest had detailed only fifty tons of this metal. This type of discrepancy was not unknown during war, when opportunities were taken and additional cargo was loaded at the last moment. The rumour, he said, was that she had been carrying about the same amount again, which put the estimated recoverable cargo at £150,000.

Enquiries to the Salvage Association of London revealed more information, but no stowage plan, as this had been destroyed in the lapse of time. In listing the other cargo, the documentation that was held encouraged a sense of romance, rather than promising any further reward – cocoa, coffee, gum, shellac, bark, lemons, lanterns, laurimite ore, antimony and wax. What an eclectic and spell-binding list. Raw materials and luxuries stowed together, held until they would be despatched to factories and dining tables, across the vastness of Imperial Russia, the world of Romanovs, Rasputin, Lenin and Molotov. What had been the fate of their recipients, poor souls, in the years of war, turmoil and revolution that were to follow?

Up until this point, we had been involved in wreck demolition and the casualties from which we had profited had been sunk by navigational error, at no loss of human life. In this respect, their respective fates had been regrettable, but without trauma. Our research into the *Guido* soon revealed that cargo recovery was a far harsher form of salvage. There was not one aspect of the loss that did not have the imprint of war, not even the paperwork. During the First and Second World Wars, British merchant ships and their cargoes were indemnified by the War Risks Insurance Scheme. If this property was sunk by enemy action, the owners were reimbursed by the State in exchange for title.

Opening the mail after breakfast one morning in early July, with our new daughter, Rachel, fed and cradled in one arm, I flourished a letter from the Salvage Association. 'You'll never guess who, or I should say, what owns the cargo on the *Guido*, now, Alec?' I asked almost seventy years to the day after its demise.

'Tell me.'

'The Department of Transport.'

He groaned. There had been a reorganisation of government ministries. The Department of Trade had ceased to administer shipping matters in theory, but in practice, this was just our old oppressors under a new guise.

'You're joking!'

'No ... but fortunately the Salvage Association act as their agents, so let's keep our fingers crossed that common sense will prevail.'

Mr Nicoll, who looked after Salvage Sales, remembered us from the days of the *Malin Head*, and could not have been more formal, or efficient. We were asked to make an offer in writing, stipulating the amount we wished to receive as a salvage award; this had to be given as a percentage of the net salved value. On considering the proposed operation, we decided that eighty per cent would be equitable and suggested this amount.

Mr Nicoll referred it to the Department of Transport with his recommendations, and it was accepted. An agreement was duly drawn up and signed. We paid the £400 fee to cover costs, and set off for the wrecksite. It was as simple as that.

The smoothness of these negotiations is, no doubt, a measure of the Salvage Association's long history. It was incorporated by Royal Charter in 1867, and since then has overseen thousands of cargo recovery attempts. A high proportion of them have ended in failure, which is to be expected with the risks involved. In perhaps as many as nine out of ten cases nothing of any value will ever be returned to the surface. Consequently, reality has taught them that whilst the contractual side is important, it is undoubtedly the easy part and legitimate salvors should not be hamstrung in their salvage attempts. After all, the cargo was to all intents worthless on the seabed.

We knew this, but it did not stop us from completely underestimating the difficulty of what we were trying to do on the *Guido*. In the event, this was probably just as well, or we might never have embarked on our fabulous quest.

Only working for Risdon Beazley Ltd could have prepared Alec for working in the position and conditions in which he found the wreck, yet in technological terms, he was aeons ahead. Our dinky, diesel-powered ship was a fraction in size of the ex-Naval vessel they had employed. The steam-driven *Lifeline* had had a massive crew, Alec had designed the *Redeemer*, so that she could be run with a compliment of five. Each mooring winch did not have to have its own operator, a man did not have to descend in a claustrophobic chamber, with another taking his directions over a telephone link. His cumulative weeks of work with the hydraulics, running pipes throughout the ship, would allow him to control the entire operation by himself from the wheelhouse; where he would sit with fourteen winch controls at his fingertips; the video monitor in front of him, displaying underwater images; and a clear view of the entire deck.

In detail, there were few similarities between us and our predecessors, apart from purpose and only the taut-leg mooring system remained the same. Alec had modernised cargo recovery practically single-handed.

Our first job was to lay our four anchors, two forward of the *Guido* and two aft. These were jettisoned off the stern of the *Redeemer*. Each was shackled first to a shot of chain, then a length of wire. This extended to the surface, where it was attached to its own large and soft, yellow buoy, which took the weight and absorbed the motion of the waves.

We would tie up to these. A wire would be run from each quarter of the ship to its respective buoy, be attached, and winched tight, so that we could manoeuvre ourselves in position above the wreck.

Even during surveying, precision of movement was crucial as none of the underwater equipment had any independent movement; both the camera and the grab being vertically suspended on their own wire, over the side. If we wished to look a metre to the port, for example, *Redeemer* would be moved a metre in that direction on the surface, by altering the tension of the wires to the buoys; the camera and grab would then quickly follow.

We may have understood this in theory, but what we had to learn for ourselves was that mooring systems were not inanimate objects – they had minds of their own, and temperamental ones at that!

The conditions would be ideal; we would lay the anchors with their buoys, run the surface ropes to the ship, pull these together so that

Redeemer was in place ... an anchor would drag. We would have to let all the ropes go, lift the offending anchor, drop it in a different position, tie up again, pull the ropes in ... only to find that the tide had turned and the current was strengthening, taking us far off the wreck ... we would have to wait.

Eventually, a couple of hours later, there would be a period of slack water. We would manage to get the camera into the water. The system was still extremely experimental and there would be a fault. It would take the rest of that day and the whole of the next to fix. Alec would go to his bunk looking forward to a fresh start, early the following day, only to be rocked in fitful sleep as the weather conditions worsened.

By 3.00 a.m., the motion would be so severe that he would be up. The rain would be sheeting, interspersed with lashings of spray. They would have to wait impatiently for dawn. As soon as the light broke insipidly and it was possible to see the rubber inflatable, it would be launched over the side, bucking with the waves, as Alec went to cut the lines to the buoys. These would then have to be caught and lifted, as we had to remove them when we vacated the site. The anchors, unreliable when we needed them, would now be reticent to give up their grip of the seafloor, and had to be wrenched free in a rising swell.

Soaked despite his oilskins and numb with cold, Alec would collapse in the mess without even bothering to take off his lifejacket. Here, he would recuperate, utterly fed up, as Giffy would give the main engine a 'kick' in the wheelhouse, above, heading for the shelter of Fraserburgh. In this recurring pattern, frustration and disappointment became the norm during those summer months.

When we eventually did get into position, with the camera working, we found that the *Guido* was lying upside down, at an angle of forty-five degrees, with her port side completely buried in the seabed; so that every surface was on the tilt and her double-bottoming was largely exposed. Her bow and stern were covered in lost fishing nets.

The water was turbid, and the underwater visibility was about six metres at best. As the results of Risdon Beazley's work became evident, we could see that however much had changed above the water in the quarter of a century since they had been there, little had changed below.

Half the side plates and the double bottom from No. 2 hold had been removed from the 'tween deck to the keel, leaving a yawning and cavernous hole. To gain access to the remaining lead, we would have to do a similar job in No. 1 hold, from the bulkhead forwards. This would mean cutting through two layers of heavily framed steel, that lay obliquely, just under a metre apart. It was neither a beginner's job nor a beginner's wreck.

Nevertheless, in our enthusiasm, we embarked on a learning curve that took off skywards with the impetus of an Air Force jet.

Progress was almost non-existent. There were perpetual problems with the electro-mechanical hoist system, none of them were insoluble, but they were not the kind to be sorted out in indifferent conditions, far offshore. Consequently, the days slipped through our fingers and in the end, we had to face facts – we had got nowhere. We had no choice but to give in, we had no money coming in. Downcast and temporarily beaten, we gave up in favour of a contract laying concrete risers for a sewage outfall off Lossiemouth, to get ourselves back into funds.

All through the job, the big question was – which wreck to attempt afterwards? We went through the list repeatedly of the potentially viable ones. The *Davanger* with tin, aluminium, copper and nickel, lying twenty-five miles west of the Flannan Isles? Again, not a beginner's choice. The *Iona*, with antimony? We had gone to the extent of negotiating a salvage agreement on her, but her position, forty miles off Fair Isle, was also a godless place to start. The *Oldfield Grange*, with copper and lead on board? It was in the Channel, and lay in one of the busiest shipping lanes in the world, operating there in the middle of winter seemed positively suicidal.

There was another option, however. We had been contacted shortly before Rachel was born, by the owner of a rubber factory in Cheshire. He had a salvage agreement on a wreck lying in the Sound of Mull. This had thousands of tons of pig iron and latex on board, but he had been unable to work the *Buitenzorg* because he could not get public liability insurance and this had been stipulated by the Salvage Association as part of their agreement. Hearing on the grapevine about *Redeemer*, he had approached us about the possibility of a joint venture.

By now, this overture was five months old. Alec and I had gone over its pros and cons at the time, but quite simply thought that we would make more money on the *Guido* – how wrong can one be?

This Rattray Head fiasco, coupled with the dull nature of the work off Lossiemouth, had determined Alec's resolve.

'I'm going to succeed, there's just no question about it, but I need a sheltered wreck in order to perfect the underwater system. This one's so protected in the Sound of Mull, it couldn't be better.

'We could begin working her as soon as we're free in November and would be able to continue right through the back end of the year, unhampered by gales.'

I had to admit she was unique in this respect.

'Further,' he continued, 'we'd be close to Oban, where we could get any electrical and mechanical parts we might need. It might be a risk going into business with a stranger, and we would undoubtedly lose some of our independence as well as half the profit, but it's worth a shot.'

Accordingly, Vince was invited to Kilburns. We sat with him over a light lunch, chatting measuredly over the soup, in that getting-to-know you way. As three people attracted to the sea and wrecks, our lives could not have been more diverse, and yet there was an affinity.

In his mid-thirties and youthful looking, with short-cropped fair hair, Vince was dynamic, enthusiastic and confident. He spoke with decision, in what to our ears, tuned to Scots, was a distinctive, but nonetheless pleasant Northern accent. He was modest. There was no boasting, just an innate grit, instantly recognisable like an old school tie, as identifying a fellow entrepreneur.

To all intents and purposes it was a two-way interview, but as we knew less about him than he did about us, we began by asking many of the questions. He was obviously very successful, but what had led him into manufacturing in the first place, as opposed to the service industries, such as banking, or law? His answers were engagingly frank.

'My father was a rubber broker in Dukinfield. He'd been well respected in the industry, but hadn't encouraged me to join him, as he'd said that there wasn't much money in it.

'When he died – it was very unexpected as he was only in his early fifties – I asked my mother if I could take on his company. She gave me the chance, even though I was only twenty-one. For a year, I continued as he had, buying and selling, but by then I had seen what the rubber was used for and realised how simple manufacturing was. So, I decided to go into it myself, as it was where the big profit margins seemed to be.

'It was only in a small way to begin with, but the two companies I've got now, Rubber Reclamation and Sovereign Rubber, have been built up over the years, and now the works in Stockport employs around fifty people, making everything from mud flaps for lorries, to the bases for synthetic tennis courts and ships' fenders. We export all over the world.' At this he shrugged his shoulders, as if to say, 'Not very much to it all, really.'

'But why the *Buitenzorg*?' I asked.

'Two things: diving and rubber. I've always been a keen SCUBA diver, but get fed up with just pottering around. So I thought that if we could set up a small salvage operation on the wreck, we could lift the latex, which is pure rubber and use it in the factory. That way, as long as the costs were right, we could enjoy ourselves and get a return at the same time.

'But, as you know, I couldn't get liability insurance for the job, because I didn't have a track record. The wreck's also too deep for air and so that would mean using mixed gases, which economically is out of the question and so that's why I contacted you. If we did the job together, I could either buy the rubber myself at a fair price, or sell it within the trade, which would solve the problem of marketing it.'

It all sounded encouraging.

Before Vince left, Alec took him to Dundee to show him over *Redeemer*. He was impressed by what he saw and dispelled any final reservation we might have. 'Look, this project is a fantastic challenge. I'm sure we can make it work. I can deal with the rubber – that's no problem. I don't know much about salvage, so I would be foolish to interfere – but I'd really like to be actively involved.'

Alec would not let the opportunity slip a second time. They shook hands on the fifty:fifty deal, then and there. It was a concord that in later years would write salvage history.

From the very start, pen-pushing was kept to a minimum and half a dozen lines, repeated and exchanged by telex outlined the joint agreement and as soon as Vince relinquished the salvage agreement in our favour, we were able to begin accessing information about the aged Dutch steamship.

A factor which has always impressed me about wreck research, is how it animates history by putting past events in the context of people. A ship lying on the seabed, broken and forgotten, is only part of the equation; it is finding out about the character of the souls on board which sparks the imagination and invariably, it is their very ordinariness that reinforces the drama.

Though cast in the central role, the *Buitenzorg* appeared to be something of an enigma. Initially, we tried to solve it by tracing her plans. If the ship had been British, the procedure would have been very simple. Lloyd's Register of Shipping, or a maritime museum close to the yard in which she had been built, would have been contacted and for a modest sum a copy of the original drawings would arrive in the post.

In this instance there was no such luck. All the records that had been held in the Rijkswaterstaat in Rotterdam had been lost when the building was razed during the Second World War. Helpful officials suggested that we try the head offices of Bureau Veritas in Paris, which had registered the ship when she was built in De Shelde, Flushing in 1916. Some missions are blighted, and it was no doubt inevitable we should be informed that they had destroyed all their information on the ship just months before.

Eventually, the giant Dutch shipping line, Nedlloyd, came up trumps. It had gained title to the wrecked hull when it had taken over Rotterdamsch Lloyd, and it managed to find a simple layout, giving hold, bunker, ballast and fresh water capacities. This scant outline proved to be a godsend, providing the only reference points.

The most puzzling thing about the *Buitenzorg*, however, was that we could not find anyone in the Netherlands who had been on her when she hit the Grey Rock at 1600 hours on 14th January 1941.

She had been en route from Madras and Calcutta, to our own home port of Dundee. We knew from records of an extraordinary investigation by the Dutch Council of Shipping, that when leaving Oban as the last of a convoy of six, the first mate had cut a corner and she had struck the rock, ripping open her port side. A slight element of the absurd was introduced into the incident when the message, 'S.O.S. AGROUND, SINKING FAST' was broadcast.

In the normal way of things, it should be difficult to be doing both simultaneously, but the *Buitenzorg* managed to do so by hitting a pinnacle that rose from eighty metres of water. Within fifteen minutes of striking the charted rock in daylight, her funnels disappeared beneath the surface in a commotion of exploding boilers.

Fortunately, all the sixty-six crew were picked up. They were a mix of officers, firemen and seamen, plus cooks and cabin staff. Some of them would have been young at the time, so there should have been a chance of finding some survivors forty years later, but we had been unable to trace a single one. A Dutch friend eventually sent an article from his local newspaper and the dismal account explained why.

After the *Buitenzorg* had sunk, and the enquiry into her loss was completed, these men were transferred *en masse* to another ship on the East Asia route. There, they had the fatal misfortune to be caught by the Japanese, who boarded and put them all to the sword, apart from two, who preserved themselves by hiding in a life raft. We never knew their faces and had only ever learnt the Captain's name, but the wreck had woven our lives together, and I have always felt appalled by their savage and unworthy end. It seemed so unjust to the natural law of the sea, which is to save lives – even those of enemies.

That autumn and winter of 1986, Alec set about dismantling the *Buitenzorg*'s superstructure of wood and riveted steelwork. He was aided in this by Giffy Sutherland, who had joined us as Master after being a captain in the BP tanker fleet, Brian Houghton, who had helped build *Redeemer*, and Tony Long, a diver whom we had known for years. They had located the wreck using the echo sounder. The moorings had been laid on 26th September. The camera was down on the wreck just after nine o'clock the next morning, and they were satisfactorily positioned by half past ten.

The visibility was not as good as we had expected, because it was darkened by the peat water from the Highland rivers. Inching the camera around in the resulting obscurity, was like feeling one's way forward, somewhere unknown, on a pitch black night.

The wreck lay with a slight list to port. Following her contours from aft, the decking was traced slowly to where it met an empty lifeboat davit. A little further on, there were a couple of valve wheels, followed by two vents. These swiftly gave way to the corner of the deckhouse, rising angular and vertical, which came as a distinct surprise to Alec at the monitor, and the camera had to be lifted abruptly to clear the top of the aft accommodation. Continuing, the remains of the large, broken funnel came into view and another fifty feet revealed the bridge. Forward of this was a broken mast and derrick, plus two drum ends and a cargo winch. Going sideways, over the ship's rails, the outside of the hull was examined.

Alec deduced that she was lying north-east/south-west; and now that he had been over her once, he could begin to get his bearings. Accordingly, the camera was raised and moved aft.

Before five in the afternoon, he was in No.2 hold, which was one of the most accessible. It had three internal decks and the cargo was level with the top of the second, the 'tween deck. Achieving such a feat so easily after all the hassle of the *Guido*, leant a great air of expectancy. The sheltered waters of the Sound of Mull made everything so much easier in comparison to the open North Sea. There was no swell with which to contend and the current, though noticeable at peak times, was tolerable. A marker buoy was dropped in preparation for the next day and it was a happy mood on board that night as Giffy made a supper of thick stew and apple crumble.

The next morning, the grab went down at twenty to ten and within half an hour it was back. Rotted tea, seaweed, wood and a hatch board, were clamped within its six heavy tines and it opened to deposit *Redeemer's* first ever haul on the aft deck – a valueless and evil smelling mass of anoxic decomposition.

Down the grab went again and up. This time it spewed a cubic metre of crushed and battered tea chests, which oozed a black slime, that forty-five years ago might have been much sought after Assam or Darjeeling. Within a space of moments this erupted in a mass of tiny, leaping shrimp-like creatures that were clearly put out at being so rudely transported. The process was repeated. A steel hatch beam was wrenched away, and so on, until twenty-four hours later, the latex was partly exposed. It lay buried beneath a heap of wire, stowed for sweeping mines. With little difficulty, this was lifted above the height of the wreck; the stern of *Redeemer* was slewed ten degrees North, using the aft winches; and it was dumped.

Everyone was preoccupied with the process, but as the grab was being swung back over the hold, a miraculous thing happened. To universal surprise, Brian, who was on deck, spotted a yellowing shape, some two feet square, bobbing leisurely along the starboard bow. It was all but submerged.

'Look Alec!' he demanded, shouting up to his open window, 'it's a bale of rubber!'

With the weight of the mine-sweeping wire removed, the natural buoyancy of the latex had taken over. We had wondered if it would float and now had our answer.

The crew, in a party, leant over the side as Tony tried to secure the surprise with a boat hook. 'Bloody marvellous,' he cried in his Cockney exuberance as Alec joined them, 'the salvor's equivalent of fish jumping into a net – if only gold bars would do the same!'

At first, this bale appeared to be a stray. The top layer of this amazing raw product was hard to dislodge. It had no edges on which the grab could grip and remained jammed solid. A hole had to be made in the bundles of hessian sacks, stowed alongside, in order to gain access. Ironically, these came up by the tonne, dripping and in shreds.

As the excavation progressed, the occasional 'floater' would emerge. A look-out was kept. 'There's one,' the cry would go, with almost as much fervour as a hunt for a great white whale. Tony and Brian would hop into the rubber inflatable and go after it. Had they not been in an air-filled craft, we could perhaps have completed the imagery by giving them a harpoon.

The tally went steadily up from thirty-two bales in a week, to twenty-eight in one day. Then, without warning, it was like pulling out a plug and so many bales came up at once, that Tony and Brian could not keep up with them all. Like a game from 'Gladiators', they rushed to and fro, throwing them into an oblong net affair, that had been rigged to the side of the ship. Some got away and had to be pursued down the Sound as the current abducted them. A few eluded capture and were borne away on a journey of their own.

Vince, who had joined ship just as soon as he could get away from his factory, was now one of the crew. He was not only a great help on board, as he could turn his hands to most things, but knew all about latex and whereas one bale looked very much like another to us, he informed us otherwise.

The bales were made of sheets. The outer layers, especially the ones from the top, were discoloured with rust or filth, the inner ones were like new. 'It's easy,' he told us, splitting a bale, 'these ones, which are crinkled and creamy white, they're known as crêpe because of their texture.

'After the tree sap is tapped and collected in cups, it's taken to the refinery in churns, where it's mixed with water and acid in baths and stirred. The rubber coagulates, so that it comes out looking like tripe. It then goes through rollers to squeeze the water out. This makes it into sheets, which are quite literally pegged on a washing line to dry. This rubber has nothing more done to it. It's just cut up, baled and sold. This makes the crêpe a poorer quality.

'But this honey coloured stuff here, which is much thinner,' he said, reaching for another, 'is called Ribbed Smoked Sheet and it's premium grade, because it has been through more processes. After the washing line, it goes on to be cured over fires, so it's really dry. Then it is pressed through rollers and baled while it is still warm; this is why it's so flat and dense. Look, here's the name of its producer.'

The legend, 'Stork Brand', was stamped in every centre and continued throughout the bale, like a lump of flexible seaside rock.

Tony, lifted a sheet to his nose, 'Well isn't that something. You can still smell the smoke, even though it has been submerged for all those years.'

The latex might have been destined for Vince's factory, but as a place of labour, the wrecksite could not have been more different from the red brick of 'England's dark, satanic mills', and that was part of its attraction for him. The Sound is incredibly sheltered. It runs from the south-east to the north-west along the Morven Peninsula and is blocked off from the Atlantic by the large lumps of mainland at both ends; Mull, itself, protects it to the west.

On some winter days, when the light was clear and the snow in the clefts on the nearby mountains glowed pink in the shadows, the sense of liberty there was inspirational. A small ship, a handful of crew and the elements. No hassle. No frenzied ringing of telephones. No speeding around. Just peace, nature and an incredible technical goal.

And then, during darkness, a new weather front would sweep in from the west. The barometer would swing and a spangling universe would be replaced by a nimbus veil. Daybreak would rise late, not putting in an appearance until at least ten o'clock, as if it, too, was demoralised. The downpour would beat with all the relentlessness of a drum tattoo.

It was as if the scenery had been changed during the interval of sleep, for the topography had disappeared. Everything was transformed, even the mood. Each had gone to bed keen, expectant and reappeared groaning and ill-disposed. Giffy, who was always first up to make breakfast, would stand beside the galley, mug of tea in hand, surveying the outside world through the open steel door. Swarthy, and moustached, his normally jovial face would say it all.

'Scotland,' he greeted Alec without patriotism one morning, after there had been nothing but torrential rain for days, 'the land of the mountain and the flood. I think we've just got the flood part' and his large frame heaved as he laughed, despairing at the miserable vista. 'It's fit for Noah.

You'll have to get Moya to bring the children, and the animals from the farm.'

Every surface ran with wet. Puddles formed in the creases of the hatch tarpaulin and anywhere that had a lip. A cascade fell before their eyes, like the emptying of a child's pail, as the water poured off the wheelhouse roof. Giffy turned in disgust. What an appalling way to start the day.

To work in such conditions, albeit in oilskins and wellington boots, was to be perpetually sodden. The moisture content of the air was so high, that it was absorbed inside as well as out. The heater in the mess hardly reduced it at all. Condensation trickled down the portholes and on any bare piece of painted steel. When everyone sat round the table for teabreak, pressed close together with the rustling of yellow jackets and leggings, the aroma of clammy flesh and drenched hair was overwhelming, and curiously reminiscent of a pen of warm, damp sheep.

Yet, when the rubber was coming up, the climate did not matter a jot. Each was caught up with the almost primeval thrill of delving into a hidden hoard, and there was not a soul on board who would have swapped their demanding and uncomfortable job in favour of a tamer occupation, elsewhere.

12

BUREAUCRACY

The rubber was a bulky commodity. Soon it filled up the hold of *Redeemer*, and began to be stacked on the top of her hatch boards, like a bouncy haystack. Rather than sell it in small quantities, we had arranged with a friend, Winston Moll, to store it in a quarry just outside Oban, until we had sufficient to get a good price.

Our only problem was one of formalities; although the rubber had been insured through the London market and its loss had been reimbursed in full, the paperwork had been lost in the intervening years. This meant that the Salvage Association were unable to prove ownership and being honest agents, relinquished any claim. This was not necessarily a problem, as there was a well tried and tested process for just such circumstance. The rubber would have to be declared to the Receiver of Wreck as it was landed. It was his duty to safeguard it, and then if no one came forward within the period of a year and a day, it would become the property of the Crown under the 1894 Merchant Shipping Act.

The Receiver of Wreck at Oban was also the Customs Officer, and could not have been more helpful; to the extent that he designated Winston's quarry a duty free zone. This meant that we did not have to put down a financial bond to cover the rubber's value, because strictly it was an 'import'. He also accepted that an owner was not going to appear within the 366 day period. Accordingly, we would be allowed to sell the rubber quickly, as having being cured, it would begin to deteriorate when exposed. These dispensations were within his power.

He had been so decent, and had made all the paperwork go so smoothly, that we were caught by surprise when he came rushing down to the North Pier, as *Redeemer* was being relieved of bales.

'There's trouble,' he explained apologetically to Tony, who was unhitching the loaded cargo nets and throwing the contents onto the lorry. 'It's the Department of Transport in London. They represent the interests of the Crown and they're making a fuss.'

'It's the Tower for you, mate!' the Cockney joked, as Alec appeared from the winch controls to see what the consternation was about. 'The Department of Transport are saying that you've stolen the Queen's rubber and you've got to put it back exactly where you got it.'

As this was not what the official had said at all, he tried to look cross, but they all laughed. Alec a little nervously, because he considered that in the light of past behaviour, such perversity could be a little too near the truth. 'I thought everything was sorted ...?'

'It was,' came the dismal reply, 'but not any more.'

There was general dissent. 'Typical,' muttered Giffy in disgust, 'We should have known this would happen, as soon as we had heard they were involved,' and the murmur made it clear that this was the unanimous point of view.

'I'm sorry, lads.'

'It's not your fault,' admitted Alec, his face instantly shadowed with weariness and his demeanour sagging visibly, with the weight of another burden. 'Can you give me a number? I'll go and phone as soon as we have finished here. At least then we'll have the rubber off *Redeemer*. Thanks for all your help.'

'Right, Brian. Better get that hook and lift this net up,' he ordered, pointing as he turned to make his way back to the wheelhouse. 'We'll be another half hour. Then I'll have to change and take the truck up to Winston's to phone.' The words were without rancour, yet there was a dullness in his measured tones, that let his disappointment show.

Glencruitten, the family house in which Winston lived, lay in amongst secluded parkland high above the back of Oban. A substantial Victorian house, it was the creation of the Scottish architect Robert Lorimer, and had been paid for by investment in North America. The belipsticked and outrageously camp matador which hung in the spacious hall, had been painted by Cadell and reflected the name of a highly prosperous land company. It also confirmed the naïvety of the sober and speculative forebear.

Winston, who was factoring the estate, was an ever welcoming host and greeted Alec warmly as he drew up on the gravel, even though the latter was not a little incongruous in his battered, blue Ford Transit truck. He was one of that rare breed of people who, when they say, 'if there is ever anything I can do to help', genuinely means it.

'You want to phone. Sure. No problem. Use my office, I'll just move some of the papers. Would you like to stay for something to eat when you've finished?' He and his wife, Nicola, both had a gift for making their friends feel at home.

Alec dialled the Department of Transport. The civil servant who picked up the receiver somewhere in the rat trap of Whitehall, was superior and abrasive when he spoke. 'Our position is simple, Mr Crawford. The rubber is our property. We do not want it lifted, so you will have to leave it where it is.'

Alec always played to win, and was deceptively polite. 'It's not your property, yet. It may well fall to the Crown, but we still have a right to lift it.'

There was some blustering at the other end, 'I don't agree ... but even if that were the case, we would keep hold of it for a year and a day.'

This was just a spoiling tactic, as few cash flows could tolerate such a stopper bottling up their income.

Alec's voice deepened, as he suppressed his rapidly mounting fury, and when he spoke again, it was slowly and with alarming resolution. 'The Receiver of Wreck has agreed that we can sell the rubber because it is of a perishable nature ... however, if you want to keep it, there is about twenty tonnes of it now being delivered to a quarry along the road here. If you give me your address, we won't bother unloading it, but will get it sent directly to your offices, where you can look after it ...'

At this point, he was cut off and there was an inordinate amount of back-peddling. 'Wwwell', the man babbled, 'wwwee ssshall just have to settle on a salvage award, if that's the Receiver's view. After he has taken his seven and a half per cent handling charge, the Department of Transport will take a standard fifty per cent before costs,' with which he hung up.

Treated in such an offhand manner, Alec was exploding with anger, and vented it to Winston, as soon as he found him in the old kitchen.

'God, these people make me so furious! It's not even the Department of Transport's rubber, it's the Crown's – to my mind there's a difference. What's more, there's no such thing as a "Standard Salvage Award"! That's just sheer rubbish. Each salvage agreement is based on the circumstances of the case, and takes into account the risk that is taken; the equipment that is used; and the skill of the salvor, amongst many other things. Even if the salved property reverts to the Crown, it has no more entitlement than the original owner would have.'

'I'm sure you're right, Alec, but come on, you've been on the boat for days. Sit down and we'll have some tea, like civilised gentlemen, and you can tell me all about it. Nicola's made some cake.'

Winston, who despite what his Christian name or impeccable English accent might lead one to believe, is a tall, blond and incredibly fair skinned Italian aristocrat. He speaks five languages fluently; has an extremely quick brain; and true to national stereotype, in at least part of his character, revels in all the passion and angst of a rightful argument. Accordingly, he had considerable experience of disputes, especially with petty government officials, and sympathised with Alec's predicament wholeheartedly.

'The trouble is,' he asserted, pausing to draw on a newly lit cigarette and waft away the wreath of smoke before his face, with a vague sweep of his hand, 'these civil servants are such idiots. I get it all the time. They think they can wield such tremendous power, and yet they're invariably so stupid and lazy that they can't even be bothered to learn the law they're supposed to administer. It's a jolly good thing, too, or else with all the rules and regulations these days, it would be like living in a police state. You'll win. You'll just have to stand firm and sort them out.'

'Thanks, I will,' replied Alec gratefully, 'but that bloody Department gave us so much trouble with *Redeemer*, and we've overcome that, yet now it still seems to do nothing but stand in our way. I've no time for conspiracy theories, but if I did not believe in incompetence, I would think that there was a vendetta against us!'

'There, there, my friend. It's nothing personal. It's called bureaucracy and effects everyone who turns his back on the norm ... Now forget about it all for a very short while, before you rush back to that filthy boat of yours and all your duties at the pier. Even you need to relax. Tell me, how's your family? I haven't seen your parents for a while ...'

Reluctantly accepting this incurably Mediterranean advice, even if it were for only twenty minutes, Alec was to feel its benefit later that evening when Vince arrived and they were wandering along the harbour front together to have a beer. Dallying at Winston's had gradually subdued his ire. Now, showered and with a clean change of clothes, he found himself feeling so much better that the matter was clear in his mind.

'The Crown has the right of "Ultimus Haeres", final owner, but no more,' he told the other. 'I see no reason why they should expect to keep any more of the rubber's value, than the Salvage Association has agreed for the pig iron on the *Buitenzorg*.'

Vince thrived on problems, and treated them like a batsman at the wicket, frequently swinging for six. 'Well, if you're sure that's the case, you recap your conversation with this fellow at the Department of Transport, to Moya, and get her to respond with a telex giving our legal position.

'Meanwhile, I'll put pressure on my end to get the bales shifted immediately. There's no doubt that they will begin deteriorating in the quarry. I'll go round first thing tomorrow morning to the Receiver of Wreck and emphasise that if the Department of Transport doesn't get its finger out, the rubber will soon be worthless.'

With tough talking from Vince, some stiff telexes from us and much official humming and hawing, a deal was eventually struck. The episode should have been a salutary lesson in our dealings with this particular government department, but ever preoccupied with the wreck, we more or less forgot about its machinations, as soon as the furore was over. This was a mistake. It had not finished with us by a long measure.

The *Buitenzorg* was so old that she had been designed for being loaded and unloaded by hand. In many foreign ports there would not even have been any cranes, and dock labourers would have toiled in ant-like droves to shift the cargo. It would have had to have been tightly packed, and little consideration would have been given to the effort required to fill the deep recesses of the wings.

This area could not be reached with the grab. Soon, the camera began to descend into the void we had created in the centre of the hold and transmit pictures of scores of ghoulishly white bales of rubber, trapped either side. These were floating and were pressed hard up against the underside of the deck, as if glued by their own buoyancy. The images were surreal. If we had been able to peel back the steel deck, akin to opening a tin of sardines, they would have risen balloon-like. Some parts of the superstructure were so rotten that they could be torn off with the grab, but this corrosion was very patchy. Many of the heavy frames and beams retained their integrity and only the impact from several pounds of underwater explosive could demolish them.

Alec had had to learn so many new skills recently, that it was almost therapeutic for him to go back to blasting again. Albeit that he would not be diving to lay his charges, the techniques were just the same as he had employed on the *Oceanic* and *Argyll*. For the *bangs* to work properly, they had to be placed in direct contact with the metal. Pieces of broken hatch beams or overburden that had been scattered during the excavation had to be removed, as the hessian sacks in particular acted as a very efficient dampers.

Precision was vital and at first it was frustrating for Alec not to be able to use his own hands. He solved the problem by suspending the explosives below the camera cage. They were attached by their own their lightweight detonating cable, which ran through a shackle as a guide. In this way he found that he could keep the neatly bundled charge, with its primer and detonator firmly secured, constantly in view. Sometimes, several attempts were needed to get the *bang* in exactly the right place. It would have to be deftly manoeuvred, with a combination of manual jigging over the stern of *Redeemer* and shifting of the camera cage, using the ship; but on the whole the method was so accurate, that he was able to drop a nine inch diameter package down a twelve inch diameter vent. As he became more confident, he practised with long, thin, shapes, attached to condenser tubes to make them rigid, so that they were custom built to sheer the flat decks.

Once Alec was satisfied with the placement of his long distance handiwork, the camera would be hauled to the surface and the detonating wire transferred to the rubber inflatable. This was in order that *Redeemer* could give up her moorings and move away. Our explosions were never so great as to put her in any danger, owing to the cushion of water at that depth. The smack of the shockwaves against the bottom of the hull, however, had the tendency to sheer the joints in the water cooling systems, especially at the inlets and outlets.

In any event, it was not as if predicting the effect of marine blasting was a precise science. Mistakes could not be sanctioned and we used to take warning from the tales told 'out of school' by Risdon Beazley men, who used to calculate the kick of the charge, by the number of rivets that they sheered in their own hull. A diver would have to go down and tap in bungs made out of a broom handle, as a temporary measure to keep the water out and their maximum score was twelve. This story always gave us good amusement, but springing a plate in a welded bottom was altogether a far more serious matter, and one piece of excitement that we sincerely wished to avoid.

Within a milli-second of the lone salvor plunging the handle on the dynamo, and despatching the electrical trigger, a violent thud would smite the floorboards beneath his feet, and the whole craft would lift with a judder. That was it on the surface. The release of energy would dissipate almost as quickly as it had arrived and within moments, it was as if nothing had ever happened. Any seabirds that had been alarmed by the dull noise or shock, would cease cawing and settle down long before Giffy steamed *Redeemer* back to hitch up to her buoys. He was in no hurry, as they would have to wait for the underwater visibility to clear and this took anything up to an hour.

On the wreck, as the dust quite literally began to settle and the camera was sent down, a very different aftermath would begin to emerge. In the pocket around the explosion utter devastation filled the video monitor, and it was like a flashback to the Blitz. A crater had appeared in the deck, a torn and jagged puncture surrounded by buckled steel. All was topsy-turvy, and bare metal gleamed ragged and tooth-like. Every fragile piece of superstructure had been obliterated along with all the powdery sediment and fauna it supported.

'The trouble is, where to start?' Alec told Giffy as they viewed the demolishment. 'Those distorted beams look as if they should come free, but

I shall just have to be incredibly careful that I don't get the grab wire caught. All these pieces are razor sharp. Any one of them could cut the hoist wire in half, and then we would lose the grab.'

Proceeding tentatively, at first, he picked his way amongst the debris like a faddy eater; raising a warped deck plate, here, to see how firmly it was still attached; teasing out a crumpled strength member, there. Gradually, as the easy bits were removed and dumped over the side of the wreck, he got bolder as he made more space. Sometimes, a large section would be all but ready to come away, held tenaciously by a small flap. To wrench it free, Alec would have to get a firm hold with the grab and haul in with the Clark Chapman winch until the hoist rope was bar tight over the pulley on the 'A' frame. The Gardner engine would growl under the strain of a thirty tonne pull, as the stern of the vessel was pulled down into the water.

For what seemed an interminable while, nothing would happen, and *Redeemer* would sit, bow raised at a noticeable angle, as if riding a petrified wave … Alec would just wait. He had admirable sangfroid and gave a good impression of being nonchalant, but his old quirks gave him away. He never spoke and one could perceive him straining to listen for the slightest sound that would indicate danger … Suddenly, the hoist wire would jerk, vibrating as it went slack. The main winch would rattle into action and *Redeemer* would plunge forward, slap down into the water, as an enormous lump of wreckage was broken away.

To enter into No. 3 hold, the entire bridge and accommodation had to be removed, which meant taking away two layers of superstructure before even getting into the ship. It was a laborious job, fraught with peril each time the grab disappeared into the *Buitenzorg*; swallowed like a doctor's probe. The levels of steel were devoured relentlessly, until we eventually reached the rubber.

Unwanted cargo is termed overburden. Removing it invariably causes a blackout, but working amongst the parcels of tea was by far the worse. As soon as the plywood chests were disturbed, the leaves would go into suspension and it was like trying to see inside a swirled teapot. The hessian, too, broke into pieces the size of cornflakes and wafted about, so it was all very allusionary to breakfast.

Digging, digging, digging. The grab would take a bite, be lifted, slewed over the side and opened. It never came to the surface and soon the whole operation became fluid, subconscious even, like a digger driver guiding his bucket. In all, over two thousand tonnes of rotting dross was removed, along with the deck, the upper 'tween and 'tween decks, in order to reach the pig iron that had been stowed in the bowels of the *Buitenzorg* forty-five years before.

The weather in the Sound of Mull was so calm that we could salvage continuously, hardly moving for days at a time, almost becoming part of the landscape. The inter-island ferries plied their way, fishing boats and the occasional yacht passed by, but we were such a fixture that the image of the surrounding coastline was burnt into the radar screen, like a ghostly apparition, it was so continuously scanned. We were so close to land, that Alec had given up using the Decca Navigator for positioning in favour of medes, the same as he had used on the *Oceanic*. To be over No. 4 hold, he had to line up the waterfall on the Morvern Peninsula with a nearby house. There was nothing very exceptional about this, except that in certain conditions the wind gusted so peculiarly around the contours of the hills that it would force the cascading torrent back up into the air, like a fountain.

After many weeks, when eventually the first grabful of iron was deposited on *Redeemer*, the pigs were black and pitted. They stuck out of the glaucous ooze, like charred sausages buried in a heap of mash. Lustreless, they were our debut in recovering sunken cargoes of metal. The rub was that it would had taken just as much work to salvage ingots of zinc or tin, even gold.

They were worth about £60 per tonne, or so we thought. When the first load went off for sale, the analysis revealed that they were of poor quality as they had a high sulphur content. This demolished their value by half, as no modern foundry wanted them. As life's jokes would have it, this meant they were destined for ships' ballast.

With the future profitability in doubt and all the rubber gone, there seemed little point in carrying on with the salvage. Accordingly, it was agreed with Vince that the project should be terminated at a point when it would still 'wash its face'. His skill in his own industry had made the whole thing viable, by getting the highest returns.

I asked him once what he thought had happened to the bales. 'We used some ourselves to make everything from fenders for lorries to backdoor mats. The stuff that went abroad went mostly to Spain, where it was made into shoes, I think.'

Thus, I cannot look at the rear end of a truck or the crêpe soles on a pair of desert boots, without thinking of the *Buitenzorg*, even now.

We could not have done without Vince. We had begun our joint venture, with an imperfect recovery system that did not fully work. Six months later, aided by his constant support, we could have operated our grab down to three hundred and sixty metres. A depth that was beyond the limit of Risdon Beazley Ltd.

It was with this quiet, little publicised achievement, one which had been carried out almost unnoticed in the stark winter beauty of Scotland's west coast, that we joined the ranks of our salvage heroes, SORIMA and Sir John Williams. It was a cut off point. There could be no turning back, for the transition from diving to remote operation had been unequivocally made. Vince had shared in all this and had helped make it possible. So it was with memories of trust, faith and a unique time shared, that our ways parted in the late spring of 1985. He, to press on with his own business and us to set our sights north for Cape Wrath and the wreck of the ss *Manipur*.

The period, however, would long be remembered; and the friendship would establish the basis of our greatest successes to come.

CHAPTER

13

STRUGGLE

Of all the difficult times I spent with the children as an almost perpetual 'single parent', the week that we spent in a corrugated iron hut in Kinlochbervie was one of the worst. We had made the long haul northward to this isolated fishing port in the expanse of north-west Scotland, by train as far as Lairg. We had then caught a decrepit bus, the round-bodied sort, with faded plushy seats, that is only extant in the Highlands and Islands, to complete the final tiring leg. The day had been as draining and interminable as only travelling alone on public transport with four children, aged seven, four, two and one can be.

Set down outside the township, I was appalled that our destination should be the end of a steep track, that led up to what looked like a small, black, lambing shed with windows and a door. Our haversacks bulged despite being stuffed with the barest of childhood necessities, and were taken out by the driver, who solicitously placed them on the verge. It was obvious that he felt sorry for us, thus making the whole scene even more mortifying, as if we had been abandoned.

With the baby on my hip; Patrick held firmly by the hand; and the other two running amok, exuberant, we crossed the road to investigate our 'holiday home'. From the general air of anticipation it was apparent that only I had a heavy heart. The flimsy, see-through curtains that hung at the square windows did nothing to relieve the gaunt facade. The door, set into the peeling corrugated iron, was unlocked. Turning the handle, we found two rooms and an ancient loo. One bed and a sofa between five of us. Rachel would have to sleep in the bottom of a drawer. 'Great!' cried Rob with genuine enthusiasm, 'Let's find Dad! He could be in at the pier ...'

I did not consider that this would be the case for one moment. Given past experience of family occasions, which perpetually saw him absent, I believed that he would be out on his wreck. 'The weather will be calm – we shall not see him for the whole seven days and I shall be stuck by myself,' I thought bitterly. Thus, to walk down, round the bend in the road, and catch a glimpse of *Redeemer* below, as she entered the shelter of the natural harbour, was to get that unmistakable start, which was the recognition of our very own ship.

'There she is!' the children yelled, pointing down to the distinctive, sea battered form that was slipping in beside the quay. 'Can we run down to meet Dad? ... Yerrrrr!' Whooping with glee, they tore off. The noise only ceasing when they eventually greeted their father. Then, as if in mime, I could see them burst out all their news, interrupted only when he gave orders for the securing of the ropes.

Alec waited patiently for me to arrive, and took Patrick and Rachel instinctively, as if in exchange for our modest public kiss. It tasted pleasantly briny, like a salted cocktail glass.

'How are you? I'm so pleased you've come. Things have been very tough.'

This was an understatement. The ss *Manipur* lay seven miles off Cape Wrath, in open water at the north entrance to the Minch. If she had been just two miles further in, we should have received some protection from Lewis, the largest island in the Outer Hebridean chain, where I used to live. As it was, the spot was exposed to much of the force of the Western Atlantic. The current, too, was incredibly strong, running predominantly from the south-east. This was counter to the prevailing swell, which meant that keeping *Redeemer* in position on her moorings had been nigh impossible. She had dragged the anchors continuously.

To cap it all, the climate was invariably disagreeable and the weather forecast would reinforce this daily. At the height of summer, when even the rest of Scotland was basking in sunshine, one would hear, '... and the coldest place in the British Isles, today, at nine degrees Celsius, overcast and raining, is Cape Wrath', leading me to wonder if *Redeemer* did not have her own depression, attached to the top of her mast.

The 8600 ton *Manipur* had been sunk on 17th July 1940. Owned by Brocklebanks of Liverpool, she had been bound from Baltimore for London with a general cargo, including the various parcels of metals she had picked up on the eastern seaboard of the United States. Crossing the open ocean as part of a convoy, she had escaped the perils of the long daylight hours, only to be picked off by the German submarine, U57, in sight of land. The torpedoes scored a direct hit. She broke in two and sank in thirty-three metres of water with the loss of fourteen lives.

In such shallow water her severed hull with its towering superstructure created a navigational hazard and so she received a second pounding, this time from the Royal Navy, in order to reduce her to seabed level. Risdon Beazley had spent two years working the remains in the late fifties, but

Salvage Association records indicated that they had left behind one hundred and ten tons of copper and five hundred tons of zinc. This put the potential value at just over £350,000, which was a lot of money to us, at the time.

We had located the stern, but found it utterly decimated. Everything was flattened, obliterated by the enormous blasts. Plates lay splayed and scattered in amongst the shingly sand. Lengthy steel billets, as long as a double-decker bus, formed rows either side of the propeller shafts, resting in the position in which they had been stowed. The engine room bulkhead had been ripped off, falling to one side. Using the general layout like a map, Alec had navigated the grab to where he thought No. 3 hold ought to be. Working when conditions allowed, he had picked his way through the confused debris. In amongst casings and plates, a few copper ingots were prized from their hiding places. They were cast in short, undulating bars, like rounded Toblerone, and came up with a thin, patchy film of verdigris, though never in the quantity expected. It took days of searching to uncover a handful. Similarly, the flat encrusted slabs of zinc were all too scarce.

Alec thought that the remainder, which equated to over a hundred tonnes of copper alone, may have fallen through the double bottoms and began blasting and tearing up the buckled steel floor, but to no avail. Where had all the cargo gone? With the floor of our own hold hardly covered, the great success we had been anticipating, had turned into an unmitigated disaster. All his hopes had been shattered, along with any promise of financial reward. No wonder he had become demoralised.

We had arrived to give him moral support. He looked tired and haggard. His spirits were extremely low. 'Come on,' he implored gently, 'let's go for a walk. There's a small beach, just round the corner. I just need to get away from the ship.' He raised his voice, 'Can I leave her with you, Giff?' It was not really a question, for hardly had the reply been acknowledged, than he had turned his back and was off, sick of it all. How do you console a man who has done so much, yet considers himself to be a failure?

During those weeks on the *Manipur* and the many ghastly months that followed, I had never admired Alec more. No exertion was too much for him. He would persevere at sea, physically working himself to the point of exhaustion, as he commanded the salvage operation and kept all the equipment running. When the grab was down, he would sit all hours of daylight beside the monitor. If there were breakdowns, he repaired them. Only when the weather deteriorated into a gale that looked as if it would last, would he give up, put the ship on a mooring in Loch Bervie and haul his weary body home; stepping out at Kilburns absolutely drained.

It was up to us, his family, to help him recuperate. At home, he could immerse himself in the chatter and chaos of domestic life, and forget about the hardship for a few precious hours. There was laughter, noise, a hot bath, a seat by the fire, and a meal that did not have to gulped down in between pressing jobs, from a table which kept still. For two or three days, as long as the wind blew, he would try to recover his strength and soothe the dull ache from his muscles and bones. During those times we often discussed the salvage operation and its meagre progress, but never did he complain or blame anybody else. More often than not, he would apologise and tell me how sorry he was that money was so short and he was away so much; making everything so hard on me and the children.

It was – but there was nothing more that we could ask of him. Everything that could be done, he did without prompt. We were all proud of him in our various ways; adventurous and competent, he was the boys' hero and I have to say, mine too. I often marvelled at his achievements with *Redeemer*. The vision and determination he had to lift her and fit her out, still amazed me, even though I had been party to the process.

There had been times, I openly admit, especially when we had been labouring to get the electro-hydraulic system to work, that he had infuriated me. We were pioneering on not even a shoestring, but part of one, trying to operate down to three hundred and sixty metres with a completely new concept, while the oil industry with all its resources was hardly contemplating a third of that depth.

'Why, when Risdon Beazley could work with a two-wire grab, Alec, can't we?' I had demanded. 'We've spent a fortune on this electro-hydraulic system to improve things and it doesn't even work properly yet!'

'It's the only method that's got any future,' he had replied with his maddening logic, but with bills and reminders turning up by the handful in every post, I had been more concerned about settling today's debts, than fuelling tomorrow's dreams.

He had been right, however. The cruel twist was that I had recognised this fact at a time when he felt that everything had gone so disastrously wrong. Money was at the root of it all. *Redeemer* was functioning well and her lifting system was a triumph, but because we could find little copper on the *Manipur* and were so desperately strapped for cash, Alec chastised himself for taking us along this route.

'Never mind,' I consoled him, 'things could be worse' – and soon they were.

There was no remission in the sea conditions. We kept on dragging our moorings and had only a few tonnes to show for all our efforts. Gutted, emotionally and financially, defeat had to be admitted and we gave up;

proceeding to search for the ss *Clan Mackinlay*, on the other side of the Pentland Firth, knowing that the best part of the summer was already gone. We found her easily in those precious days that ticked frantically away, but she was untouchable, covered from stem to stern in snagged fishing nets. For the life of me, I cannot even remember what was on her, she made so little impression – rubber, comes vaguely to mind.

Thwarted and hard-pressed, there was hardly pause before we headed down the coast in search of the ss *Cape York*. This Second World War casualty was to prove far more illusive. She had been bombed just weeks after the *Manipur*. Her position of attack had been forty-five degrees, ten miles from Kinnairds Head, just north of Fraserbugh, but she had drifted for hours before sinking in an area that was literally strewn with wrecks. Armed with only the echo sounder and the Navy Hydrographer's print out, we attempted to pick her out, with no more certainty than playing 'Lucky Dip'.

Careful to be methodical, we began a structured sweep and for once, it seemed that the gods were on our side. Almost immediately, we came upon a mark that was exactly the right size and close to the last reported position. Alec laid his moorings and began a survey.

As the camera descended and in the clearest visibility, he came across the most perfect specimen of a sunken vessel. Made from riveted steel, it was lying upright on the seafloor and loomed out of the darkness. Piece by piece, he began to explore, being able to see in a six metre radius. It was like putting a jigsaw together, without ever seeing the picture as a whole. The funnels had gone, but the central bridge stood erect. All the hatches were off and he could drop the camera deep inside. Like the setting for a 'B' movie, interesting objects caught the eye. A spare cast-iron propeller remained secured at the bottom of the derrick, the lashings withered, but still in place. A capstan winch, with its twin, cast barrels seemed to have lost none of its promise for hauling in ropes.

All that she lacked to satisfy Hollywood was a treasure chest in the captain's cabin and a giant, man-eating squid. She was an ideal wreck, but had nothing to make her distinguishable from any other. She was right length and breadth, as far as could be judged, and had the correct number of holds, but was she the *Cape York*? It was like being landed in a city centre without any street names or signposts, and looking for some unmistakable feature.

Ponderously, they hovered around the stern to look for clues. 'Look at the rounded lines,' commented Giff, 'they're very attractive,' and he mocked his own nostalgia with heavy sentiment, 'och, they just don't build ships like this anymore.' He was right.

Alec ran his hand across his beard, and rubbed the hidden chin in a gesture that signified puzzlement. The wreck seemed to be just the ticket, but earlier he had found something that ought not to have been there. It was an insignificant piece of machinery that lay under the broken deck, just forward of the engine room. It had been almost indiscernible in the shades of grey that filled the video monitor, but he had known exactly what it was and perturbed, he returned to it, now.

'See that,' he explained, 'it's a steam donkey engine. You can see by the valves and piping on top. The *Cape York* ran on oil – she had combustion engines!'

Giffy sucked in his breath. 'Who would have thought it.' Up until this point, every detail had seemed to confirm the identity, but not any more. 'Do you think that she would have had it just to do the auxiliary work? It's very unlikely.'

'I know ... I know, but she's so similar.' Alec paused, 'Let's see what else we can find.' Panning through three hundred and sixty degrees, they spied a heap of what looked like silt-covered rubble. Inching the grab towards it, Alec flicked the switch and the tines closed. The flashes of reflected light, as it raked in its load left absolutely no doubt what it was. 'Steam coal. What a bastard! I don't think that this is the *Cape York*.'

'What are we going to do?'

'It's simple enough. I'm going to search for the name on the bow. I couldn't find it on the stern. I couldn't face digging to the bottom of this wreck, only to discover it's the wrong one.'

Manoeuvring forward, the camera was dropped over the side in search of the proud lettering. The contours soared downwards in a cliff-like edifice. The surface was covered in dead men's fingers that had all the appearance of inflated surgical gloves, the colonies so thick that it was impossible to know if they were looking in the right place. Using the edge of the camera cage as a hoe, Alec scraped them off, by jangling it up and down. Gradually, the creatures came away, revealing the shapes hidden underneath.

'Look, there's an "O",' exclaimed Giffy as it emerged.

'That's fine,' Alec agreed, with roused spirits. 'I could be wrong about the donkey engine, ' but then, minutes later an 'S' appeared next to it. All his expectations were dashed. 'Hell's teeth – does nothing go our way?' and in accepting that they found an impostor, his tone became empty and flat, as he reconciled himself to the worst. 'Come on. Let's see which vessel this really is,' and he snorted with disgust.

With a little more half-hearted abrasion, it was not long before *PORT DENISON* was spelt out in bold. 'Surprise, surprise,' muttered Giffy sarcastically, 'gotcha, that time' and his shoulders heaved in caustic laughter. Alec joined in, a knife edge from despair. This cargo recovery business was as loaded as a roulette wheel. Like the old gambling joke, 'How do you make a small fortune out of salvage? Start off with a big one'.

'I'll call up Moya to see if there is anything worthwhile on this one before we lift our moorings,' he announced, but even as he spoke, he knew by the way our luck seemed to be running, that this would not be the case. While he waited for the confirmation, he prepared mentally to press on and put down the grab to occupy himself. When he returned it to deck, his bitterness was clear. 'A trophy – some of the most expensive steam coal in the world!'

After a month of searching, the *Cape York* was located ten miles further out to sea than her reported sinking position. She was lying upright, with her holds full of thousands of tons of timber and grain. It would all have to be removed in order to get at the lead stowed in her deep tanks, and it was not as if this was a very valuable commodity. Our hard knocks had made us better judges. She was a non-starter – a dead loss. Alec tied up *Redeemer* among the fishing boats in Fraserburgh and came home a beaten man.

Having had such high hopes at the beginning of the salvage season, we now viewed the rapidly approaching winter with considerable alarm, appealing, 'Hasn't Risdon Beazley left any decent wrecks on which we can make a living?' If this were truly the case, the consequences were unthinkable.

Those months from November onwards, when we could not operate in open waters, had to be endured rather than passed. So frantic were we to gain an income that we even contemplated recovering slates from a small coaster and anthracite from a collier lying not far from the *Buitenzorg*, in the Sound of Mull. It was all so hopeless.

Alec, more to keep himself busy, rather than from any great conviction hired a magnetometer and attempted to locate an historical wreck. After all his endeavour, he was devastated that things had turned out so badly and when at Kilburns, he frequently spoke of giving up salvage altogether. We discussed the options, 'There are not very many for a failed, thirty-eight year old salvage engineer with a Diploma in Agriculture,' he surmised.

Mercifully, the friend who did our research, Jonathan Miller, suggested that the ss *Parthenia* might have a viable cargo to salve. And so it was, by committing ourselves to this vessel in the north Irish Sea, which had sunk following a collision en route to Glasgow from Baltimore on 29th November, 1940, that we sealed our fate.

I have no inclination, now, ten years on, to go into many of the details. Suffice to say, that she was another ex-Beazley wreck. They had removed forty-four nickel billets from No. 1 hold, leaving seven hundred tons of zinc. She was lying reasonably sheltered in one hundred and twenty metres and we could get both ship and stowage plans. In theory everything stacked up in our favour – or so we thought.

Onsite early, in the weeks of a bleak February, we quickly found a very different state of affairs; the underwater visibility was often down to hand's breadth, due to the vast run-off of ground water that poured down from the surrounding coasts of the entire United Kingdom and Eire; and even though we were seven miles south-west of the Mull of Kintyre, far from the mouth of the North Channel, the amount of water that was sucked in and out of this bottleneck, four times a day, made the currents vicious. For once the non-ferrous metal had been stowed in the upper 'tween and 'tween decks but as sod's law would have it, we found her lying on her side. This meant that there was no easy access, and explosive charge after explosive charge would be required to blow through her hull and frames. None of us had been optimists, but she proved to be far beyond our worst apprehensions.

To compound problems our overdraft had been mounting steadily for the past eighteen months. The Bank of Scotland had been patient, but it had been made clear that we just could not go on accruing debt. Three properties on the boundary of the farm at Nether Kirkton had to be sold. They raised over £120,000. This assuaged the immediate problem, but that was all.

Alec had rallied after his low point, but from the outset things had looked pretty grim on the wreck. Increasingly, our accountants and lawyers were making mutterings about voluntary liquidation. Any hopes that the *Parthenia* would be our easy salvation were rapidly dashed, she would be just another bloody struggle.

In the late spring, when the wind was blowing on the west coast and Alec had returned, we sat at the kitchen table as directors of Kilburns Salvage Company and discussed the future. Normally so direct, he began with a preamble that I knew meant awful news. 'I've been thinking about it long and hard since I've been in the Irish Sea, Moya. There's been practically nothing else on my mind, all the time, so that I begin to worry that I shall start to make silly mistakes, I'm so preoccupied.'

He paused, looking me in the eye. 'We seem to be cursed not to succeed and in many ways have gone backwards over the last year. It's quite clear that all the easy and profitable cargoes in shallow waters, especially around the British Isles, are gone. That leaves us little option ...'

He drew breath, gaining his courage. I knew that the crunch was about to come . . . the end.

'The only way that I can see us getting out of this mess is by going deeper.'

I was stunned. Speechless. We were broke and taxed beyond belief by worry. Of all the bombshells I had expected him to drop, this was the last.

14

A LUCKY
DEBACLE

I can remember exactly what I was doing when the telephone call came – vacuum-cleaning the office floor. It was not just because this was a chore that I did so seldom that it stuck in my mind, but the manner in which the Naval officer launched into his tirade without even ascertaining my name or position. I could have been the cleaning lady for all he knew – in fact, at that moment, I was.

The ancient, upright Hoover had taken a few moments to slow down when I switched it off, and I had to wait for the noise of the motor to subside before picking up the receiver. I did not have time to open my mouth, when the voice at the other end demanded, unmistakably cross, 'Is that Kilburns Salvage Company?'

'Yes.' Hardly had the confirmation been given, when it continued, 'This is the Harbour Master from the Nuclear Submarine Base at Faslane, here. Do you know that your company sent back two submarines into dry-dock, yesterday?!!!'.

My brain whirred, as if in overload ... That was news!

Obviously, he did not think so, or else he would not have framed a rhetorical question. It did not matter, for even if I had known, every instinct in my body would have warned me against admitting such guilt. As things stood, however, I was oblivious and replied, 'No,' with intuitive calm.

This was true. I did not have a clue. I had known, though, that there was something strange up. Alec had put in a radio link call the day before. He would not elaborate on the open air, only warning that there might be 'a small problem'.

'Ominous,' I had mused, 'I wonder what it is this time?' But as he got us so regularly into deep water, the sort of incredible adversity that only he could muster, I had long since given up fretting what the next complication might be. Thus, shrugging my shoulders rather philosophically, I had just waited for this one to turn up – which it had just done in rather full force . . .

'How on earth could you let off explosives in the middle of a Submarine Exercise Area without informing the Navy?!!!'

My initial shock had subsided and this was not such a fast ball. We had been letting off explosives on the *Parthenia* for the past two months and I had seen with my own eyes the small, mauve capital letters on the chart, printed, it seemed, somewhat vaguely over the expanse of the Northern Irish Sea 'SUBMARINE EXERCISE AREA'. We had even pondered at length the Note to Mariners, which cautioned, 'Submarines exercise in the area covered by this chart. A good look out is to be kept for them when passing through these waters'. We had wondered how it might effect us, but as it appeared that it was they who posed a threat to us, and not the other way round, we had merely concluded that they were just one more hazard with which we would have to cope. Besides, they knew all about us and so I asserted, mystified.

'But we did inform the Navy. Commander _____ at Taunton has the details of our operation. It's a requirement of all our salvage agreements to inform the Naval Hydrographer when we begin working a wreck. And I spoke to Commander _____ from the Clyde, only last week. He asked how much longer we would be working on the *Parthenia* and I said another couple of months. I'm sorry, there seems to have been some problem in communication – we thought that you all knew about what we were doing and didn't mind . . .'

These junior officers with whom I had dealt, had always sounded so charming and efficient, that I had assumed there would be stacks of memos in triplicate all over the country, keeping trace of what we were doing. The muffled choke I had heard as the defence sprang from my lips, told me that this was not the case, and I might as well have clapped them in irons with my own hands.

The Harbour Master's assault, bullish at the outset, petered out in the face of explanation and it was not altogether begrudgingly that he announced, 'I'll look into this – but don't think that this is the last you've heard'.

The phrase, 'If only,' came to mind and I was never more grateful to hear a line cut off.

Vaguely comprehending the ramifications of damaging Her Majesty's submarines, albeit unwittingly, I just prayed that we were not going to be sent a bill. 'Oh Alec, what have you done, now . . .?'

He, the perpetrator, was going to arrive home late that evening. Our professional advisers had become increasingly uneasy about our financial situation and had called a meeting for the following day. Alec was to attend as we knew they wanted to discuss voluntary liquidation.

Mine was an uncomfortable wait, for it had not taken long for me to conclude that his was probably a treasonable offence and I did not know quite what to expect, next. Every time the phone rang again, I suffered grave foreboding and with my imagination running riot, I would not have been surprised, had burly marines kicked in the front door.

Lights flashed in the yard around 11 p.m. It was the yellow Austin Maxi and I hastened to meet it.

'Thank God you're here – I've been so worried!'

'Have you found out what the flap's about?'

'Flap, Alec! … Flap isn't the word.' Enlightening him, I repeated the exchange I had that morning verbatim, in an urgent, irate whisper.

It took a moment for it to sink in. He stood in silence in the cool of the late spring evening. Then he burst out laughing; that half embarrassed, half jubilant laugh which just welled up inside him, when he knew he had done something absolutely awful. Covering his eyes with his hand, he shook not with shame, but mirth.

It was infectious, cathartic even, for the enormity of the 'crime' left no illusion. We were in profound trouble – and fell on each other's shoulders in hysterics, until self control could be regained.

'What do you think's going to happen about it?' he enquired, sobering up.

'Who knows? For crying out loud, what did you do?'

Little prompt was needed. The words spilled out, like a confession that had to be shared with an accomplice. 'Well,' he began excitedly, as we crunched over the gravel on our way inside. 'It just happened out of the blue. We'd been on the wreck, as usual, for a couple of days minding our own business. We were trying to make the hole into the side of No.3 hold bigger, so that we could have more space with the grab and had just set off two *bangs*, when suddenly a Navy helicopter buzzed overhead, really low, like there was no mistake it was us it wanted. The pilot broadcast over Channel 16 – which can be heard by every fisherman up and down the entire Irish coast – interrogating, "Did you just set an explosive charge off twenty minutes ago, at 1220 hours?" The only thing I could do was say, "yes", there was no point lying about it and then he asked, "Did you send another one off at 1140 hours?" and I said, "yes", again. Then he just flew up and went away and I called you.

'We did not know what it was all about, but we knew something was up.'

Adding, as if an offhand remark, 'we see submarines on the surface almost every day. I reckon they sometimes hang around the moorings, and pretend to use us a target because we're stationery for such long periods of time.'

The image of *Redeemer* as a sitting duck for novices was a startling one, all the more so because one could believe it to be true.

It was hard to sleep that night, and when the alarm bell for the telex rang in the early hours of the morning, it was a matter of seconds before I was out of bed, pulling on a discarded jumper and clattering downstairs. I knew exactly what the incoming message would be about. In the dark of the office, I could hear the bold, black letters beginning to be hammered out by the machine and felt my heart pounding against my ribs. Breathing heavily, I fumbled for the switch on the Sten gun light which stood on the desk, and watched as the imprint appeared in full, dogmatic and uncompromising:

COMSUB G
ZNR UUUU
R 2816057 MAY 87
FM COMCLYDE
TO KILBURNS SALVAGE CO TELEX 76421
BT
UNCLAS
1. YOUR SALVAGE OPERATIONS ON THE SS PARTHENIA ARE TAKING PLACE WITHIN AN ADVERTISED SUBMARINE EXERCISE AREA. UNDER NO CIRCUMSTANCES ARE UNDERWATER EXPLOSIONS TO BE INITIATED WITHOUT FIRST HAVING OBTAINED POSITIVE APPROVAL FROM MY OPERATIONS ROOM OR VIA COASTGUARD. SUBSTANTIAL DELAYS MAY BE EXPERIENCED BEFORE APPROVAL IS FORTHCOMING.

2. IN ADDITION, BEFORE INTIATING EXPLOSIONS A WARNING SECURITY BROADCAST IS TO BE MADE ON VHF CHANNEL 16

BT
NNNN

Grasping the thrust of the message, I snatched the copy from the roll and my limbs shook with adrenaline as I bounded back upstairs. Alec was alert, his hand outstretched, 'What does it say?'

'Not good news – the Navy are effectively going to stop us working the wreck.'

He swore, read the telex as I climbed in beside him and swore, even more passionately a second time, as he concluded the same. 'If we can't work the *Parthenia*, we're finished.'

'I know.'

'How do we turn this situation around?'

'Beats me.'

Sitting upright in our marital bed amongst covers that were a homage to restlessness, we thought long and hard to no avail. The only immediate measure we came up with was a holding reply, just to let the Navy know that we were on the ball.

'You'd better send it.' There was not an engine that he could not strip and rebuild, but he had never come to terms with equipment that was even remotely secretarial.

Unchastely dressed, and shivering with cold and tension in equal proportion, I returned to the office to type the non-committal response. A sequence of button pressing and the rejoinder was on its way. It travelled from a dimly lit room in an isolated farmhouse, to some bustling, illuminated military base on the other side of the country. At that moment, two corresponding organisations could not have been further apart, or more ridiculously matched.

FROM KILBURNS SALVAGE CO LTD / A.C. CRAWFORD
FOR COMCLYDE
YOUR REF: R2816052 MAY 87
SALVAGE OPERATIONS ON S.S. PARTHENIA

WITH REF TO YOUR TELEX TIMED APPROX 0136 BST 29.5.87. WE CONFIRM THAT WE SHALL BE CONTACTING YOUR OPERATIONS ROOM LATER TODAY.

A.C. CRAWFORD
29-MAY-87 02.44 A.M.

Using those stillest of the day's hours, we thrashed over the issue again and again, until somewhere around dawn Alec managed to formulate his thoughts. He had not been brought up in a military family for nothing, and taking the old maxim that 'attack is the best form of defence', he had overthrown concern with justifiable indignation.

'Firstly, we sit over the wreck when we let off the explosives, because they're going off over a hundred metres below and the water absorbs practically all the impact. We've sustained no damage yet – and nobody's closer to them than we are.'

'Secondly, they can't expect us to broadcast on Channel 16 every time we set off a charge. That's the last thing to do. When the Police gave us the explosives permit for this wreck, they told us to be as discreet as possible, because we were working so close to Northern Ireland. The safest code, they said, was not to tell anyone we have them on board. Now this COMSUB CLYDE wants us to publicise that we're using submarine blasting gelatine to the entire radio carrying population of Ireland, from Malin Head to Waterford.

'I'll put him, right,' and with this statement, I felt a glimmer of hope. His blood was up.

The exchange that he held at nine a.m., on the dot, with the bearer of the cryptic title, was robust to say the least.

'You sent my submarines into dry-dock.'

'You've compromised the safety of my entire crew.'

And within a period of minutes, each understood the other's position. Whereas one was incensed that a civilian should have caused such disruption, cost, and kicking of backsides; the other was furious that the Naval response had been so public and against all security advice. In a word – 'quits'.

Now that these views were aired, Alec enquired if the submarines had been damaged. They had not. Taking them into dry-dock had been a precaution. Both had reported impacts at the same time and the concern had been that they had bumped into each other.

'Perhaps, it was good practice for being attacked?' he suggested pragmatically. To which the clipped, but not altogether unfriendly retort was, 'It's quite terrifying enough, thank you' and the 'permission', that only hours before was going to be onerous to gain, was gentlemanly bestowed. Over the broadcast warnings, however, there was to be no concession and we were limited to twenty-five pounds a detonation. The Security Forces, however, 'would keep an eye on us'.

The British often complain about the way they are governed without giving credit for any of the good things. It is precisely because the Armed Forces are controlled by the State, that our freedoms as individuals are protected against their might. We had caused an incident, but had not broken any law. In the first few hours of investigating the matter, Admiralty lawyers would have informed COMCLYDE of that. Neither did they have any authority to ban us using explosives on the wreck and they would have been told that, too, although others could revoke our licence. This course could be pursued, but it might prove a very messy business if we put up a fight – not least because it was three weeks away from a General Election and the story had every potential for sensationalism – so, the best course was to appear magnanimous and compromise.

For our part, we played the game, accepted the terms and kept our mouths shut, without the slightest temptation to sneak to the Press. Besides, now that this little hiccough of depth-charging British submarines had been successfully dealt with, we had other potentially terminal things on our mind. At eleven o'clock, if our solicitors and accountants got their way, we would have no business at all.

Unlike our Naval conflict, we had seen this one coming a long way off and how we had feared this battle of wills – but that was yesterday. This morning, with the euphoria of surviving the onslaught of such a formidable opponent as the senior service, we were so buoyed up that the opinion of bankers and accountants seemed irrelevant. This feeling of elation was not just mental, it was physically all-consuming and so pleasant that we could not, would not, help it. Joking and chatting, we drove to our local market town and parked the car. When we happened to overtake the financial contingent, wandering morose up the street, their faces were incredulous. We entered the Georgian building and were shown to the conference room with all the usual pleasantries.

To this day, I believe that our sense of joy was the only factor that got us through the ensuing showdown. With the submarine denouement resolved, we were left feeling so invincible that words, which only twenty-four hours earlier would have sounded stilted, now carried weight and confidence.

Alec had spent weeks doing calculations and drawings, ever since our private deliberation on going deeper, and now expounded on his plans. 'There are virgin wrecks in the Mediterranean lying in up to 1800 metres of water which Risdon Beazley has never touched. For once, we will be looking at whole cargoes – not just at those they didn't want or couldn't get. Quitting British waters will also mean that we won't be so hamstrung by the weather and tidal conditions. The engineering is sound – what we need is outside capital.'

'Whose going to put money in a company with accounts like yours?'

'Someone will,' I countered, with not just the night's events, but all *Redeemer*'s achievements clear in my mind. 'We've been through too much to give in now. There will be someone who will support us and we'll find them. If not in the UK, then in Europe or America. We'll get backing even if it means going to someone like Richard Branson.'

With the mention of this multi-millionaire, who was a bye-word for high-flying, risk-taking enterprise, it was obvious that we had lost all reason. This was a rural backwater in which we were having this debate – nothing out of the ordinary ever happened here.

Nothing? Alec and I knew different due to the *Parthenia*, but kept our own counsel. This inner knowledge was a formidable weapon. We were staunch that we would succeed and because of this the insurrection was quashed.

We left victorious, but cynical. The pangs of being forsaken bit hard, however glad we were that the Company had survived to fight another day. It was to be the first major stand in a long and gruelling campaign.

CHAPTER

15

PENURY

Conviction is such a mysterious force, as invisible as the electricity that eighteenth century scientists generated and collected in Leyden jars and just as forceful. A power that can withstand misery, suffering and pain, brooking no resistance – but what is it, faith or delusion? One never really knows, because the conclusion is dependent on the result.

Ours, I considered to be a sort of projected belief. There was no rational explanation for it. We simply knew that we could solve the engineering puzzle of how to provide lift and power at depth, given time, money and a little luck. There were no cast iron guarantees. In fact the odds were quite unfavourable, but this made no difference. It was a challenge, which like a calling, seemed impossible to shirk. Oh, into what catastrophe this virtuous ardour led!

'We must be so stupid,' we told each other frequently as it seemed our perspective was so contrary to every trend. It was the 'eighties boom and monetarism ruled. Yuppie fortunes were made on share-dealing and speculation; and a fast mouth, a fast car and a mobile phone appeared to be all that was required in the slick service industries. By these standards we had failed miserably. There was no champagne lifestyle; our capital investment was incredible and our income paltry on 'No Cure/No Pay'.

After years of funding our entire design and development programme ourselves, the toll was clearly manifest in our private affairs and even though our indigence was never openly acknowledged, we knew that it was frequently discussed. Many people were very considerate about it and their solicitous enquiries were well meaning, but this was not always the case. A disquieting report came back from our researcher, Jonathan Miller: There had been a professional leak and he had been given a 'friendly warning' by a mutual acquaintance, 'be careful what you have to do with Alec Crawford – he's going to go down.' It was a piece of subversion that could prove self-fulfilling if it were spread around and so a word about client confidentiality had to be whispered in the miscreant's ear.

143

As the summer passed on the *Parthenia* and the zinc seemed no easier to winkle out from amongst the cargo of crated trucks, boxes of fuses, birchwood and ordnance stores, despite having blown an enormous hole in the side of No. 3 hold, Alec took time off the wreck to begin scouring the country, looking for investment.

The pattern became all too familiar. We would make a contact in a merchant bank or pension fund, prepare all the presentation and supporting documentation and Alec would set off on the sleeper to London. 'Fascinating, Mr Crawford. Extremely enterprising, but it's so high risk.. If it were my own money, I'd give it to you tomorrow – but we have our shareholders' interests to consider.' The whole thing was so aggravating; financial blob after financial blob could be made in property; millions could be lost on purchasing a chain of estate agents or investing in iffy shares; but if you wanted to create something new, especially something mechanical that was oily and greasy, you had not a chance.

The list of sources that we approached to take the business forward grew and grew. We tackled merchant banks, like Hambros, Morgan Grenfell, the British Linen Bank and Noble Grossart. We held meetings with pension funds, such as the Prudential, and small, medium and large venture capitalists, alike. Companies with an interest in ocean mining were contacted, including RTZ. Government funds were targeted. We even engaged the expertise of David Walker, the Chief Executive of the Bank of England, through a relation by marriage, who was the chairman of United Biscuits, but all to no avail.

By the time winter came, the *Parthenia* had been long abandoned, *Redeemer* was inert, laid up in Victoria Dock, Dundee, and even Giffy was paid off. We were struggling for our very survival.

In the harsh financial jungle, forbearance came from a surprising quarter. Willie Nicoll, the senior manager at the Bank of Scotland in Cupar was a taciturn, stocky man, with rosy cheeks and jet black hair that gave him a perpetual six o'clock shadow. This, coupled with the broad pinstripe suits he wore, made him look like a Chicago gangster, so much so that one almost expected him to talk down his nose in mobster slang, when interviewed in his office.

He might look intimidating and his manner was certainly forthright, but there were no such threats. His advice to us was simple, 'Don't ask for another penny from the Bank – and you'll be all right', he proved to be as good, if not better than his word. Far from calling in our debt, he stuck up for us, lending truth to the adage, 'you can trust a strong man, but never a weak one.' We did our best not to give him cause to foreclose on us.

Never before had we subsisted through a soulless period, nor faced such appalling prospects. For months we had survived on what little rent came from the farm after its overdraft was paid, supplementing this income by breaking up and selling the leftover scrap in the yard. In spending terms this meant that a budget of thirty pounds a week kept a family of six.

Anyone who uses a phrase that equates to 'money does not matter', has never been short of it. It is the lubricant of almost every single activity and transaction, however small and insignificant; from heating a room, to buying thread to mend clothes, to paying twenty pence to park the car. It is the grease upon the wheels of life. Without money aspect after aspect of everyday existence grinds to a painful halt and all the finer things, like pleasure are locked solid – seized by penury.

The one single claim that we could make, each night, was that we put the children warm, fed and content into their beds. In order to achieve this everything was measured, including ourselves. This self-discipline begat austerity. By necessity, everything became so utilitarian that the issues of taste or liking no longer arose. The only question was 'Do we really need this … I mean really'. If the answer was not in the affirmative, then it did not get bought. No treats. No indulgence. No outings. No chocolate biscuits. No beer or wine in the fridge. No nice clothes, cast-offs for us as well as the children. If something got broken it was only replaced if it was vital and then with the cheapest possible thing.

It was like living in our own private communist state. So much so, that I knew years later when I walked through the streets of St Petersburg, why the population's eyes were downcast and they shuffled as if the weight of the world was on their shoulders. It was the burden of endurance that they bore. Ease and grace were such unobtainable goals, that resignation had stolen into their hearts.

Our only salvation was hope. A wraith whose dim light stopped one putting an end to it all for good. Some days were so dark, that on occasion one could not see it at all and it was if there was no future. For long stretches I could not bear to tend the garden, with all the old-fashioned roses and cottage flowers I had planted, because I thought that it would be taken away.

There were ups as well as downs, and our doggedness was sure. When I had announced those words about getting support from the multi-millionaire, Richard Branson, everyone in the room, apart from Alec, had thought the idea fantastical. In June the following year, we were searching for an anonymous, rickety wooden gate that led to his houseboat, on the canal in Little Venice.

The breakthrough, which had come in January, had taken a long time to achieve. A first approach, written in the style of a personal advertisement in *The Times*, is one of the few things that I have done, which makes me cringe with embarrassment. As in advertising, the task was not only to reach the person being targeted, but to grab his attention with something snappy, in order to avoid the waste paper basket. Faced with such a predicament, I had come to the conclusion that sincerity sucked, and plumped for an audacious approach. This is how I came to send a telex with the following parody, 'Twenty-nine year old female director of a marine salvage company, into rubber and heavy metal, seeks entrepreneur for exciting business relationship with view to profit'.

The telex machine, which had been bought at vast expense in order to receive shipping casualty reports from Lloyds of London, had never been a great success in its true capacity, suddenly paid for itself overnight, because there was a response. I had got my foot in the door. The play on words was apt, but anyone less like a 'hippie-chick' is hard to imagine.

We did not get very far, however, until a new managing director was appointed to head Branson's private company, the Voyager Group, early in the New Year. David Benson had come from the shipping world of P & O, and because their ferries ran up and down to Shetland, he was familiar with all the islands. He had even been to A.K. Reid's shop in Walls, where the Foula mailboat picked up its post and stores. We therefore found that we had much in common and the deep water project fascinated him. Reasonably quickly, the whole thing developed.

A shipping company from Glasgow was also involved. It was agreed that they would manage Voyager's interests and a shelf company, Pacific Shelf 150 Ltd was formed. An offer was then made for research material that had flowed from Risdon Beazley in order to give continuity to the new company and some naval architects were commissioned to upgrade *Redeemer*. For once, it seemed that events were going in the right direction. We were cautiously optimistic and then in mid May, everything fell apart.

David Benson was extremely decent and came up to Fife especially to break the news. He sat tall and slim at the end of the kitchen table and had the courtesy not to beat about the bush. 'We have undertaken a reassessment of our investment strategy in Voyager for the short to medium term, and I'm afraid that with our decision to concentrate our resources on expanding Virgin Atlantic Airways, we can't consider investing the proposed £500,000 in the salvage project, any more. It's nothing to do with the concept or personalities, the "people chemistry" is still good – it's just business, I'm afraid.'

We were devastated. It would not have mattered so much if our expectations had not been raised, but we had expended so much credence and energy pursuing this avenue, that it was crushing to lose it all in one fell swoop. A meeting was set up with Richard Branson, to see if anything could be reprieved.

Alec and I sat in subdued mood in the sitting room of his houseboat, waiting for our appointment upstairs. How different it was from *Redeemer*. Sofas, pot plants, coffee table, books and carved parodies of green tropical frogs, instead of a steel, Class A20, fire-retardant laminate and horse hair seats. I could see a stain on the varnished wooden floor where the deck above had leaked. The windows were the sort that one propped open using the handle. I had noticed the crumbling putty that held them in, when I had stood to take in the view, of stagnant green water and leafy skyline, the situation was obvious.

There was nothing arduous or industrial about the surroundings. In fact the very opposite, they were suffocatingly tame and suburban. I knew at that instant, that despite all the panoply of the Virgin empire, all the hype about ballooning across the Atlantic, risk-takers though we might each be in our individual ways, we had nothing in common at all. The record world might be profitable, but it was totally ephemeral. With our unsophisticated ways and matter of factness, we were oddities, here, for sure.

A tight spiral staircase wound up to where Richard Branson had his desk. One of the two girlie secretaries who ministered to him showed us the way in a manner that suggested we might be impressed by the novelty of the arrangement. He rose to meet us as we cornered the upward bend. Towering above us, as we rose to his level, gave him a carefully managed, but less than subtle advantage.

Having seen his face frequently in newspapers and on television, I thought I knew what to expect. There had appeared to be a striking resemblance to the late Charlie Butterworth and I had anticipated a similar boyish charm and natural good humour. There was the same bearded face, fair curly hair and broad mouth. The height almost identical, but this man was far more thickset than I had imagined. I took in the pastel, 'V' necked jumper and open shirt, which showed the promise of a surprisingly hairy chest, but what staggered me were his eyes. Wide-set, they were of such an intense blue, that they made me start. In retrospect, I think they must have been tinted contact lenses, because cold and non-reflective, they were void of all emotion. They held no spark, no humanity, nothing but icy cobalt – and in that split second, ping, like reception of a transponder signal, I was overwhelmed by the most profound and instant dislike.

Inevitably, it was downhill all the way. He appeared totally disinterested and the nadir came when as Alec was explaining some details, he said, 'Do you mind if I sign these papers while you speak to me?'

It was such rude, arrogant behaviour that the retort, 'Yes, I do actually …' was out of my mouth without a second's thought. In all my years with Alec, whatever the circumstances, I had never known him anything less than polite and I was damned if he should be treated with such contempt. Only then, was there a glance that showed any trace of civility.

Two men could not have been more similar in age, social background, education and enterprise, but the thought of them being in the slightest way compatible was an abortion it was so ill-conceived. 'How could we have ever dreamt such a thing ... Poor old David Benson. He's going to be unpopular,' we agreed as we poured out from the 'secret garden' and into the warm, stucco-terraced street which smelt of drains.

We caught a bus and headed vaguely in the direction of the Thames. We had nowhere particularly to go, and eventually called a halt on its banks to hold a makeshift post mortem. As we overlooked the filthy grey water eddying past and carrying the flotsam and jetsam of the city in its flow, a used French letter swept along, transparent and bloated like a pallid jellyfish. Given that it was the time of Richard Branson's 'Mates' condom campaign, it seemed strangely apt – spent and down the drain. I snorted with derision.

Salvage is all about being dogged, persistent and above all, positive. In the past months we had approached over seventy sources of finance, producing summaries, cost analyses, engineering appraisals, budgets and cash flows. Figures, figures, always more figures and yet nobody wanted to know. Our quest went on.

Then one day we had an unexpected visitor at Kilburns. It was Vincent Snell, with whom we had carried out the venture on the *Buitenzorg*. He knew that we were still looking for backing and had wanted to meet up again. Sitting, having lunch two years on, it was as if nothing had changed.

'Look the rubber factory's done well recently. I can't afford the whole amount that you're looking for, but I've got a £100,000. Are there any good wrecks that we can get to with that?'

The *Glenartney*' replied Alec. 'The others we were looking at were deeper and worth more, but we built *Redeemer* to work that wreck. I would need to upgrade the lifting system, because it would be almost at its very limit, but it would be a fraction of the work.' This ship was like a siren, wooing him still.

The project was established over the remnants of crockery and coffee cups. With a minimum of fuss, mutual trust and a legal agreement double spaced and hardly filling two sides of paper, Deep Water Recovery & Exploration Ltd was born.

I did not feel foolish any more.

CHAPTER

~~~

16

ARREST

We had just had tea and were saying 'goodbye'. As I stood with Rachel on the North Pier at Oban in the drizzle of an early September afternoon, there was no hint of the trouble to come.

If the scene had been part of a film, the sound track would have already begun an ominous roll. The first few notes would have been heard in the spring, as we busied ourselves getting *Redeemer* ready for sea. That was when our dealings with the Foreign Office over the *Glenartney* were abruptly curtailed, but absorbed in our goal and not working from any script, we had no inkling of our fate. In the wet and deserted holiday resort on Scotland's west coast, high drama seemed absurd.

When Risdon Beazley cast off their moorings from around the *Glenartney* for the final time in 1978, they had lifted a total of 750 tons of tin. This had taken them two seasons and they had intended to go back, as there was good reason to believe that there was the same amount, again. Economics, however, had caught up with them and they never returned. The wreck lay unmolested for nearly ten years, until a newly formed consortium appeared onsite, in the wake of euphoria following the salvage of HMS *Edinburgh*'s gold. The diving support vessel involved was the Norwegian-owned *Wildrake*. She hovered over the wreck, her dynamic positioning system consuming hundreds of dollars of fuel a day, seemingly doing little. The size and modernity of such a ship, stationed eighteen miles off their coast, was not lost on the Tunisian Navy, especially at a time when the Americans were having a bash at General Gadaffi in Libya, next door. As no one had thought it politic to inform them what was going on, already sensitised minds ran riot. The *Wildrake* was arrested despite lying six miles outwith Tunisian waters and a brief diplomatic incident ensued.

We had watched all this theatre from the sidelines with relish, rather grateful that the prize for which we had lifted and refitted *Redeemer* had not been wrested from our grasp.

The *Glenartney* was a First World War casualty and had been insured under the War Risks Insurance Scheme. Title to her, therefore, belonged to

~~~

the Department of Transport and we monitored the developing situation closely by liaising with the Salvage Association, which acted as their agents. The reports we had been getting had gradually improved through the winter. In December, a month after we had formally asked for an agreement, we were told, 'the Department of Transport are still considering the 'Glenartney case' in the light of problems which the last operation caused and we will write to you again when they feel able to enter into another agreement'. Matters churned on. In late January, after a technical meeting, we were asked to submit a salvage plan, giving our proposal for the salvage award.

The Salvage Association's records showed that there was still 752 tons of tin and 581 tons of wolfram to be raised. Jonathan, our researcher, could confirm neither figure as there were discrepancies between the Ministry of Shipping's Weekly Schedule of Losses and the Ministry of Munition's List. The former referred to a total cargo of 5984 tons, which did not include 915 tons of tin, 63 tons of wolfram, 2 tons of scheelite and 892 tons of rubber, itemised on the latter.

If the two inventories were amalgamated, the total amount of cargo onboard equated to 7829 tons, agreeing almost exactly with the figure given by the Master, but it did not take into account the extra 535 tons of tin, that the Salvage Association believed to have gone down with the ship. A further anomaly arose in that 792 tons of tea, which had been insured under the War Risks Insurance Scheme, had not been claimed for, suggesting that it had not been loaded. It was frequent practice during war time, for cargo that was urgently required to take precedence and therefore it was reasonable to assume that the parcel of tea had been bounced at the last moment and the extra tin, wolfram and other small consignments mentioned above, had made up the balance.

Jonathan's research was meticulous, and his patient assimilation of information from the various incomplete and mouldering archives, scattered throughout the country, was the principle element in deciding the percentage of our salvage awards.

In the case of the Glenartney, although we all yearned for the extra tin to be on the wreck, we had no concrete evidence that it had been loaded and therefore could not take it into the equation for doing our sums. The salvage attempt would have to be viable on the lower figure, or not at all and accordingly, the workings were based as follows:

Tin (90% recovery rate) 150.03 tons @ £3,800/ton = £570,114
Wolfram (70% recovery rate) 30.8 tons @ £2,000/ton = £61,600

TOTAL = £631,714

With costs estimated at £222,180 for a year's work, there was margin enough for error. All this was discussed with the Salvage Association, who forwarded the details to the Department of Transport, from which there was no response.

At the end of February, we were told that there was some concern over the status of the previous salvage company, as they might have some claim if an agreement was given to another firm. This was highly implausible as under the usual terms agreed, the Secretary of State had the right to terminate his relationship without giving any cause. Nevertheless, in order to allay any fears, we asked our accountant to investigate the other salvor's financial position. The evidence was incontrovertible. The company was in Receivership, with a Liquidator approved. The coast now seemed clear. Another month passed and still nothing. By mid-April, with our refit for the deeper water of the Mediterranean two-thirds complete, we were beginning to get desperate. It appeared that although the diplomatic problem had been resolved since early in the year and all other loose ends had been tied up, there was another log jam. A policy review regarding all the wrecks and cargo to which the Department of Transport held title was being undertaken and until it was completed, 'no new agreements could be considered'.

In the privacy of the kitchen at Kilburns Alec went berserk. 'It's just ridiculous! This government prints articles in the papers about promoting enterprise and encouraging industry to invest and take risks. We do all those things in spades. We work our guts out; risk every single penny we have; pioneer new technology; replace the capability of a 1300 ton ship run by a thirty-five man crew with *Redeemer*, and what do they do – tell us that they're having a policy review.

'Well it's very simple. We have every right under British law to carry out a salvage operation without an agreement, if they can't get their act together, we shall just bloody well go ahead without them!'

Which was what we did.

How any bureaucracy conceived that businesses could turn their revenue-making activities on and off, according to its whims, left us both incredulous. We had agreed numerous salvage agreements with the Department of Transport through the Salvage Association and now, suddenly, the whole protocol had changed. We knew exactly why. Ignorance, greed, and the dogma of competitive tendering to which the incumbent administration was wed.

Their bean-counters had been at work. In a frenzy of monetarist orthodoxy, they had been calculated that there were millions in sterling lying in wrecks. This included the large number of War Losses, which they deemed rather callously for merchant shipping that had gone down in the struggle to save Great Britain from tyranny, as assets. Some were even sold like car registration plates. Until one was bought as a wedding present because it bore the name of the bride, and the relatives of a man who died when it sank, complained. Glossy government publications even fuelled the notion of untold fortune, there just for the picking, with phrases like '£'s in sunken treasure'. How they arrived at this deduction seemed so crude and simplistic, that it was pitiable – add up all the non-ferrous metal that the War Risks Insurance Scheme paid out on, adjust for inflation – and hey presto!

What the would be profiteers did not take into account, nor even wished to be told, was the reality of how this 'wealth' rested on the seabed. The vast proportion of it was encapsulated in thousands of tons of steel hull, that lay at any angle from upright to upside down, in positions that were sometimes so vague as to be given as 'in the Northern Atlantic'. It was dotted in small parcels among hundreds and thousands of tons of overburden, ranging from tinned apricots to munitions, for which there was no surviving stowage plan. It lay in conditions that guaranteed invisibility, because the underwater equipment was streaming away in the current, from a surface vessel that was pitching and tossing like a bucking bronco. Commercially, all but a fraction had a negative value, which meant that it was written-off in insurance terms. We knew about this, because we had recently added our costs in attempted salvage to some of the original pay-outs.

There was a more unsavoury aspect, too, which the whole concept of competitive tendering exacerbated. There were always parties who were more than willing to offer low salvage awards, as a means of getting their hands on agreements. They would then term these as 'contracts' and try to use them as collateral for raising finance. Over the years we had seen this gambit repeatedly, in what we estimated to be a three-year cycle – just long enough for new suckers to come along. A new company would spring up with a gleaming prospectus, promising enormous returns from sunken wrecks; it would have no ship, no equipment, no experienced personnel, but ... if it could raise a colossal sum from special sorts of investors – ones that wished not only to get a high return that would reflect their risk, but share in all the excitement, glamour and romance – then there was a killing to be made.

When sufficient money had been sucked in, a spending spree would take place, as much on salaries as anything else, and a half-hearted attempt at salvage would be made. No recoveries of any value would hit the deck and horrendous debts would be left behind. The absolute mockery of it all, was that the owner never benefited a sou. Without salved goods, there is no salved value. An owner may strike a deal that entitles him to retain thirty, forty, fifty even sixty per cent of his property's value, but the proportion is academic unless the salvor fulfils his part of the agreement.

We could give the Department of Transport the benefit of our advice until we were blue in the face, for want of a better phrase, but competitive tendering had become an unquestionable doctrine. Ever since the Tories had entered their second term with a swingeing majority, it had been applied to every aspect of contracting, from emptying bins to tug-handling aircraft carriers. Any dissent was considered tantamount to heresy, especially with such an ardent Thatcherite as Cecil Parkinson as the Secretary of State. There was no way that we were going to be allowed to undermine this cornerstone of policy – or so it was thought

We knew our salvage law. *Redeemer* was a British registered ship. The *Glenartney* was a wreck lying in International waters and had no salvor in possession. We could begin a salvage operation on her without an agreement, but we could not sell any of the recovered material. If equitable terms could not be agreed, they could be imposed on both parties by the Admiralty Court. We had nothing to be frightened of – or so we thought.

Ignored by the Department of Transport, which was 'too busy dealing with a Nato exercise' to cough up the outcome of its unconsultative pow-wow, we were more concerned by practicalities, such as not sharing the fate of the *Wildrake*, and planned to inform the Tunisian authorities of our intent.

Not ones for pulling strings normally, we succumbed to using the family network when faced with the prospect of approaching such a vast and auspicious body as the Foreign Office. Alec had a first cousin, once-removed, who had recently retired as the Second Permanent Secretary. We had never met him, but wrote all the same. In his reply he told us that he had heard all about our doings from a favourite aunt, Nancy Bampton, who often used to invite us and the children to lunch. She had even lent him her copy of *The Other Titanic*, Simon Martin's book, which he really must return. Yes, he would be more than happy to put us into contact with the Marine Section, and things went swimmingly, until one day, the woman who had been dealing with us, informed Alec that she 'could not help him any more as the Department of Transport had informed her that we were not acting in the best interests of the Country'.

Our reaction was immediate and ballistic was not the word. Alec hit the roof, 'How can anybody say that about us? The bastards!'

An incandescent telex of complaint, demanding retraction, was sent to the Minister of Aviation and Shipping, Lord Brabazon of Tara. The opportunity was also taken to make our position regarding the wreck clear, at the very top. His response was sent by a minion, and contained a denial that any such statement had been made. 'We have however advised the FCO that as a result of difficulties arising on another application for a salvage agreement we have been asked by Ministers to review our policy on salvage. Until this work is completed no new agreements can be considered … Your interest in the *Glenartney* is noted and I will contact you again in due course.' The tone of complacency was nauseating, and we consigned it to the file, disgusted.

July passed and August found us undertaking trials in the smooth and supposedly bottomless waters of Loch Ness with a completely new crew. Among them was Rodney Hopkinson who, with his Master's Ticket and considerable foreign-going experience, was a great replacement for Giffy, who could not join us because of ill health in his family. Steven Moyes from Tayport was a time-served welder, who had badgered us regularly for months to get a job. Both had put their weight behind the preparatory work, but it had taken us longer than expected. Had it not been for a number of apprentices, Steve's friends, who had come to give us a hand every weekend, free, we would never have coped. Even with Vince's money, things had still been tight, due to the size and scope of what we were trying to achieve. *Redeemer* had had to be refitted to operate in the Mediterranean; all the accommodation had to be revamped to cater for the warmer climate; the explosive store had to be upgraded, so that it could be certified for international use, her machinery had to be overhauled, including installing a new Lister generator to provide the necessary power; and her recovery system had to be extended to 660 metres.

This last job involved designing and building our first underwater hydraulic pod in order to power the grab. This was crucial, as hydraulic oil could not be pumped through such long lengths of hose, due to friction. To get round this problem, current had to be supplied to an electric motor, which ran in an oil-filled container. It was mounted on the grab and drove the hydraulic pump. The whole development, involving a combination of electrics, electronics and fluid mechanics, had proved far more difficult than Alec had envisaged and we experienced yet another learning curve.

There was an unexpectedly high voltage drop on the electrical cable, and a transformer had to be installed alongside the electrical motor in order to compensate for this. In addition, and for no explicable reason, the first hydraulic pumps we chose worked on the deck, but obstinately refused to perform as soon as they were submerged. Their replacements, however, birred away quite happily on the bottom, without appearing essentially different at all.

There was nothing that we could copy. Everything was trial and error. Without fail, as soon as one problem had been eliminated another reappeared. The numerous Allen-headed set screws on the watertight lids, had no sooner been tightened than they had to be undone again, in order that remedial surgery could take place. *Redeemer* would sit off shore on one mooring from dawn to dusk, with Castle Urquhart as a distinctive canvas, while Alec tried to get the grab to operate in the pitch dark of the loch, three hundred metres below.

A bitter setback came when the newly purchased generator blew up, and had to be totally rebuilt from the bottom shells, and pistons upwards. I ran backwards and forwards to Fife collecting spares, repairs and last minute items. It was like preparing for an expedition due to the complexity of essential items involved. Food, tools, welding and cutting gear, ropes, medicines, charts, lubricants, mooring buoys, anchors, ropes, chain, the list seemed endless and there hardly seemed a place on deck, or in any locker or drawer, that was not stuffed to the limit with something vital.

By the time it came to say farewell at Oban, we were mesmerised by exertion. Soon, we promised ourselves like battleworn infantry, we should be victorious and then we would be able to slump zombie-like and rest.

I had made the three hour journey across Scotland to give a final hand. The boys were all at school and Rachel had been delighted to be singled-out, by being packed into the front seat of the Maxi. After one last big shop at the supermarket it was time to go back. My parting from her father had been inept and awkward. So much to say, but so few words would come out of either mouth.

'Look after yourself, Alec.'

He shrugged. 'I'll do my best to succeed.'

'I know you will.'

'Take care of the children for me.'

'I promise.'

A final wave. Driving off I had left him standing plaintively among the puddles in the rapidly fading light.

We had been separated frequently before, but seldom for longer than two to three weeks. During these spells, never more than a few days passed before we would be in touch. The telephone would ring, 'Hello, it's Alec. I'm calling from ...' the place could be anywhere, but we would chat, discussing any problems to do with either business or home.

Much of the time I knew exactly what to do and it was only the very technical issues which foxed me. For years I had written all the company correspondence. Sometimes Alec would check it and make a comment, but more often than not it was by my hand alone. We were in tune from hours of talking to each other. I knew my job, yet there was a comfort in knowing that he was there to consult. As *Redeemer* headed down the west coast of Great Britain this link slipped away, released like a hawser from a bollard.

Workington in Cumbria was the last port of call in order to pick up five hundred kilograms of Plaster Gelatine, one hundred Hydrostar detonators and three reels of Pentaflex at a designated pier. More legislation had come into force since we had left the *Parthenia*, and now only specifically licensed quays could be used for the loading and unloading of explosives. Long gone the days when quarrying *bangs* could be bought over the counter at Stove & Smith's in Commercial Street in Lerwick, along with paraffin, spades, pots and pans, and any other ironmongery one cared to mention. The twenty wooden boxes, with DEEP WATER RECOVERY & EXPLORATION LTD stencilled in black, were loaded in torrential rain.

As *Redeemer* plied down the Irish Sea, I sent a telex to the Foreign Office to let them know that our British registered ship would arrive off Cap Bon, in Tunisia, in approximately fourteen days, in order that they could inform the authorities in Tunis of our arrival. We had been asked to do so by the Department of Transport, with which we were still at odds, but just on speaking terms. A link call through Land's End Radio in Cornwall, saying that they were leaving the English coast, was the last I knew I would hear from Alec for six days. The children and I got the atlas out during homework and began plotting their course.

It was only later, as his letters began to arrive that we could begin to picture in our imaginations what the journey was really like. His simple phrases, coupled with his almost constant use of the present tense made it seem as if he were in the room with us, making up for not actually hearing his voice:

Redeemer
Off Southern Portugal
September 5th 1989

At last, we are making the end of our journey. Another twenty hours should see us at Gibraltar, if all goes well.

The trip, so far, has been considerably better than expected. After a delay in leaving Workington, and having to take a pilot onboard, we set off into foggy conditions, which gradually got better as we went south. Except for today, we have had a moderate swell all the way and little wind, which has made the decks wet all the time, as we have such low freeboard. Today, there is hazy visibility and a light breeze head on – can our luck hold out?

The machinery has performed well so far. Our only breakdown being the fuel transfer pump, which we now have to transfer by hand pump. It takes about ten minutes every one and a half hours.

We run the watches six hours on and six hours off, which works quite well and no one seems tired. We have seen a few porpoises and dolphins, but not as many as we have seen off Shetland in the past – rather disappointing as I thought we might see many more. We have not even seen much of the coast, and what we have seen has been hazy. Just a long slow haul to get to Gibraltar, I'm afraid. What little time off there is, I have spent reading. There is little chance of doing any real work, while we are en route. The deck is always awash and the engine room is like an oven.

That's me off watch, again, and the end of this leg is starting to get very close. We now have the wheelhouse and mess fans working all the time, and to pump the fuel in the engine room's a very hot job.

Gibraltar at last – the weather finally gave out on us and the last six hours were the worst, as we ploughed head first into a possible Force 7 going through the Straits. It is once more compulsory pilotage – what a rip-off for a vessel of our size – and eventually we get tied up alongside. It was such a pleasant feeling to shut down the main engine, which had run trouble free for the last six days; and the generator we rebuilt in Loch Ness has only used two pints of oil. We are tied up just ahead of 'Samson', one of the largest tugs in the world, owned by Bugsier of Germany.

Now all the officialdom starts with lots of men in uniform, and all the ship's papers being looked at. I find it very intimidating, setting me quite on edge after such a long haul. I have to surrender all our paperwork, as we have no agent, yet. I try and snatch an hour's sleep – not very successfully – and then the agent comes down. Back to work. When there is someone on your side it is not so bad and the officials seem more relaxed.

We had spoken together shortly after this and the main topic of conversation was inevitably what we referred to as 'The Situation'. Things had moved apace since Alec had left the UK. To a large extent we were forcing everybody's hands.

There had been a missive from the Department of Transport stating that 'We maintain our claim to ownership of the *Glenartney* and reserve our rights'. This was fine, as we had never disputed their ownership. The Foreign Office had also been in contact. It was a chap this time, who had been really friendly. He had said that our telex had not arrived on his desk and he was acting on instructions from the Department of Transport. I therefore had to repeat our enquiry about the Tunisians' conditions for salvaging the wreck, as these had been vaguely mentioned earlier in the year. He had replied that he knew nothing of them, but would find out. The whole thing seemed quite positive.

Gibraltar was once described to me by a retired naval friend, as being like Portland in the sun, not necessarily a compliment to either place. For Alec there was no break to look around and explore.

With the elation of the morning's arrival quickly forgotten, toil began in the bright Mediterranean sun to get *Redeemer* ready for the next stage. Water was taken onboard for drinking and filling up the double bottoms as ballast. Maintenance was begun. Alone and far away from home, a stilled bunk was the only meagre comfort of being alongside. First thing the next day, a hired crane arrived to lift the moorings from the hold and onto the deck, ready for laying and the ship was refuelled. By the following afternoon, Friday, everything was lashed and the hatch covered, set to go.

We spoke again. 'What news?' he asked.

'A message has been prepared and will be sent by the British Embassy, informing the Tunisian Authorities that we are going to the *Glenartney*.'

'That's great. You've done really well. What do you think we ought to do? Do you think that we ought to wait for a reply from the Tunisians, or just turn up and begin working the wreck?'

'I really don't know, Alec ... I think waiting would be better.'

'It's so difficult to know ... Look, what I'll do is steam to Pantelleria, it's an Italian island that lies between Cap Bon and Malta. The journey will take about another four days, by which time matters might have moved on a bit. I can go ashore there, and contact you to see how they have progressed.'

He set sail at 1700 hours GMT exactly. I knew because the agent sent notification of his departure. This had arrived whilst I had been haring around Dundee, picking up the boys from disparate activities all over the city; banging open the office door, feeling jaded because it had been such an excruciating week, I had found it awaiting me. I looked at my watch – 5.15 p.m. This was British Summer Time. It meant that he had left over an hour ago. 'Thank God, he's got away,' I thought, because it had been our worry that there might be some official ruse to keep us tied up indefinitely.

Having checked that there was nothing awful on the answering machine, I switched it off and relaxed for the first time in days. As far as I was concerned, this was my cue for the weekend and gratefully sank into motherly mode.

In the kitchen, all was normality. The biscuit barrel had been raided, the dog was being petted and the small, portable television had been switched on. The children had arranged themselves on the chairs and sofa, packed together at all angles as if they were a litter. They were staring at the flickering screen in various states of disorder; Robert was filthy and still in his rugger kit after practice; Drew was in his school uniform; Patrick was in his kilt after attending the party of a female classmate; and Rachel was in her jeans, sucking her thumb. Everything was perfectly relaxed and I was about to join them, when the phone rang. Blast! There was no ignoring it.

The melodic voice had a slight, but unmistakable Welsh lilt and introduced itself as belonging to the Head of the Marine Department at the Foreign Office. 'You spoke to one of my colleagues earlier in the day – I was just phoning back for a little chat.' Having secured my somewhat dulled attention, what followed could only be referred to as a verbal bruising. A premeditated and brutal, one-sided conversation, akin to that French style of Apache dancing, where the man beats up a vulnerable woman and drags her around the stage by the hair.

Whallop. 'I hope that you appreciate that the Foreign Office has severe reservations about your proposed salvage operations off Tunisia.' Whallop. 'I also hope that you realise that it is entirely likely that you shall be arrested if you go to the *Glenartney*.' Whallop. 'I also have to inform you that in setting out in this manner, you shall be operating entirely at you own risk.'

Shaken but defiant, I replied, 'But we do everything at our own risk'. I sensed a slight stumble here. After an almost imperceptible pause, he continued, 'Nevertheless, don't you think that it would be sensible to keep your vessel in Gibraltar until this matter with the Tunisians has been completely settled?'

I had anticipated this line of attack, 'I can't, I'm afraid – she's already gone. I have a telex here saying that she left over an hour ago.'

A slight note of alarm had set in, 'Can't you stop her?'

'No, the message says that she will probably be out of range until she reaches Pantelleria . . . We made the decision for her to go after speaking to your colleague, this morning. Tell me. Has a message been sent to the British Ambassador in Tunisia?'

Experiencing some resistance, albeit feeble, the onslaught became more subdued. 'Yes, but we haven't had a reply yet. I'll give you a ring tomorrow to give you an update,' and with this I was left in a heap.

Badly mauled, I went over the attack again and again, wondering how I could do better next time. No public servant, I told myself, especially one from the Foreign Office phones on a Saturday, but I had to be ready this time, on the off chance. The one thing I felt that I really must not show, was how much I had been rattled. Confidence was all. Practising my opening remark whilst lying awake at night, I repeated the phrase, parrot-like, with all the pleasantry I could muster, 'Hello – how nice to speak to you, again!' . . . 'Hello – how nice to speak to you, again!'

Sure enough, late in the afternoon, long after I considered that the beach at St Andrews had been scratched for no good reason, at all the phone rang. It was him.

'Hello . . . how nice . . . to . . . speak to you . . . again.' Despite all my rehearsal, the words stuttered out unconvincingly, they were such a palpable untruth. We both knew that he had been beastly to me, and for a brief moment he forgot himself, laughing in surprise. This put him off his stroke, so that he was not so stern as he might have been, otherwise.

'The Ambassador has not as yet received a reply to his Note. He will, however, be making personal representations on Monday. You will have to understand that when he does so, he will be representing the interests of the British Government and the British Government, alone.'

This left me extremely concerned. The whole affair was escalating and becoming extremely impersonal. This was our livelihood, our ship, our crew we were talking about. Decades of our ambition were in the balance. We were acting entirely within British Law, and yet we seemed to have forfeited all its protection, for having the temerity to question the arbitrary policy of a government department.

On the basis that it was better to be hung for a sheep than a lamb, I got hold of the Ambassador myself. From the very outset, Steven Day could not have been kinder. He did not wish to give us any false hopes, but he would do his best for us. He also asked for details of *Redeemer* and everyone onboard. In the hands of this man, the villainy that seemed to have enshrouded us was removed and we became citizens again. For the first time in months, we were treated considerately.

Meanwhile, onboard ship, life had become pretty grim during her long haul eastwards. They had put to sea too early, without any proper rest. The forecast had been for following winds, and with such a heavy deck cargo it had been a window that they could not afford to miss. The weather had held until the end of the second day, but had broken that night, producing a short, steep swell that churned the guts. Alec, who was exhausted after working for months without a day's break, was incredibly ill and this further drained his strength. Tension was compounded by the radar going on the blink. He took it apart, but could not pinpoint the fault. In all the heat, toil, strangeness and distance from home, one of the deckhands, who had come to us from working on a fishing boat off Rockall, decided he could not take it any more, and demanded to be put ashore as soon as possible. By the time they arrived at Pantelleria, and anchored off Punta San Leonardo at 1030 hours, he was so uptight that he had eaten his fingernails to the quick.

Alec came ashore as soon as the Customs launch had visited, to find that the Port Captain would not give *Redeemer* admittance to the harbour because it was full due to ferry traffic. When he called me from the telephone box outside the bank to get a bulletin, he sounded all in.

His main concern was about sailing directly to the site without having come to some sort of understanding with the Tunisians, albeit that he would be operating in International waters. My view was that we had suffered from such conflicting attitudes and pieces of information – or misinformation, if one wanted to be precise – that there was no way of resolving the issue apart from putting into Tunisia, and sorting things out for ourselves.

'Look ... it's important for us to get started and establish ourselves as Salvor in Possession. Tunisians or no Tunisians. I'm going to go to the wrecksite tomorrow, lay the moorings and begin lifting. We should surely get a few days grace before we are discovered, and could call into Tunis in approximately two weeks, as a courtesy call, when we would need to refuel.'

The Foreign Office were duly informed of these plans and asked for any update. Their response which came at 6.30 p.m., was stark:

WE HAVE NOT RECEIVED ANY REACTION FROM THE TUNISIANS TO OUR NOTE INFORMING THEM OF YOUR VOYAGE. AS I SAID DURING OUR PREVIOUS TELEPHONE CONVERSATIONS THERE REMAINS A RISK THAT THE REDEEMER MAY BE ARRESTED. YOU WILL WISH TO KNOW THAT OUR AMBASSADOR BELIEVES THAT YOUR SHIP IS LIKELY TO BE ARRESTED AND HAS ASKED US TO REMIND YOU AGAIN THAT THE TUNISIANS ARE VIGILANT. HE HAS ALSO ASKED US TO TELL YOU THAT THE TUNISIANS MIGHT OPEN FIRE IF THE REDEEMER DOES NOT COMPLY WITH TUNISIAN ORDERS.

Alec was devastated when he called back. 'Shit! All this should have been sorted out months ago, and would have been if the Department of Transport had not told the Foreign Office we weren't acting in the best interests of the country ... I'm just sick and tired of the whole bloody thing! We can't get a berth. The anchorage is useless, we're continually dragging and have to keep a watch round the clock. I've been doing Stuart's stint too because he's just a bundle of nerves, asking to be put ashore all the time – he says he'll make his own way home! Everyone's worn out.

'I'm not too bothered about being shot at by the Tunisians, but I can't risk them cutting the moorings. We'd lose all our chain, blocks, wire, everything and it would take me weeks, plus another arm and leg, to replace it in the Mediterranean, – we've no contacts here.

'What we'll need to do, is find a port which we can enter and tie up. We can send Stuart home from there and sort out a replacement. I'll get the radar repaired and take on more fuel. Then I'll be able to leave Rod in charge of *Redeemer*, so that I can go to Tunis and sort things out. There are ferries from both Sicily and Malta – I'll look up to see which would be the most suitable choice.'

Fateful words.

We knew that all explosives had become classified as Dangerous Goods under new International Maritime Organisation regulations, because this was why we had had to take on a pilot when leaving Workington. It was irrelevant that one of the recommended ways to dispose of these 'tools' was by incineration.

Alec scanned the Admiralty List of Radio Signals, Volume 6, 1989, Part 1: Port Operations, Pilot Services and Traffic Management. Valletta in Malta required seventy-two hours notice before arrival with dangerous goods. Bizerta in Tunisia stipulated twenty-four hours, but he was not too sure that we would be welcome there. Italy, however, with which the United Kingdom was a European Community partner, mentioned no notification period at all.

We spoke again, first thing the next morning. 'Can you get hold of Winston Moll and see if he can arrange for us to go into either Marsala, or Mazarra del Vallo? They're both small ports on the south coast of Sicily and I'm not sure that anyone will speak English. Have you got a pen, I'll give you the telephone numbers. He needs to arrange for us to come in, but we'll call up the harbour office on VHF to make sure that everything is O.K., before we arrive.'

I tried repeatedly to get hold of our Italian friend the next day, but to no avail. In the end, by a tortuous route, involving an associate of an associate, the harbour master at Mazarra del Vallo was contacted, entrance secured and a ship's agent appointed. It was arranged that *Redeemer* would berth at 0700 hours.

When it came to seven o'clock at night, I had still not heard from Alec and I began to become concerned. This time, I managed to get hold of Winston, and gave him the telephone number. He called back fifteen minutes later to say that the reason that Alec had been unable to contact me was because he was in jail.

I could not believe it.

What followed was a baptism of fire for working abroad.

In the sleepy backwater that morning, nobody would admit giving permission for allowing *Redeemer* to come alongside and the officialdom that had turned up to go through formalities had seemed unhappy because she was unannounced. A passing Italian American from Boston, was commandeered as an interpreter, and through him Alec apologised. Matters were under control and they were waiting for the agent to arrive, when the Customs boarded in their immaculate white uniforms, pistols packed in their holsters. 'Had *Redeemer* any explosives or firearms onboard,' they asked Alec as Master.

'Yes. She's carrying five hundred kilograms of plaster gelatine, three roles of Pentaflex and one hundred Hydrostar detonators.' He showed them where they were.

Things got worse.

At 1445, owing to 'irregularities with her arrival', *Redeemer* was ordered out of port and told to anchor off, in order to 'undergo formalities'. Under escort, the local armed Caribinieri supervised. Twenty minutes later, totally unsuspecting, Alec was taken ashore, photographed, finger-printed, and his boot-laces and belt were removed. Led to a police cell, the portal clanged to, the grill was shut, and he found himself facing nothing but a bed with bare boards. Nobody on the ship knew where he was, or what had happened to him.

Events in Sicily got rapidly worse. Next day, the local newspaper printed an article expounding how the police had caught 'suspected terrorists'. The Customs brought our agent, and an elderly doctorre from Tuscany who was supposedly an expert to examine the explosives. On opening the store he found the wooden boxes damp. This was because they had been loaded during a cloudburst in Workington, that pelting, globular sort of rain which is all too familiar in a maritime climate. Since then they had been stowed in accordance with international regulations in the store, which was heavily insulated and dogged shut.

'This is why the moisture has not evaporated,' explained Rod the First Mate, through the agent, who acted as interpreter.

'No, no, no.' The doctorre looked up at the cloudless Mediterranean sky above and felt the intensity of the sun's heat. He shook his head and his declaration was immediate. 'They are weeping and dangerous ... You have put the entire town at risk!'

Our agent resigned on the spot.

Shortly afterwards Rod was instructed to take *Redeemer* five miles offshore, where she and the explosives were sequestered by court order. They were under armed guard.

Had it not been for a courageous young woman, who worked for the competing ship's agency and agreed to act for us, we would have had no local assistance at all.

At my end, things were no better. I rapidly learned that Alec had broken the law of 2nd October, 1967, No. 895, Disposition for the Control of Arms and Munitions, by which he had introduced explosives into the Italian State without permission. For these purposes the Italian State included their Territorial Waters, commencing at the Twelve Mile Limit. It did not matter that they were still onboard. The minimum penalty for this offence was two years imprisonment and the maximum, sixteen, both plus fines – but that was not the worst of it. Under Italian Law, you were guilty until you were proved innocent, and because there was no judicial discretion, if you were not acquitted, the minimum sentence had to be imposed. I had managed to contact Winston, who had appointed a solicitor in Palermo through a firm of Genoese marine lawyers, he knew. He had also got hold of the British Consulate in Naples.

In Scotland, I had been used to scrapes, but never anything like this. It was all so appalling and confusing. When something awful happened, like the *Parthenia* debacle, we would reach a hiatus reasonably quickly. One of us would get on the phone or telex, and with explanations, a mixture of contacts, experience, and good humour, the matter could be usually be ironed out. This was quite different. Instead of improving, Alec's chances of liberty seemed to be deteriorating at an alarming rate and, for the first time in my life, I understood what it was to be truly foreign. I did not understand anything: the law: the procedure: the culture: the language – they were all completely alien. Having consulted the Admiralty List of Radio Signals, we called into this country because of our bond as fellow members of the European Community – we might as well have come down from Mars.

For three days I was wracked, hardly sleeping, not eating. The phone rang at all hours of the day and night. The Italian authorities wanted every bit of information about us: our ship: our company: and what we were doing: photocopies of ship's documents: Articles of Association: and a chronological breakdown of events, all had to be furnished. Then, they wanted the chemical composition of the explosives, which was the manufacturer's trade secret. The stream of demands was never ending.

Alec was eventually allowed back on board, having been taken to the local magistrate and formally charged. This time, he was accompanied by a second explosives buff, who took samples. *Redeemer* was still sequestrated and under armed guard.

By the time Monday came, my nerves were so fraught that I was terrified by what was going to happen next.

There was talk that Alec might be released on bail, but it was also suggested that the Italian Government might, in addition to prosecution, take out a civil action to sue for reparations, due to all the cost. This would mean an inflated claim of tens of thousands of pounds.

Nobody doubted that he was guilty. Our Italian advocate telexed:

ALL BEING WELL, THE JUDGE WILL APPLY THE GREATEST OF LENIENCY, AND ON TOP OF A FINE – ANYTHING FROM ONE MILLION TO TEN MILLION LIRE (£400 – £4000) THE MINIMUM SENTENCE WOULD BE IMPOSED. UNFORTUNATELY HOWEVER, BEING TWO YEARS, IT WILL NOT BE SUSPENDABLE.

I was horrified. Our life lay in ruins. This meant certain jail for a man I knew to be completely innocent of anything evil at all.

What could I do?

Redeemer, the *Glenartney*, marine salvage – none of it mattered any more. It was him – his liberty I cared about most. Everything else was irrelevant. It did not matter a jot about it being our life's work. We could pick up the pieces and cope with anything if he were free, but not if he were behind bars.

I knew that the Foreign Office did not care. They were probably sitting in London thinking that we had got ourselves into a right pickle, and that it served us right. I was also aware that if I contacted them, they would try to make us go back to Gibraltar, and with all the cost and hassle, it would use up our rapidly diminishing budget. I could just as well violently sweep my arm across the length of my desk and consign every aspiration to work in deep water into the bin. Commercially, we might never recover from such a setback.

If this was the sacrifice I had to make to secure Alec's freedom, so be it. I dialled the direct number at Whitehall, expecting the worst.

CHAPTER
17
TUNISIA

'How are things going?' the melodic voice asked. I gasped in incredulity. Surely he was aware? There had been telexes containing the slightest details about *Redeemer* being despatched all over the Foreign Office. I had found this out due to a chance oversight. The circulation list had not been removed from a simple communication, answering my query as to where we could obtain a copy of Tunisian Customs regulations, and there had been this most disturbing addendum:

MAJOR
YYYY
(GOBLE)
MAIN
LIMITED 6
MAED 6
NENAD 6
CONS DEPT 6
LEGAL ADVISERS 6
PS/LORD BRABAZON
PS/ MR WALDEGRAVE
MR BAYNE
MR GORE-BOOTH
MR SLATER

ADDITIONAL
MRS BOUNDS, DPE/DTP
OCMIAN 3689
NNNN

'If,' I had wondered, 'a copy of this innocuous response has been sent to the parliamentary secretaries of two government ministers, as well as all these other departments, what on earth else is going on?' The episode had quite jolted me at the time. It was as if I had glimpsed into some covert, intelligence network and now, for the Head of the Marine Department to be supposedly in ignorance of our arrest – the situation seemed quite unreal.

'Don't you know …?' I faltered in amazement. 'The Italian authorities have sequestrated *Redeemer* in Sicily, because she has explosives on board. She's being held five miles offshore under armed guard. Alec's been charged and is going to have to stand trial. The British Vice Consul in Naples has been informed – I thought you knew …'

'Noowwww!', caught off guard, a strong Welsh lilt burst through as he reverted to the modulation of youth. For the moment it took each of us to gather our wits, it was impossible to gauge who was the most shocked.

For my part, up until that instant, I had considered the Foreign Office stern and uncaring. All knowing, if no longer all powerful. Only torment beyond endurance had forced me to seek its assistance. I had anticipated a renewal of its calculated censure, numbing myself to accept whatever terms it dictated in return for succour. Now, finding it to be in total ignorance of our predicament, and the individual who had previously given me such grief both friendly and concerned, was all too much. The relief was so unforeseen that its effect was painful. For the first time in my business career, my self control gave way. I let out a sob.

It was followed by an awkward pause. 'I'm sorry. It's just been so awful. I thought that you knew about our trouble and just weren't prepared to help.' The intonation which had once been so disapproving, grew gentle.

'Not to worry – I need to know what happened?'

As I narrated the woeful tale, he listened with the silence of an intelligent man, making notes. After I had finished, there was only one matter left to be resolved. 'Tell me. If the Italians release the *Redeemer* can she get back to Gibraltar?'

For all the new found sympathy, I had still anticipated this question . My reply was as honest, as it was quietly firm. 'No, she can't. I discussed the possibility with Alec, when he was in Pantelleria. She's not got enough bunkers and the Italian authorities won't even allow her back into port to refuel. They're also saying that they're going to telex every port in the Mediterranean to make sure we're not let in anywhere else.'

'They can't do that.'

'That's what we've been told.'

'Why?'

'I really don't know – we seem to have made ourselves very unpopular with someone'.

'Whom?'

'I haven't a clue.'

'Put everything that's happened down in a telex and I'll get back to you. Also you must find out if you'll be allowed into Bizerta and, if so, how long it will take you to get there. I'll get on to our Embassy in Tunis and seek their advice.'

'I'll do that,' I promised, adding a tentative, 'thank you . . .'

The turnaround had been so immediate, that I felt dazed as I replaced the receiver. 'How can I rely on a word of it,' I puzzled, ironing tense brows with my fingers

It was probably a ploy, or there would be a catch. He would go and speak to his superiors, or the Department of Transport would become involved, and our treatment would change again – flipped, coin-like. I could not let myself hope for the best, only to be deceived. Having no doubt that we would be recast as the bad guys, if it were at all expedient.

'Why had I phoned? I had just played straight into their hands! That's what they had wanted . . .'

Wandering through to the kitchen, alone, I was so worn out and uncertain, that I crumpled into a dejected heap on the sofa. I had thrown everything that we had ever worked for away. It was obvious. Some deal would be done behind our back, and we would be forced to Gibraltar. 'All that work raising *Redeemer*, and fitting her out for the *Glenartney* – all lost! We'll never get to her, now,' I declared to no one at all. The tears that followed were heartfelt. The worst thing was not comprehending what was happening in Sicily. If only I could speak to Alec. We were so apart. What I wanted more than anything was just to hear his voice, and have him reassure me that I had done the right thing.

Far removed from this solitary anguish, under constant guard and stripped of any autonomy, his conditions could not have been more different. He had been released back to the ship and perched uncomfortably on his seat in the wheelhouse, he was trying to occupy himself by dipping into the short stories of Saki.

The weather five miles off Capo Granitola was 'fine and clear', according to Rod's early morning entry in the Log. There was plenty of work to be done, but little which did not require a great deal of activity, like starting the Gardner generator for welding, or using the derrick to lift chain out of the hold. Such industry, Alec had surmised, might upset the armed Caribinieri tied alongside, not least for its inherent presumption that they would soon be free. It had thus been a conscious decision to allow the atmosphere onboard to become lethargic. After everyone had dawdled through a few essential chores, the crew had been left to sleep and sunbathe on the hatch cover. On which surface they now lay, protected by their towels from the sizzling rays.

Above left SORIMA's Artiglio on RMS *Egypt*.

Above right SORIMA's Eye and Tool recovery system, pioneered in the 1920s and operated until 1978, on the ss *Glenartney*.

Right Diver emerges from his one atmosphere observation chamber – we replaced him with an S.I.T. low light level camera.

Above The author, with mother-in-law, Philippa, and children aged 10, 8, 6 and 4, at the beach, 1989.

Right Electro-hydraulic lifting system, designed to 660 metres, lifting on the ss *Kohistan*, Sicillian Channel.

Redeemer equalling the world depth record for commercial cargo recovery, 1990.

Lifting on the ss *Kohistan*.

Steve Moyes with one of the lead ingots from the ss *Kohistan*.

First Mate, Rodney Hopkinson, supervises unloading at Marseilles.

Comex II, whose world record we equalled, Marseilles. *Redeemer* is on the right.

Alec with the new high speed winch with Lebus grooving.

Developing the electro-hydraulic system on the grab for the *François Vieljeux*.

The *Redeemer* at Vigo, May 1991.

Preparing one of the moorings on the wrecksite, ready for laying.

Above *Redeemer* on her four-point mooring system in 1250 metres of water.

Left Keeping good crew can be quite a problem!

Below Frank and Henry work on the electro-hydraulic pod, which powers the grab.

In this torpor, with the still water absorbing the blue of the limitless sky to make it the purest sapphire, there was a timeless quality. Everything had changed and nothing. To human eyes the distant rocky shoreline was identical to centuries before; so that one could easily perceive *Redeemer*, as just one of many vessels that had been caught up in incidents between mariners and coastal states through the epochs.

Sicily had been the battleground of countless causes, straddling as it did two continents and bisecting the Mediterranean into east and west. In their ascendancy, the Greeks, Phoenicians, Romans, Saracens, Normans, Spaniards and French had all let blood there. Even the great mathematician Archimedes, whose quantification of shape, volume and density we used in our everyday engineering calculations, was run through the guts whilst doodling in the sand around the coast, at Syracuse. Historically speaking, in the age-old situation of captive and captor, we may have drawn the short straw, but our treatment was by no means bad, for being the oppressed.

Whereas the atmosphere on *Redeemer* was subdued, the contingent on the small Caribinieri launch were enjoying good humour. The uniformed men, all at ease, lounged with their feet up and their stubby machine guns sported, somewhat disconcertingly askew. They idled away the time by chatting and smoking the strong, rich local cigarettes; but for the want of strong drink and some bikini-clad nymphets, theirs would have been the lifestyle of millionaires. There was no pretence whatsoever that we were hardened criminals, in fact quite the reverse. We had blundered into their lives, giving them all a bit of excitement followed by a few days off from more dangerous duties. Now they would just have to wait for the bureaucratic system to deal with us. Whether or not we would get justice was out of their hands. In their own minds, at least, we did not pose any threat.

Even as Alec considered it, the whole situation was laughable in many respects. The two explosives experts who had escorted him back to the ship, one naval and the other civilian, had seemed similarly bemused. After a studied examination of the offending articles below, which they had carried out much in that serious vein of generals inspecting the Boys' Brigade. There had followed a learned debate on deck. The motions had been gone through, but it was apparent the last thing they wanted was to take half a tonne of explosives ashore.

It was never said in so many words, but organised crime was a consideration. With the presence of the such a quantity of blasting gelatine having been so widely broadcast, it appeared that discretion was going to be the better part of valour. Alec was duly informed. For the moment, at least, unless they received orders to the contrary, this part of our property would not be removed. Far from being cheering, this intimation had caused him further anxiety. If they did not want to take responsibility for the bangs, the logical thing to do would be to let *Redeemer* go and detain him. How easy it would be to become totally forgotten under such circumstances and moulder in jail.

Now, on the day pending his Hearing, he had been mulling over the problems of being separated from the ship so hard, without getting anywhere, that he had tried to absorb himself in his favourite short stories. Long minutes elapsed and looking up from a page in *Tobermory – the Cat that Speaks*, he found that he had not taken in a word.

The children, me, home; he had been dwelling on all he had forsaken and happy memories had been flitting through his roving mind. Pray to God, that he would not be made to give us up.

Separated we might be, but in this sentiment we were as one. To say that fortune had not been favouring us of late, would be a little understated.

Pulling myself together, I reviewed my latest conversation with the Foreign Office. Things had gone so badly wrong recently, I had become cynical and decided to vest no faith in its auspices. To my astonishment, within an hour of putting down the phone, the Harbour Master at Workington was in contact, saying that he had had an official approach to check up on us. This was followed shortly afterwards by the local police knocking at the door, just to let me know about Alec's situation abroad. In the course of that day, it appeared that the whole of our lives was being vetted and our recent movements retraced. By late afternoon the Head of Marine Department came back and said that he would help us get into Bizerta. I could hardly credit it.

'This seems something of a turnaround.'

The retort was cryptic, 'Circumstances change'.

'That's good, because I've heard that the port will let us in.'

This disclosure, completely underplayed the resolve it had taken to organise *Redeemer*'s entry. The simple enquiry to the Lloyd's Agent had taken much deliberation. I had felt so guilty, as if there were a giant hand pointing down from the sky declaring our ship to be a travelling trouble zone. 'Never explain, never complain,' I had to remind myself, suffering waves of despair. Either, the Tunisian authorities would take a hard line and prevent us from entering their waters, or whoever it was in Sicily we had upset, would carry out their threat to make things impossible. Whichever, it hardly mattered – we would be unwelcome.

Again, when the response arrived, I felt humbled.

FURTHER TO YOUR TELEX TODAY, PORT AUTHORITIES DO NOT SEE ANY OBJECTIONS TO ALLOW VESSEL TO PROCEED

ALONGSIDE WITH EXPLOSIVES AS DESCRIBED IN YOUR MESSAGE. PLEASE CONFIRM ETA IN ORDER TO TAKE NECESSARY STEPS.

This could not be right. It was the Tunisians we were dealing with here. The unreasonable nation that would shoot us up at any given opportunity, or so we had been warned. They must have misunderstood. I made sure by asking about special procedures due to hazardous cargoes, and back came the assurance that apart from an embargo on night manoeuvres, there were none. After all the trouble that we had with our European partners across the water, the contrast seemed unreal.

Following on from this progress, telexes and phone calls continued to arrive into the evening. Even after seven, when I was making supper and overseeing homework, I had to go back through to the office, for what I thought would be a quick, two-minute conversation. Half an hour later I came back to find the book-covered table abandoned of children, the television on, and the peas I had been boiling a charred and welded layer on the bottom of the pan. Mercifully, however, the nadir seemed to have been reached and that night, I slept for the first time in days.

In Mazarra de Vallo, positive Consular overtures had begun to be made. They cut in with all the decisiveness of the clutch of the Lister generator and out of darkness, there was light. The whole local mood abruptly changed, to the extent that it was absurd. Alec was sent ashore to attend his Hearing on charges of terrorism in the rubber inflatable, with nothing more than a friendly wave from the commanding officer of the Caribinieri. No guard to accompany him. Hardly a backward glance. The inconsistency of it all was so disorientating. On a personal basis, there was such courtesy and an almost child-like trust; yet on a public level, especially once the judiciary had become involved, there was the severest protocol which had to be obeyed at all cost. It was the antithesis of everything at home.

Making his own way up to the ship's agent, he was met by their interpreter and taken to the Summary Court. There, in the presence of our Sicilian Advocate, whose address Alec nominally took as his own, a single judge arraigned him for trial on the promise that he would return. Out of the courtroom and once alone, the interpreter made her opinion on the matter quite clear. 'My father has been in prison, awaiting trial in Sicily for five years. They do whatever they want, here. There is no justice. Take my advice and don't come back.' Her words were to haunt us for months.

At last, with these formalities over, it was possible for us to speak to each other. I had waited for this for so long, but nothing could prepare me for the utter joy of hearing those easily recognisable tones. 'Hello ... I'm phoning from the agent's ...' and he paused, hardly daring to anticipate the response.

'A-lec! Thank God. I've been so worried ... How did you get on?'

'Fine' and he laughed expressively, more relaxed. 'That's the court bit over for now, anyway. I'm free to go at the moment, but there's going to be a trial. I don't know when. We'll just have to take it as it comes. *Redeemer* and the explosives should be unsequestrated this afternoon, if there's such a word, and then I hope we'll be able to go.'

'It could be worse.'

'Yes,' he agreed ruefully and all too soon we were aware that there were more pressing issues. 'How have things been developing . . .?'

'Surprisingly well. The Foreign Office have been very helpful, and you can enter Bizerta. I just need an ETA.'

'Gosh.'

This was the information he had sought, and with it the conversation faltered as he grappled with his newest concern. 'I need to ask you – the advocate from Palermo has been discussing the situation with Winston. They both think we've made such a mess of things here, that we'll do the same across the water and should just get back to Gibraltar, somehow. Give up. Retire to the farm. Do you think that we still ought to try for the *Glenartney* . . .?'

Winston had said much the same to me, too, thereby promoting some long and serious thought. 'We can't go back, Alec . . . what good would it do? It would just let Vince and everybody else who's helped us down. There's nothing for it but to press on. We'd never forgive ourselves if we gave up now, when we're so close.'

He sighed, relieved, 'That's what I think' and there was a short conspiracy of silence. The forces against which we were pitting ourselves were formidable, indeed; the disapprobation of the Department of Transport; the jurisdiction of the Tunisian government; trial by the Italian State; a shortage of money, which had been made even worse by the thousands of pounds I had just had to send in agent's costs and legal fees. On top of all this impersonal resistance, could be added the sanction of a trusted friend. It carried most weight of all, but was set aside, nevertheless.

'I'll ask the agent to let you know when we're out of Italian waters.'

'Understood. I'll let Bizerta know you're coming.'

A ten minute conversation to organise so much and say so little of what we felt.

Before Alec was permitted back to *Redeemer*, there seemed to be one final hurdle as he was directed to the Harbour Master's office. Presuming that it was going to be a dressing-down, he braced himself for the tirade. With the greatest humility, the Harbour Master apologised for all the inconvenience that he, as a visitor, had suffered and expressed a sincere hope that everything would be sorted out in due course. As a parting gesture, a medallion bearing the relief of Santa Barbara and the inscription, Capitaneria di Porto, Mazara del Vallo, 4-12-1988, was bestowed. It commemorated a battle, he was told. How unprecedented. Alec would never be able to fathom these people; and after taking his leave with the shake of his hand, he quitted the building, with a shake of his head.

It was after four in the afternoon before *Redeemer* was allowed to lift anchor. Two armed patrol boats escorted her to an imaginary line, reportedly twelve miles off the Sicilian coast, and in a piece of sea that was no different from any other, a voice in broken English called them on the VHF radio to advise that they had just left Italian waters.

'Thank you and goodbye. *Redeemer* over and out,' as his hand clicked off the speak button, Rod punched the air in jubilation, 'Whoopee! We're out! When that old doctorre said that we'd put the whole town in danger, I thought we might have to make a run for it and leave you behind, Alec.'

'I can imagine,' he agreed with a grin.

' Now it's off to the land of the Kasbah, camels and souks. I'll change course. After this treatment in Sicily, Tunisia doesn't seem so bad after all.' He could not have been more right. Such had been the twists of fate, that we could hardly wait to get into the jurisdiction of a country that had bedevilled us for months.

Steaming west-south-west at a constant nine knots, the glimmer of Bizerta rose on the horizon before dawn. An historic port, its position on the most northerly tip of the Tunisian coast, had made it ever strategic for trade. As the town gained relief from its hilly environs, a modern swing-bridge dominated the vista, until more subtle features appeared. Like a slowly opening pop-up book, the solid buttresses that defended the entrance to the Old Port, became apparent behind the long, north-running beach. There, in the distance was a fortress, and in amongst the flat roofs of the more recent French centre, minarets, punctured the skyline like the jagged blips of a cardiograph

They anchored off the breakwater until around nine. The commercial wharves lay down the east side of town, sited along the bank of an ancient canal. This had been originally cut by the early Phoenicians to give access to a large inland lake, which now formed the country's main naval base. This restricted area seemed particularly active, if the number of small grey craft that were continually zipping in and out was anything to go by.

As soon as permission to come alongside was granted, a pilot came onboard. A Greek cargo ship was waiting ahead in the roads, and by following in its wake a very grand entrance was bestowed, as the swing bridge graunched through ninety degrees to let it through. *Redeemer* was a minnow in comparison and required no such headroom.

The ropes were caught and tied, and it was so long since everyone apart from Alec had been ashore, that the keenness to get Clearance was unconcealed. When the Customs officials duly arrived, the outcome of their search could not have been more unexpected. The 'bangs' were of complete disinterest to them, but Alec was in bad odour for not declaring the ship's supply of teabags, the crews' personal cameras, a knackered black and white television that had not been able to receive a proper signal since it lost reception from the UK. They were also displeased because he had not separately itemised the drugs held in the Ship's Medical Cabinet, including morphine, which he was required to carry by statute.

It seemed that we could not win. The hard and fast rule, we had found since leaving home, was that there were no hard and fast rules. Everything had to be accepted as chance, like playing *Monopoly*, and however hard you tried, it was part of the game that you perpetrated infringements and suffered penalties, simply by moving round the board. Based on this new found philosophy, we found it easier not to care about the five hundred dinars fine, especially as we had only just been released from jail, relatively free, a few squares before.

To get to the office of our new ship's agents, Alec had to cross the rail tracks that interlaced the concrete hinterland. SOCOTU's tall manager, Noradeen, guided the way, pointing out the necessity to keep a keen eye out for the shunted wagons. As they stepped out from behind the large piles of wood, they were faced by a hive of activity. Lorries were being loaded by hundreds of stevedores, toiling in their wrapped and knotted clothes and certainly Alec felt that it would be easy to be knocked down in the stramash. Stopping by the sentry post under the shade of two enormous palm trees, his passport was briefly inspected, and they cut a dog leg into the dust blown Rue d'Algers.

SOCOTU's front door may have been unprepossessing, but it belied the calibre of the people inside. Anyone fond of reading *Our Man in Havana*, would have revelled in the character of Monsieur Mohammed Bejaoui, who could be found only by entering his shaded, inner sanctum, tucked away beyond the high, front desk. Alec's pupils were still small with the bright sunlight, and only gradually did his vision adjust to the gloom. A propeller blade fan whirred lazily, suspended below the ceiling and dull mosaiced linoleum covered the floor. The gentleman he had come to meet rose purposefully from his leather chair, his back lined by a small library of reference books.

Short and stocky, which was typical of the indigenous population, his dark olive skin and black-rimmed lips made him at first unusual to Northern European eyes, as he stood wreathed in the smoke of the cheroots he inhaled. A small, thick glass of cold, sweet tea, the colour and consistency of cough linctus, sat by his hand. Everything about him, except his conventional linen suit, was painted from a sombre palate; so that one felt slightly unnerved as to what to expect from such a very different person. Then he spoke. Gravelly-voiced, with perfect erudition, it was clear that Mr Bejaoui was as engaging as he was wise.

He inspired trust and Alec explained our predicament.

He smoked as he listened, considering all the factors carefully before he replied. 'I foresee no real difficulty with the wreck, as you describe it, because there is no Tunisian control that far off. However,' he shrugged expressively, 'things have a habit of changing here. So to make sure that you don't get into trouble, like these previous salvors you have told me about, we must write to all the relevant people. Give me the details of what you propose to do and I shall translate them for you, this afternoon. We should get a reply over the weekend.'

Le Commandant de la base Navale de la Maritime Nationale, Le Chef de Poste de La Garde Nationale Maritime, Le Chef de Quarter de la Marine Mechande, Le Directeur du Port de Bizerte, Le Reserveur des Douanes de Bizerte and Le Chef de Poste de Police were all contacted, our intention was stated, and the *Glenartney*'s position in International waters and its distance offshore were confirmed.

Saturday and Sunday, which are working days in Arab countries, came and went. As the new week began to disappear, Alec tried hard to conceal his impatience by busying everyone with preparing the moorings. So much valuable time had been lost already in Sicily, that it was hard to tolerate this slow consultative process. There was sign for encouragement, however, when personnel from the Merchant Marine turned up on the quayside. At least it signified that something was happening.

Increasingly, the word returning to Mr Bejaoui from all those contacted was that the matter was out of their jurisdiction. This was good news, but the advice we had been given from the British Consulate in Tunis, with which we had established tentative links, was to get this confirmed in writing. We suspected that it knew best, and so we waited and waited.

The wind, blowing from the north, whipped up the sea into a fierce choppy swell and it helped not to be missing any good weather on the wrecksite. Then, once it became calm, again, and there was still no reply, we began to grow cross. Operating a ship was like having a taxi meter running. This sitting around, twiddling our thumbs was costing us dearly.

On the twelfth day after our arrival, an officer from National Security called in at the SOCOTU office, asking for confirmation from the British government that we were a bona fide salvage company, that *Redeemer* was a British registered ship, that Captain Alec Crawford was a known individual, and that it was our company's intention to work on the wreck of the *Glenartney*. This was no problem, as I was by now on first name terms with my contact in the Marine Department. As soon as this reference had been delivered, then we could get going, or so we thought.

It had no sooner been despatched, when another telex winged back asking for assurance that the British Government was happy about what we were doing. This was much more difficult. The Department of Transport most certainly did not approve of our proposed operation, because it was still considering its policy on the award of salvage agreements. Keeping our fingers crossed that it would be accommodating in the circumstances, and give a message that at the very least would wish us luck in developing our technology, we made an approach through the Foreign Office. The rebuff we received sent me into paroxysms of anger:

WE HAVE NOT ENTERED INTO A SALVAGE AGREEMENT WITH YOUR COMPANY AND REGARD DEEP WATER RECOVERY AND EXPLORATION AS HAVING NO RIGHT TO RECOVER CARGO FROM THE *GLENARTNEY*.
FOLLOWING OUR RECENT REVIEW, THE POLICY OF PUTTING CARGOES OUT TO COMPETETIVE TENDER HAS BEEN REAFFIRMED

'How could they!' I ranted at the children when they came home from school, as there was no one else to tell. ' We're entirely within our rights to begin our recovery operation without a salvage agreement. It's not a legal requirement to have one – even the Department of Transport's own literature says so. Therefore, the matter's extremely simple. They have not changed the law, and so whatever policy they wish to implement, in a choice between policy and law, law comes first; and they should give us their support'.

My good nature snapped. Fit to bulldoze through any barriers, whatever the resistance, I got through switchboards and secretaries to find out the Secretary of State's number. Channelling my ire into an incandescent telex, one metre long, I made sure that his office had received it by speaking to his Parliamentary Private Secretary. I also raised the stakes by tracking down our new MP, who on the basis of my outraged phone call, gave his support in the form of a hand-delivered letter, that same afternoon.

It was all or nothing. The onslaught may have been considerable, but the cause was lost. As a champion of the whole pedantry of competitive tendering, the Right Honourable Cecil Parkinson was unmoved. The following day, his underlings bleated the same stupid cant:

WHEN THE DEPARTMENT ARE IN A POSITION TO GO OUT TO TENDER ON THIS CARGO, YOU WILL BE ADVISED.

I was devastated. As a decision it was not only totally illogical, it was constitutionally wrong. For all our good intentions and endeavours, I might as well have pleaded with the tide.

Meanwhile Vince had flown out to join *Redeemer* as he had wanted to visit the wreck. I felt awful. Gutted. There would be no way of spurring the Tunisian authorities, without the message they required and we would probably have to wait months for this competitive tendering document to come out. The farce was that there were no other salvors interested in the *Glenartney*. How long were we supposed to survive without any income, to bid against nobody else? I had failed everyone. 'What am I going to tell Alec, when he phones this evening?' I bemoaned.

The events which transpired next, were so totally unanticipated, that it was he who found out first.

'We've got the message we need!' Alec cried.

'How?' I was incredulous. 'The Department of Transport refused point blank.'

'It didn't come from them, it came from the Embassy and was sent to SOCOTU! I've got a translation from Mr Bejaoui. Look, I'll read it to you, it says' and his voice was slightly breathless with excitement, 'following our conversation of today, the British Ambassador to Tunis, confirms that on the eighth of September he informed the Tunisian Government of the intention of Captain Alec Crawford's company, to carry out a salvage operation with his ship *Redeemer*, on the wreck of the *Glenartney*, eighteen miles off Cap Bon. The operation does not raise objections on the part of the British Embassy. There – you've done it!'

I could not believe it. I had only spoken to Stephen Day, the Ambassador, once and that was before Pantelleria – but what a saviour. How humane of him to help us in this way. I was staggered and hardly took in the rest of what Alec said. The release of tension was so overwhelming, I felt ill and just plonked into the chair.

'Now we can get back to salvage,' the distant voice continued. '*Redeemer*'s ready. The camera's working and the moorings are all prepared. I intend to go out first thing tomorrow morning, as soon as it's daylight and we're allowed to move the ship. This is what we've been waiting for.'

The lucky break was to be short-lived.

18

THE GLENARTNEY

The heat was palpable as I stepped out onto aircraft steps at Monastir, like walking into a warm, moist wall and the dusk-time breeze from the Gulf of Hammamet billowed my flowing skirt. The aroma, the sounds, the temperature, it was so long since I had been abroad, it felt magical, as I literally entered a whole new world.

In amongst a motley assortment of tourists, I crossed the open aerodrome. The charter flight had been packed. How out of place I had been, seemingly the only person onboard not wearing their flesh-revealing beach clothes and laden down with sun hat, camera, and tanning lotion, amongst all the other essentials for six days' budget price, ultra-violet exposure. We should have arrived at 3 a.m., but there had been more than eighteen hours delay at Manchester. Being put into a central hotel, overnight, had been no consolation, despite the fact that other travellers had not been so lucky. I had not seen Alec for nearly two months and this hold up was like theft, cutting into our precious time together.

How hard I had worked to get away. Even the fare had been a struggle and my only means of raising the money had been by selling scrap in Dundee. For a whole week, I had taken the children down to Dundee harbour after school, to help me to tidy up the off-cuts from *Redeemer*'s refit. These were piled in a heap against the wall next to our old berth in Victoria Dock and we had to throw them into a skip, toiling away to glean all the oddly misshapen pieces, which looked like the leftovers from metallic pastry cutting. As customary, I followed the burly driver up to a less salubrious quarter of town to witness the weighing. Five tonnes – not bad for using child labour – and I collected my cash in a wad of oil-stained notes. I did not care. Scrap was part of our lives and it struck me as an honourable means as any, to pay for the trip to North Africa.

Passing through immigration, I found Alec waiting patiently in the void of the reception area. Any delight on his face had been worn to a weary grin by the long vigil. Seeing him, again, he looked so different. When we had parted, he had looked outdoors sort of healthy, now his skin was weather-beaten to a lustrous gloss, as brown as polished cedar wood. His beard was long and unkempt. It had been bleached in streaks by the elements, to the colour of his eyebrows. These were a vivid, peroxide blond. Large-pupilled, through the lack of sleep and slightly wild looking, in the khaki safari shirt and drill trousers he wore, he could have come straight from the desert, my own latter-day Indiana Jones.

'I'm so sorry you're late – I've been waiting ages.'

'I know. I'm sorry, too.'

'I've been looking forward to it, so much, as well.'

We dutifully embraced. Time-killing had extinguished any spontaneity in the reunion. The disappointment was painful, and unsought on both sides.

'Let's take a taxi and stay somewhere. I don't want to drive all the way back to *Redeemer*. We can get a hire car, tomorrow morning. I passed lots of hotels just along the road when I arrived in the louage – what a nerve-racking journey that was!' and he grinned, recalling the frantic, horn-blowing, swearing, swerving journey he had shared in one of the ubiquitous Citroen estates that served as long distance cabs. What a pleasure to see that smile, again.

We booked into a nearby establishment that catered for the package holiday trade. Its entrance was so vast, with a high pillared concrete ceiling, that it was a hybrid between the new Coventry Cathedral and a National Car Park. Our footsteps echoed down the endless white-tiled corridors as we were shown to our ground floor room. The humidity was so high that the walls ran with rivulets of condensation, like the public swimming baths.

With all the pressure that had been on us both, what a blessing it was to shut out the world. To be alone, at last. Together, after so much. There hardly seemed to be the words to adequately express the feeling. Events had made us such strangers, that simply to touch was sensual.

We shared a bath together and talked for hours. Such a cheap and innocent pleasure, in our hands it was like a vice. The children, family, friends, we discussed all the interests that bonded us as a couple, laughing and joking at particularly good tales. We were so late in the restaurant, that there was nothing left on the menu, but we could not have cared less. None of it mattered. We were our own luxury.

As we lay in bed, the scatter of tawdry furniture was illuminated by the bedside light. The night was warm and mellow and the mosquito net across the open louvre door rose sporadically on the light gusts of air, that also rustled the palm trees. Dogs barked in the distance and the cicadas rasped.

To be together was such heaven, that one wanted the evening to last and last.

After breakfast under an awning beside the sea, we knew that we would have to move on emotionally, every bit as much as physically and set about the formalities of organising a hired car. The prices were exorbitant and the money I had left only ran to the smallest, cheapest model, which happened to be a pale green Fiat Uno, with a slipping clutch. As we screeched off to the capital, Alec looked transformed. Some scissors he had brought had enabled me to prune his beard. This, coupled with the suit he had asked me to pack, plus his own tie and white shirt, had made him so respectable, that it earned me the reputation of man-tamer at our destination, the British Embassy. Wholly undeserved, I am sure.

Tunis is a city jumbling with cultures; not completely Arabian, not quite African, somewhat European. It is a glorious junction in the central Mediterranean, where all shades of humanity mix. Coming from the south along the coast, we kept to its seaward side and parked off one of the main boulevards in the new financial quarter, next to a building site. Tall, smoked-glass offices, constructed with Saudi investment, seemed to look disdainfully on the earthworks for the new sewerage system, that were being gouged past their frontages.

We navigated on foot, not too certain of our direction until we happened on the triumphal arch that marked the Place de la Victoire. Beside it, inconspicuous at first amongst all the hustle and bustle, sat the British Embassy. A café had its brightly parasolled tables and plastic chairs set out almost up to its arched wooden door. This together with its unimposing white walls and turquoise shutters, gave the building a quaint, slightly holiday air, like a family hotel on the Cornish Riviera. This illusion was immediately dispelled by the armed Tunisian sentries who, in demanding our reason for entry, quelled any expectation of chintz and trellis wallpaper.

This was just as well, as the stone staircase led to a first floor reception that had all the welcome of a Social Security office. A right angle of square, foam padded chairs, sat on a thin, wall-to-wall carpet, and the arrangement was completely at odds with the high, corniced ceiling and turn of the century fireplace. A framed poster of a much younger Queen hung above the mantelpiece. Another anachronism, a rural fifties idyll of a thatched cottage with a babbling brook, seemed to be the only other image of home worthy to bestow.

The sound of a manual typewriter emanated from behind the glass-fronted consular section at the far end of the room. It stopped for the vice-consul, Mrs Zaoui, to be notified of our arrival. This Englishwoman had met and married a Tunisian whilst a student in France. Now middle-aged and in a loose fitting suit to combat the heat, she sat behind her desk with a wry look, our file marked Classified, clearly to hand.

'You haven't been held by gunboat off Bizerta, again, I presume Captain Crawford?'

'No,' and he laughed in embarrassment remembering the incident all to well.

At 0600hrs, the morning after the Ambassador's message, the port authority had given him clearance to cast off. They had the pilot onboard and there was only one rope left attaching them to the shore, when a young Naval lieutenant, who had obviously been shaken from his bed, rushed up to tell them that they could not go, because the Navy had not given their permission.

Wanting to keep some momentum, especially with Vince there, they had decided to call his bluff. This proved to be a very false move, as an armed patrol boat cut across their path as they made their way out beyond the breakwater. They were ordered to drop anchor and there *Redeemer* was detained for four days, under surveillance. The north-westerly swell became so bad that she pitched and rolled. The wallowing was sick-making and the waves took one of her lifebelts overboard. It was only when her anchor cable parted under the strain, and she had to beginning zig-zagging up and down to keep in position, that she was eventually allowed back into port.

Alec had spoken to Mrs Zaoui at the time on the VHF, but other than making sure that they were not coming to any harm, she had been able to do little. Now, she regarded him with a not unkind and motherly eye, rather than disapproval.

'In your meeting with Commander Montamri, it was claimed that as the Germans compensated the British for their war losses, the *Glenartney* was no longer a British ship.'

Alec nodded.

'It was also suggested that Tunisian Customs control now extends well beyond their twelve mile limit.

'Yes.'

'And you have been led to believe that they will come to a financial deal regarding the wreck.'

'That's right'.

She raised her eyebrows as if to say, 'wonders never cease' and turned her attention to me. 'Before we go any further, Mrs Crawford, I shall explain to you, as I have your husband, that the Embassy regards what you are doing as a commercial venture. You will therefore receive our commercial and consular assistance, but because the Department of Transport has not issued your company with a salvage agreement, we cannot enter into any negotiations on your behalf.'

'I understand.'

'I've been trying to get hold of various people in the Cabinet for you, but like all politicians they're very adept at being too busy when there's a sticky issue. The Ambassador would like to meet you both, but he's attending a state function, this morning. Come and meet the First Secretary, instead.'

He, too, was very decent to us within the restraints imposed, but we were left in no doubt that we would have to forge on alone.

We sought out our motorised tin can for the final leg of the journey north. The road was straight and wide. With windows wound down to combat the heat, we hit the suburbs of Bizerta within an hour and a half. The squat, white houses with their flat roofs had a cubic charm. Crossing over the swing bridge, I could see *Redeemer* on the far side of the canal, below and it gave me the old thrill.

First, we had to call in to SOCOTU, where I had to give Mr Bejaoui my passport in exchange for a yellow piece of paper. This was printed in both French and the rounded squiggles of Arabic, and was to act as my *Port Passe*. The swap was like one of those ghastly 'what's the difference' riddles. It was of course that I could not leave the country and I was left feeling more than short-changed.

At the sentry post, a guard rummaged through my carpet bag out of sheer curiosity as much as anything else. We ran the gauntlet of the railway tracks and made our way to the ship. With a new mosque in the near distance and two boys fishing around her in a dory, catching octopi. It was in exotic contrast to the Steamers' Pier at Oban, where I had seen her last. Stepping aboard, I was greeted with open enthusiasm. Everyone was fed-up with waiting for a breakthrough in the decision-making process. It had been nearly a fortnight since Vince had left and I had arrived as a new catalyst.

One can sense, at times, when one has an effect purely by virtue of being female, and here, in a traditional corner of a Muslim country, in amongst the male preserve of shipping and Merchande Marine, I knew that my presence had caused a stir.

The very next afternoon, Alec and I were called down to the agent's office to meet two naval officers. The more senior was from Intelligence, Mr Bejaoui informed us. A few months before he had dealt with the Israeli raid just outside Tunis, when a leader of the PLO had been assassinated. I gulped. This was a bit out of my depth. My passport had been surrendered and now I was being questioned by military security. What was most unsettling was the man's seediness. Flakes of dandruff from his slicked, black hair were conspicuous on his badly fitting uniform and his eyes narrowed to slits, as he smoked compulsively. Intrigue, espionage, the investigation of betrayal, all the plots made glamorous in movies. Here was a prime mover in all these things questioning us with nicotine stains on his fingertips.

Mr Bejaoui saw the visitors out and returned. 'Not the pleasantest of experiences, but these things have to be done. I'm told that they have to compile their report and have it on the desk of their superior by 8 a.m., tomorrow. It seems that there's an agreement in sight.'

It proved to be as illusive as the end of a rainbow.

At approximately the same hour as our details were expected in some anonymous in-tray, we set off for the Embassy. Expectant because we had learnt that the person dealing with the matter, was based at the Naval headquarters in Tunis. Mrs Zaoui, who had been palmed off despite her excellent use of the local vernacular, handed over his details with the air of a minder giving two naughty children a project that would keep them occupied for some considerable while. Imagine her surprise when we bounced back, with an appointment to see Colonel Cheriff the following afternoon.

'How did you arrange that?' she enquired, impressed.

'We walked down the road and stumbled on the Tunis office of SOCOTU. The general manager there thought that Moya was from the Embassy, because she was so smartly dressed and phoned on our behalf, then and there.'

'It's like David and Goliath,' I suggested cheerfully, flushed with such immediate success.

'More like feeding the Christians to the lions, if you asked me,' she retorted a little too emphatically for it to be quite a joke, but laughed, all the same. 'Anyway, the Ambassador would like to meet you. You're invited to his Residence this evening at six-thirty. Do you know where it is?'

We had to undergo a security check and the underside of the chassis was checked for bombs, before we were allowed to whirr up to the forecourt with our slipping clutch at the appointed hour. The grace of the old colonial building was appealing and Stephen Day stood on the veranda to greet us. Relaxed and urbane in his claret cardigan, tumbler of whisky in hand, he had that quiet sort of educated charm that one fears, at times, has become totally outmoded. One could easily imagine him as a favourite uncle, of the companion kind.

What I liked most about Mr Day was that he took us entirely as he found us. No pomp, no ceremony. He and his wife treated us sincerely and on leaving, when I thanked him for the message he had given on our behalf to the Tunisians, he momentarily cast down his eyes, as if in reflection, before looking me straight in the eye. 'I was sent a copy of your telex to Cecil Parkinson and thought that you deserved a hand ... London did not tell me to help you – but then, it did not tell me not to help you, either,' his lips flickered mischievously in the shadow of a smile.

Kindness can be the most effective instrument, if only one has the courage to use it. We would not forget his deed. It had found its mark.

The office of Colonel Cheriff was located on the hill behind the British Embassy and to get to it we had to go through the steep Rue du Kasbah. A young clerk from the SOCOTU office acted as our guide through the narrow winding alleys, checking over his shoulder conscientiously to make sure that we were not waylaid. 'There are some not very nice people about,' he explained. On either side of the covered, narrow thoroughfare, vendors of every kind sold their wares: carpets, clothes, leather goods, garishly lacy lingerie, prickly pears and spices in bushels and sacks. Each salesman called out the merits of what he sold, beckoning his potential customers with samples. We wound our way through the crowded, close-knit theatre, slightly overwhelmed.

Suddenly, the market came to an end and there was daylight. The orderliness and cleanliness of the administrative centre with its substantial edifices, laid out around a formal open space, came as a shock. Worse to come was the sentry box at the Ministry of Defence. I handed over my now slightly crumpled Port Passe, none too convinced of its authority, but it hardly seemed to matter, they knew we were coming. The building was modern and air conditioned, with lots of marble and glass. We were taken up several floors.

First, there was a brief social meeting with Commander Montamri, whom Alec had met previously. He was a small, neat and very pale skinned individual, who conversed in perfect English, 'I've just been reading a book on Scotland and I'm surprised by the effect that Calvinism has had on your country.'

My mouth did not drop, but only because I prevented it. 'Yes, it's still very Presbyterian, especially in places,' I replied, staggered once again by the tremendous curiosity which these mild mannered people had for the rest of the world, even the damp, boggy northern rock from which we came. It made me feel ignorant. An ancient civilisation had thrived in their land and I knew hardly anything about it, at all.

In this state of disadvantage, we were passed on to his superior, Captain Layouni, whose interests were a little less cerebral. He was the officer who had arrested the *Wildrake*, when it was on the *Glenartney*, and so the interview was difficult to say the least. We tried not to fidget in our seats as we listened to his justification for this action. This included excuses as varied as the wreck being historic due to United Nations Heritage of the Sea, to her having nuclear material on board. We stated, rather unhelpfully, that she was modern and was carrying tin and pineapples. The nuclear part was absurd.

Finally, we were ushered into the presence of the boss, Colonel Cheriff. His room was large, newly decorated and plush. The inside of the door was covered in soft, white leather and padded and buttoned, like a Chesterfield sofa. Prints of battleships in full sail adorned the walls and on his desk, American-style, sat a trio of miniature porcelain flags, cast in a flutter. Cheriff, with his bare pate and middle years, held court in the manner of a man who enjoyed power. The long cigarette holder that he twiddled roguishly in his fingers, made him appear slightly cavalier, in the mode of Noel Coward, so that one felt as if the interview could have as easily taken place with him in a Paisley silk dressing gown, cravat and slippers, as opposed to all this gold braid and epaulettes. One thing for sure, I was glad not to be on my own.

We had brought with us a formal letter offering a percentage of our recoveries from the *Glenartney* in return for using Tunisia as a base. The amount would be decided once the wreck was located and the salvage operation commenced. It would be a unique payment. No mention of extra-territorial jurisdiction was made.

'Forget about all this nonsense about British ownership of the *Glenartney*,' he said with an expansive wave of his hand. 'The wreck now belongs to the Tunisian government and you can salvage it for us. Go away, and think about it,' he ordered. 'Make me an offer.'

It was the *Glenartney* handed to us on a plate.

We made our way back to the car deep in thought. What he asked was impossible. International Law was set by precedent. If we accepted his proposition, we would effectively endorse the Tunisian claim to a contiguous zone, by ceding to their authority over us eighteen miles offshore. This was not a position in which ordinary individuals should have been placed. The effect of the Department of Transport denying us diplomatic representation, had been to put this most serious issue into our hands.

This was how the *Glenartney*, our Holy Grail, turned into a poisoned chalice.

How long we had quested for this four hundred and fifty feet of riveted steel. All my salvage life, even on the *Oceanic*, we had marvelled at Risdon Beazley's achievements on her. All those years slogging around the coast of

Scotland, developing the cost-efficient technology to recover the remaining portion of her cargo. Now, it was within our grasp, but on such terms that we would have to dishonour ourselves to work it. What a spiteful twist.

The diesel motor ship, Glenartney, was built in 1916 at the Govan yard of Harland & Wolff, for the Glen Line, of 1 East India Avenue, London. Accordingly, in the final year of the War, she was a relatively new and glossy member of the convoy of six under escort of HMS Acacia. Starting in Singapore, she had called in at Penang and Colombo, to pick up oriental produce that was destined for a Thames wharf. The 7800 tons comprised 1050 tons pineapples, 1200 tons sago flour, 1000 tons copra, 792 tons tea, 600 tons white pepper, 220 tons black pepper, 220 tons flake tapioca, 110 tons pearl tapioca, 150 tons buffalo hides, 67 tons rattans, 57 tons gum copal, 35 tons pearl sago, 20 tons benjamin, 10 tons gum damar, 5 tons rice bran, 3 tons fish maws, 7 tons gamboge, 1 ton mace, 140 cases mother of pearl shells, 12 cases empty cylinders, 1112 tons rubber, 915 tons tin, 63 tons wolfram and 2 tons scheelite.

Steaming east and ever more northwards, she had crossed many seas before entering the Suez Canal. Once in the Mediterranean, she called into Alexandria and then the last disastrous leg of her journey began. At a quarter to midnight on the fifth of February, she was keeping a speed of nine knots, off Cap Bon, when a German submarine patrolling the Sicilian Channel fired one torpedo. It hit her engine room. Immediately all the lights went out and the engines stopped; within three minutes the compartment was flooded. The Master, Harry Henderson, went on deck and put up distress signals. The boats were lowered, filled and ordered away, in case the vessel foundered without warning.

There were twenty-one British crew on board and thirty-four Chinese, plus three Naval gunners. Finding that 4th Engineer, Hugh Holman, was missing, the Master conducted a search with the Chief. He only abandoned ship after searching all the quarters without success. The ship floated more underwater than above, in calm conditions of darkness and sank abruptly before the dawn. The only other fatality was Able Seaman Hugh Tregarthen, who drowned.

She lay untouched, far out of any salvor's reach until Risdon Beazley found her after a prolonged search, nearly sixty years later. Working to the very limit of their depth capability, they removed 748 tons of tin over two years, according to the records they had filed. Thereby leaving a balance of 167 tons. Even if we only managed to take the recovery rate up to ninety per cent, which was quite usual, this would generate three hundred thousand pounds, on which we could make a considerable profit given our low running costs. If we did this, we would also establish ourselves firmly at the forefront of the cargo recovery business – or so the prognosis had read until our meeting with Cheriff.

'What do you think we ought to do?' Alec probed, as we drove back to *Redeemer*.

'We can't work the *Glenartney* for the Tunisians, that's for sure. We'll have to get across why it's not a course of action we can take and hope that they'll at least let us get on site. Then, there might be some chance of negotiating an agreement with the Department of Transport, which will strengthen our hand, considerably.'

The letter was as courteous as my written French would allow. Mr Bejaoui helped me with some of the translation in the morning, but it was a laborious task getting the nuance right. We were now beginning to run out of time. We had a second appointment at the Ministry of Defence the following morning. Keen to get my letter delivered before four o' clock, I gathered my notes and decided to use the reception of the British Embassy to finish it off and make the only response our conscience would allow.

It was hot in the room. The overhead fan rotated as I toiled with the sleeves of my blouse rolled up. I had sheets of foolscap paper and my dictionary spread over the table. Informed that I had arrived, the First Secretary came in. He was a young, gentle-mannered man of slim build, who initially conversed at a safe distance, leaning against the wooden door surround, as if my unruliness was somehow infectious – which it was.

'You look busy.'

'I'm writing to Colonel Cheriff – badly – in French. He's told us to work the *Glenartney* for the Tunisians and make him an offer – which we can't do. I'm laying out our position in the hope that he'll allow us to locate the wreck, and then we'll be able to recover an identifiable item.'

He perked up, like a dog sniffing a recognisable scent. 'You don't have to tell me if you don't want to – but if you lift something off the wreck, does that alter your status with the Department of Transport?'

It did.

We contemplated each other. He knew, that I knew, that he knew about salvor in possession; we had given him a copy of *The Other Titanic*, which chronicled the battle with Nundy over the *Oceanic*.

'That's a very difficult question,' I dissembled, 'I'm afraid I don't think that I'd be able to explain the answer to you properly.'

He laughed at my evasion. 'Even if you did explain the answer to me properly – I don't think that I'd be able to understand ...' His subversion was so subtle, it was a conversational gem. The truth was imparted and yet nothing was said.

'Do you know of a translator who could help me finish this off? I've got to get it delivered before everyone goes home.'

'Not at this short notice. I shouldn't really, but would you like me to help?'

He translated in a quick scrawl, and I copied his words out in ink, as neatly as speed and my handwriting would allow. There was nothing in the content to offend him, in fact quite the opposite. Our stand was clear.

The problem was a difficult one, there were two conflicting views, both of which we understood. We were a small family business that made its living by salvaging cargo from wrecks, and currently we were extending our capability down to six hundred metres. The *Glenartney* posed a very delicate problem because it lay outside the limit of Tunisian territorial waters, but within an area in which they wished to control natural resources. Therefore, we understood that Tunisia had a great interest in our proposed operations there.

Given our argument with the Department of Transport, and our determination not only to prove ourselves, but make money, Cheriff's offer should have been the answer to our prayers. Explaining why his offer was unacceptable was hard, without sounding pompous or jingoistic. What I wrote was:

The War Risks Insurance Scheme recompensed the owners of ships and cargoes sunk by enemy action in the two World Wars. It paid out on the Glenartney *and her contents, when she was sunk eighteen miles off Cap Bon.*

This financial compensation represented only a small part of Great Britain's interest in each ship lost. The men onboard risked their lives serving their country during a time of deep crisis, in order to keep it supplied with vital commodities, such as food, wood, fuel and medicine. These goods, although a lifeblood at the time, were worth nothing to their insurers, now. Therefore, it was impossible to measure the contribution these brave men made by the current value of the cargoes, for the dangers in transporting items which had long been ruined, had been no less than for carrying gold, copper, zinc or tin, which was still valuable today.

The enormous contribution made by the British Merchant Fleet rested entirely in the spirit in which it was given. As British salvors, operating a British registered ship, we would be in contempt of the law of our country, if we did not admit that the Glenartney's cargo belonged to the British Government, and we were certain that it would be unacceptable to our fellow countrymen, if such a symbol of their struggle were given up in an arbitrary way.

Finally, we suggested that the best way forward was for us to go out to the wreck with any Tunisian personnel, as required, and once we had all seen the situation for ourselves, matters could be taken from there.

The letter was despatched by hand and its effect was as electrifying as a plug-in chair.

Cheriff's temper was ill-concealed when we sat down in front of him early the next morning. This time, ominously, his manner was neither suave, nor playful. In the brief encounter, high voltage displeasure zapped at us with every gesture, every look. We had openly defied him. Him, the Chief of the Tunisian Navy! His aide, Mohammed, who was also present, shuffled uncomfortably from foot to foot.

'You cannot expect me to accept this!' The letter was thrown in derision onto his desk. The matter is now closed – Tunisia claims ownership of this wreck.'

'There was nothing else that we could do,' I replied.

'But we would have agreed the same deal as you have negotiated with your own government.'

The terrible jest was not lost on us, but we did not let on. 'Even still, we cannot accept.'

'Then you're not welcome in Tunisia, anymore and shall be asked to leave the country – it's all arranged.'

I was numbed with sudden fear. It was like being caught in an open boat by a violent squall. This could turn nasty – just exactly how is one 'asked to leave' by a dictatorship? Even in the short time I had been there, we had seen the military presence. It was ubiquitous. We had even had to pull off the main highway to let a long convoy of armoured tanks go past.

Redeemer was at Bizerta, and one of the last things my contact at the Foreign Office had said, was 'I won't overemphasise the difficulties of leaving a Tunisian Naval base, against their wishes'. Now this conundrum had been turned the other way round. This was expulsion and I had not got my passport.

Thanking him for his time and trouble, and expressing our regret, we left. Mohammed showed us to the sentry post and shook our hands, 'I'm sorry,' he said with an expressive shrug of his shoulders.

'These things happen,' Alec agreed phlegmatically.

Making our way back to the Embassy, I was worried. 'What do you think is going to happen?'

'I don't know, but I'm pleased, at least we've got a decision. This hanging around has been killing me. I'll be glad to go.'

'How will we be asked to leave?'

'I should think we'll soon find out.'

'I've never been thrown out of a country, before.'

'Cheer up. I'm beginning to get rather used to it, myself' and he put his arm round my shoulder in consolation, but I was crushed. I had worked so hard for the *Glenartney*.

'It's funny, Alec, he was so sure that we'd accept his offer, and that money was the only thing that drove us, but it would have been so tainted.

'I thought of all the war wrecks that we've worked on which people have been lost – I've never considered that they've minded what we've done, because we've been honest, and have struggled to achieve something worthwhile – but I knew they would begrudge us this. We'd have given away the same sort of freedom, for which they had given their lives – all for profit.

'My father's best friend from school was killed in the Med . . . How could you buy a poppy for Remembrance Sunday, if you knew that when push-came-to-shove, you had made it all meaningless?'

'You're right. There would have been a lot of people disappointed in us, but it wasn't Cheriff's fault. Without the Embassy's involvement, he got all the wrong signals.'

When we arrived there, only the Commercial secretary was in. He was disquieted by the outcome of our audience, but tried not to show it. 'Come on,' he said, 'you'd better phone London direct and tell them what's happened.' I was shown to a small, shaded upstairs room, which can only be described as a kitchenette, it even had a sink and was cramped and austere. A formica table sat beneath the window. There was no view. We were entirely enclosed, looking out onto the drainpipe on the blank wall opposite. No one could see in here.

The handset was reassuringly chunky and a book, with a pencil attached to itemise the length and destination of the calls, sat by its side. My contact was in and I do not know why he should be so unfortunate, but for a second time in my career my voice broke as I told him the news, I felt so unjustly defeated. 'The Chief of the Tunisian Navy said we could work the wreck, if we did so for the Tunisians, but we refused.'

The sigh of relief at the other end was clearly audible.

'You know,' I continued with conviction, 'we could have sorted out this matter if we had had an agreement with the Department of Transport'.

'I know,' he agreed in his marvellously lilting voice, 'I know'.

When we had finished, the Commercial Secretary was hovering nearby, having heard it all.

'Are you O.K.?'

'Yes. Just a little upset that's all. It's so stupid, I know.'

'Not at all. When do you have to go?'

'My plane leaves tomorrow. *Redeemer* is still in Bizerta. I don't know what's going to happen about her.'

'Don't worry, we'll look after you and make sure that you all get out safely.'

Yet, all the way back to the ship I feared the worst, praying that we would not find the crew under siege. Even supposing we did get out without too much of a fuss, there was the future to consider. It looked such a void.

I stared hard as Alec slowed going over the swing bridge. 'Can you see anything?'

'No – thank heavens. Nothing.'

In the heat of the post meridian, the sun blazed in such intensity that the concrete shimmered and there was not a soul to be seen. 'What an anti-climax - I've been so worried! I thought we'd really blotted our copy book with Cheriff.'

'You never know what the Embassy has said on our behalf ... besides we've done nothing wrong, broken no laws. I knew it would be all right. We'll have to go and tell Mr Bejaoui what's happened. You'll need to get your passport back. Then I want to go up to the telephone exchange and call Henri Delauze in Marseilles.'

It was so typical of him to be developing an alternative strategy. How typical, also, that he took it for granted my conversational French would get us to the president of Europe's largest diving company, using a public payphone up the road!

'I've been thinking about it for a while, in case we did not get anywhere, here. The wreck of the *Kohistan* is just across the Sicilian Channel. Delauze's company, Comex Deep Sea Salvage Ltd, has lifted some wolfram and lead off her, but I've heard that they've now given up. Perhaps we could we could come to some agreement with them.'

'Is it worth very much?'

'Not half as much as the *Glenartney*, but at least its a wreck to which we can go'

The post office was an arcaded building just off the Rue du Mars, and calls could be made from a large, oblong room around the back. It had that over-used, uncared for look that one normally associates with urban bus stations. Dozens of men, and a few chaperoned women wrapped in black, milled in small groups, waiting for their turn in the rickety partitions that divided the black handsets around the walls. A stubbly, surly man, with all the looks and grace of Blutto, from 'Popeye', sat in at a counter at the rear, keeping a log and collecting the dinars.

Alec signalled for permission to use one of the enclosed international boxes along the far wall. It would have been slightly more discreet had the door not been hanging off one hinge. We packed in together, conspicuous foreigners.

With clicks and capricious pauses, the system eventually deigned to connect us.

'Bonjour, Comex.'

'Bonjour, puis-je parler à la secretaire du Monsiur Delauze, si'il -vous-plait?'

'Qui,' and so it went on. Pretending that I was a smart personal assistant, who was just crossing her long, stockinged legs behind a suitably large desk, I did my best to ignore the dirty, crowded annex with its hubbub of Arabic. With as much confidence as possible I plunged on with this recently remembered tongue.

'I'm calling on behalf of Alec Crawford from Bizerta in Tunisia. Could he speak to Mr Delauze, please?'

'Mr Delauze has visitors with him at the moment. Call back in about an hour.'

Alec was anxious, 'Was it just a brush off?'

'No,' she sounded very pleasant. I think it's the case. We'll find out soon enough.' The time was spent in a restive walk around the Old Port. Another suspense. We teetered on the knife-edge between having a future and not.

The second time we got through.

Henri's Delauze's English was attractively accented, with a Gallic flow. He knew about us, he said.

'We've been having a little local trouble,' Alec informed him, 'and can't work the Glenartney, at the moment, as we had planned. I wondered if I could come and speak to you about salvaging the remaining cargo on the Kohistan.'

'Monday is a holiday, but that's fine. I can see you then.'

After all the trouble with the Department of Transport, and then the Tunisian authorities, it was that simple.

We spent what part there was of our last night, before my 4.30 a.m. flight, at the same hotel and in much the same way as we had spent our first, only sadder, because we were to be parted all too soon.

I flew home amongst the band of now tanned and merry tourists with their duty free and stuffed leather camels, in tears, believing that I was going home to feed my children on principles.

HOUSE OF COMMONS

The telephone only rang twice, the following Friday. Once, at around midday, to tell me that *Redeemer* had safely left Bizerta, and then again at 3 p.m. to inform me that the date for Alec's trial as a suspected terrorist had been set, and he would have to appear in Court in Marsala in three and a half weeks. It was a case of relief to distress in three hours flat.

'What am I supposed to do, now?' I demanded to no one at all. Alec was already out of radio range. I could not get hold of him, and did not even know when he would next contact me. What if he did not ring and I could not warn him in time?

Fate was such a bitch, always meting out some form of retribution to counter good luck. This was because arranging the salvage agreement on the *Kohistan* had been so straightforward, I knew. The meeting with Henri Delauze had been on Monday. The terms had been drawn up and checked by the lawyers on Tuesday, and Alec had flown back to Tunisia on Wednesday, overjoyed at being able to leave Bizerta after forty days and eager to get back to cargo recovery. This was his forfeit.

For all this time, we had blotted out the Sicilian debacle, as if it had never happened and now it was back with a vengeance and Alec was incommunicado, again. I put my head in my hands, as the spectres of guilty until proved innocent, no judicial discretion and sixteen years' imprisonment loomed even larger than before, along with the interpreter's advice to Alec, 'There's no justice in Sicily – don't come back!'

'How on earth am I going to sort this out!'

All of a sudden I got reams of faxes in Italian, which I could hardly make out, except for certain words like 'procurator' and 'tribunal'. When communications came in English, it was no better and the term, penal proceedings, sounded as if I should order Alec's suit with the arrows on it, now. I was told everything was 'essential' or 'imperative', so that I could not get the measure of how serious one aspect was in comparison to another. This inability to discriminate or make any priority made the whole proceedings into a conundrum. Thankfully, I had already arranged a meeting at the Foreign Office to discuss the *Glenartney* on the coming Wednesday afternoon, and would raise the court case then.

I had never been to the imposing buildings off Whitehall before; a huge Victorian barrack, relieved by the odd naked bust in the name of art. The main entrance is through an archway on King Charles Street, down the side of black, cast iron gates. The security alert, the board informed me, was Amber. A guard scanned my briefcase and I signed in, waiting my turn for an elderly guide to lead the way across the courtyard, through a maze of corridors and the occasional lift. The high, wide doors and scuffed paintwork was both scholarly and municipal, reminiscent of a university. We seemed to walk for ages, down conduits that narrowed from arteries to capillaries, until I was shown into a room containing the two officials who had been just voices for so many months. The senior was the shorter of the two, and was slim-built and dark. The junior was bespectacled and slightly uncertain of himself.

I knew as soon as I entered that I was not what they had imagined, being certainly a little more formidable in the flesh, especially due to the recent strain. Ever since I had been told of the summons, I had lost my sense of humour and had become single-minded and intense. My features were taut and when I forced what was meant to be a pleasant smile, the effect was ghastly and fixed, like a grinning moray eel. From that sinister moment, it was down hill all the way. The telephone kept on ringing and the atmosphere was constrained.

First, we went over the events of the *Glenartney*. Now that *Redeemer* had left Tunisia and the pressure was off these two men, they could afford to be a little more relaxed over the affair. This was not the same, soothing, 'You don't need me to overemphasise the problems of getting out of a Tunisian naval base against their will, Moya,' Head of the Marine Department, with whom I had built up a rapport. They had become all but indifferent.

'What you need is a court case under international law to establish this matter'.

I was incredulous. This might seem a rational solution if you were a civil servant, with an index-linked pension, but I was the director of an active salvage company, that operated on No Cure/No Pay. In the first place, we could not afford such a case and in the second place, it would take years. We wanted to get back to Tunisia within months.

As the discussion developed, there was no hiding, either, that their lead ministry had been busy justifying its position, and like a fisherman, casting a fly, my contact with the lilting voice attempted a few lines, 'But the Department of Transport said that they asked you to competitive tender for another wreck, and you refused'.

I huffed at the sophistry. 'They wrote to us inviting us to competitive tender for the silver on the *Gairsoppa*. It lies in 4000 metres of water – its deeper than the *Titanic*!'

Not a syllable was uttered, but there was the most undiplomatic rolling of eyes. I could have added that it was in an unknown position, approximately 120 miles off the west coast of Ireland, but I had made my point, enough said.

Anyway, as much as we wanted to get back to the *Glenartney*, it was not my most pressing concern and I broached the awful subject. 'I've just had notification that Alec's court case is coming up in Sicily. Obviously, if it goes against us the outcome will be very serious and I want to know – because the whole issue of not being able to turn up on site, and the Ambassador sending his message that we might be fired upon, is so crucial – whether it would be possible for the Foreign Office to testify to the train of events, on our behalf?'

There was a pregnant pause, as the Welshman hesitated, 'We'll have to see.'

This lack of commitment was so unexpected, that I exhaled, as if smitten in the chest. I could hardly believe it; we had been maligned and messed around by a government department that was supposed to oversee our safety; arrested and sequestrated on the north coast of the Mediterranean; obstructed and held in port on the south; and now, as British citizens asking for simple confirmation of facts to which the Foreign Office were party, I was being informed that they would have to go away and think about it. I was aghast, shocked.

Persevering, nevertheless, 'If we can't get any help, then perhaps Alec ought not to go back – he was told, while he was there, that there's no justice in Sicily'.

'You may well find that it's an extraditable offence.'

The words were not unkindly said, but on hearing them my shutters came down. Everything seemed so hopeless, and the tenuous faith I held in what it meant to be afforded such assistance and protection as may be necessary, in the name of Her Britannic Majesty's Secretary of State expired. Gone.

Escorted by the chap in the glasses, who did his best to cheer me up, I left the building through a side entrance. Ironically, it let me into the street directly opposite the Cenotaph. The Red Ensign fluttered among other flags. 'What hypocrisy!' I thought. Few people really cared, I knew in my heart. The Department of Transport had sold wrecks, as wedding presents, on which the very men this stark memorial sought to commemorate had died, just to raise a few pounds for the Treasury. So much for the ultimate sacrifice and 'WE WILL REMEMBER THEM'. So much for being British.

I felt so disillusioned, betrayed even. We had turned down the Chief of the Tunisian Navy to work the *Glenartney* on a matter of principle, despite having striven beyond common endurance to get to her tin. This integrity had cost us dreams, as well as engineering and financial goals. Having given up all this, it was devastating to ask for a fiduciary duty, only to find it a matter for consideration.

No one cared. I despaired of getting Alec off, and everything I had been brought up to believe in – particularly that decency and honesty would be repaid – was rent as completely, as if it were *Trygg* being dashed upon the rocks. Alec would be just as much at the mercy of the Italian legal system, as she had been to the waves. We were on our own, sink or swim.

In a daze, I wandered off in completely the wrong direction and ended up catching a tube that terminated at Aldgate – not that I wanted to go anywhere near there – and it took an eternity in the jostle of rush hour traffic to get to my sister-in-law's flat in Battersea.

That night, staying with Ann, I took advantage of her concern and after supper cried, distraught. Never before had I felt so utterly powerless. In those hot tears, there was anger and bitterness, confusion and fear. I was in a swirling maelstrom in which every facet of my life, marriage, motherhood and work, was being sucked down. All depended on Alec and his liberty, yet I was so distraught and furious about all that had happened, I could not think properly.

The only avenue seemed to be the newspapers, and expose the whole sorry mess. I knew an advisor in The Mirror Corporation, and a guest of Ann's who had eaten with us, had given the name and number of the editor of the *Financial Times*, but even at my most desperate, I sensed it was not right. There would be a big brouhaha; a lot of dirt would fly and the people who would be paying the toll would be those individuals in the Embassy in Tunis, who had gone out of their way for us. Good would suffer and cynicism would triumph. As wretched as I was, I would hate that.

Raw and upset, if I could not trust my own judgement in this crisis, then I would have to turn to someone else for advice. Who was there who would understand the complexities of all this Ministry nonsense, and not be totally appalled by the frightful mess into which we had got ourselves? I racked my brains ...

Alec's cousin who used to be the Deputy Under-Secretary at the Foreign Office? Even though I had never met him, I had no doubt that he would do his best for family's sake, but what an awful imposition to put on someone so well respected. I could just hear the 'Chinese Whispers' now, going through the mandarins, 'Good Lord. Would you credit it. Johnny's cousin's wanted by the Italians as a terrorist – such a stable fellow, too. Just as well he's retired . . .'

What about our lawyers in Fife? They had nothing to do with the sea, let alone Italy, and if anyone was going to be fallible in their eyes – us or the Secretary of State for Transport – my money was on us.

Who was there, whom I would not compromise who would take our side?

Taking a sheaf of law reports with me to bed, because I knew I would not sleep, the answer came to me long into the stuffy metropolitan night, as illuminated by the bedside lamp in a pair of Alec's pyjamas, I ploughed through *Pierce versus Bemis and Others* for the second time. This dispute had been over the personal belongings on the *Lusitania*, which had no known owner, in which a salvor had taken on, among others, the Treasury and the Department of Transport and had been vindicated by the Admiralty Court. 'The government had lost,' I reiterated to myself . . . I should have seen it before. 'They had been proved wrong! The Individual had won.'

It was such a boost to my morale after all these months of being harried for our views on Competitive Tendering, that it was like a revelation and my thinking became clear, as if a light had been switched on in my head. This should have nothing to do with emotion, it was everything to do with obligation and law, and I knew exactly what I would do. Tomorrow, I would go to the House of Commons and try to contact our new MP. Intuition convinced me that this stranger had all the qualifications to be rational. If I could not rely upon my own judgement to do the best for Alec, then I would defer to his.

I had only met Menzies Campbell once, the week before, when I had arrived in his surgery hot foot from Tunisia on the warpath about the *Glenartney*, and yet I had known his name ever since I had married into Fife. Even his face was familiar. It had been blazoned across mustard-coloured election posters in a multitude of rural vantage points, such as roadside trees, in each election that he had fought as the Liberal candidate for North-East Fife. Clever and well-mannered, he had been a Commonwealth and Olympic sprinter, before becoming a successful Edinburgh QC. He had beaten our relation in the last election, for which he had not been forgiven by most of the family.

Their disapproval had made me feel slightly wicked for consulting him, but in those ten odd minutes when we sat and discussed our problems with the Department of Transport, there was something about Ming, as he is known, that left its mark. Abrupt at times, serious and professional, I was left in no doubt that he was both firm and discreet; and it was these two attributes above all others that made me seek him out.

As soon as business hours began the next morning, I rang round various numbers and established that he was in a weekly political meeting and would not be free until later. It did not matter, as I had other things to do beforehand. Taking myself back to the scene of yesterday's let down, I dropped information on the *Gairsoppa* into the reception at the Foreign Office, and gave my contact a call from the red telephone box, just down Whitehall. Now that I had a course of action, I was quite composed.

'I just wanted to let you know that I'm so concerned about Alec, I'm going to consult my MP.'

'Look, don't worry. I'm sorry about yesterday, my superior was away and I had to take all his calls. Ministers know about your case and would be prepared to meet you to discuss it.'

He might as well have tried to buy me off with a bunch of flowers. The last thing I wanted was to be wheeled in and given tea and sympathy by William Waldegrave, or some other politico. I feared it would be a cosy little chat, just to soothe me down. It was not the answer. I had to keep detached.

'I'll come if I can bring my MP.'

The offer was not extended.

'I'm sorry,' I apologised and headed across the traffic lights to Westminster.

It was perfectly true, I was sorry. I had genuinely warmed to the Head of the Marine Department. He had become a real support, so much so that I had begun to wonder if he were incredibly smooth or just very solicitous. I had settled with the conclusion that he was good at his job. He was disappointed with my decision, I could tell, but what I knew he did not understand at this moment, was that I was just doing mine.

Had the policeman standing outside the public entrance to the Houses of Parliament tried to stop me, I knew that like in some Ealing Comedy, I should have probably kicked him in the shins and made a dash for it, I was so determined to get in. Evidently, I must have looked suitably harmless, because despite not having an appointment, I was let through. After a quick search, I passed through the stall-like metal detector and was off down the long, cloister-like passage, trying not to race as if participating in the three o' clock at Kempton. My mind was so full, I felt blinkered and oppressed, the statues of distinguished statesmen passing by as blurs.

Once in the Lobby, the space was open and the decor gothic. Stained-glass windows, high vaulted ceiling, a mosaic on the floor, it all swirled like a kaleidoscope of colour and there was a hubbub of haughty male noise, from the loud coteries in city suits. Approaching the liveried office-bearer, I inquired if it were possible to speak to my MP and anticipated a long and lonely wait. Gazing around, unseeing, unhearing except for the occasional piercing comment, I was astounded when literally within minutes he was there.

Appearing to have hurried, too, he straightened his tie and came to an abrupt halt, clicking his heels as if in amusement at finding one of his northerly constituents arriving in such a dramatic and purposeful state. 'And what can we do for you, today?' he proffered dryly, as if I made a habit of it.

Debonair, and better looking than I remembered, he was undoubtedly on cheerier form, but I simply was not in the mood for preambles, and gave it to him flat. 'Alec has to stand trial in Sicily in just over two weeks. Under Italian law he's guilty until he's proved innocent. The maximum sentence is sixteen years imprisonment and I don't think the Foreign Office is going to really help.'

'This is serious,' he admitted frankly and we sat down on one of the green leather bench seats that ran around the wall.

Badly, I began to give the outline of the case.

'Wait a minute,' he interrupted somewhat testily ...' You can't go breaking the laws of other countries and just expect to get away with it.'

'But we did it.' I pathetically confessed.

'Ah ... You're going to mitigate.'

Were we? If he said so. My fuddled brain was none too sure. If there was no judicial discretion, was it an option? The advice from our Palermo lawyer was that we had to prove our passage was innocent and this was why it was so important for the Foreign Office to verify the events leading up to our call into Sicily.

Weighing up all that I told him, he lent over conspiratorially. 'I'll give you a free piece of legal advice – let's write a nice letter to the Foreign Secretary, Douglas Hurd.'

That was fine by me. Merely being able to unload my cares made everything so much easier to bear. I knew I was not on my own, anymore and after giving him a few more details, we began to part.

'Don't go that way, or you'll be a pier,' he called after me.

'Pier?'

'I used to make the same mistake myself. That's the Lords' exit. You have to look for the clock,' and he pointed overhead.

'Peer – I thought you meant a jetty!' It emphasised the very disparate nature of our lives and I smiled for the first time in days.

Not only had his quiet wisdom restored my faith in human nature, but he had helped me keep my dignity and not damage people who had given us the benefit of the doubt, like the Ambassador in Tunis. I went off to see the General Manager of the Salvage Association in Leadenhall Street, as if I did not have a care in the world.

CHAPTER

20

TRIAL

Solitary, being rocked erratically to and fro on the slow Sunday train from Leuchars to London, the first countryside we passed through was so wintry and familiar, that I found it hard to believe that by the same time, tomorrow, I would have arrived by plane in the warm, urban environment of Palermo in Sicily. 'Palermo!' The very thought of this island capital, with its Mafia and turbulent lawlessness, made me shut my eyes as the haunt of imprisonment visited me once more.

The chain of events after I had seen Ming, could only have been partly anticipated. He had written to the Secretary of State immediately, requesting that we should be given the Foreign Office's full assistance, as Alec's well being should be put above any question of policy in the Department of Transport. Whether it was in consequence of this correspondence, or not – the Minister responsible would have us believe not – the British Consulate General in Naples was put on the case. No sooner than I had begun dealing with their man, when the Advocates in Sicily went on strike and Alec's case was postponed.

This had made for a most welcome reprieve at the time, especially as I had been unable to contact *Redeemer*, but now, in early March, the winter had seemed to have evaporated and we were again facing the crunch.

For all but a fortnight of this time, over Christmas and New Year, Alec had been on the wreck of the *Kohistan*, working through the worst of the Mediterranean winter with its short, vicious peaks. It was not like winter in the Atlantic, where the reaches are so long that a heavy swell can run for weeks. It was a squally, unpredictable, bad-tempered sort of sea, that came from nowhere and was mostly wave. In it *Redeemer* did not roll, she bucked and pitched and tossed. The motion was constant. No piece of ship, hull or superstructure, stayed in the same plane for more than a second. The deck, the bulkheads, the gunwales, the partitions, the seats, they all gyrated. There was hardly a mealtime when plates could be put on the mess table, and all food was consumed in oriental style with a soup bowl inches below the chin.

A walk down the passage necessitated a series of hand holds, one after the other, this side and that. Until the exit into the loo or the forepeak was accomplished with a finely calculated lunge. This led to numerous knocks and bruises. Showers were nigh impossible and stillness a fantasy. The conditions were punishing and prison-like in their confinement. There was just the accommodation and the deck as useable space. No escape from the constant thrum of the engine and jarring swirl.

In the history of modern salvage, there could hardly have been a more hapless crew and yet the prospect of recovering the cargo kept them all going. There, 413 metres beneath the *Redeemer*'s hull, it beckoned like a temptress – available, but not quite yet.

They had pin-pointed the wreck using the Loran position that Comex had given them, and laid three of their moorings buoys within twenty-four hours of turning up onsite. Then the weather broke and they had to fare as best they could for two days, banned as they were from Italian waters and unwelcome in Tunisian ones. This set a pattern for the next four weeks, a tantalising start/stop situation that gave brief glimpses of the wreck before the weather or an intermittent equipment fault would take it away.

The 4732 ton cargo ship, *Kohistan*, began life inauspiciously as ss *No. 466*. She was launched in 1910 for F. C. Strick & Co Ltd which, trading as it did from the Far East, named all its vessels after Indian States. When she met her end, she was on charter to the Admiralty and carrying most importantly lead and wolfram for the Ministry of Munitions, along with rubber, rice, beans and band instruments from Colombo, of all things.

Late in November 1917, she was second last in a convoy of six, when a U-boat caught her with a torpedo on her starboard side No. 2 hold, which rapidly took in water. The collision bulkhead between it and the engine room was breached, the starboard jolly boat had been blown to smithereens, and the bridge and wireless equipment damaged. The sixty-five crew members were taken off by one of the escorts, HMS *Asphodel*, and a small salvage party, including the Master returned. It was found that although hold 2 with its afterpart, hold 3, were filled with water, there was only a few inches in holds 1 and 4, respectively and hold 5 was practically dry. The hope was that it would be possible to take her under tow as darkness approached, but the submarine surfaced again and fired a second torpedo at 1740 hours, which struck abaft the funnel and she sank within fifteen minutes. No lives were lost.

On the seabed she lay upright with her bow to the south-west, a mass of twisted and battered steel, due to both her violent end and the previous salvage operation. Around where the bridge should have been, plates had been bent upwards, ten metres high, to form a hazard of jagged pales. In

No. 4 hold sacks of rice could be seen through the broken decks, a derrick lay across No. 5 hatch, whilst the gun that had been meant to protect them, remained sentinel on the stern. Everything was covered with a fine, loose powder which was the remains of decomposed overburden and this billowed into suspension as the heave of the grab created a vortex, due to the poor weather above. Under these conditions – winter, no shelter, and a new underwater system to commission – stamina was the order of every waking moment.

Out of the thirty-two days spent in the Sicilian Channel before Christmas, only a third were spent working, because of bad weather and of these, six were taken up establishing the moorings.

When they quitted to come for a short break, it meant a two days steaming to get to Marseilles, which almost unbelievably was the nearest friendly port. Squeezed in amongst the glossy, tupperware yachts on the tenth of December, exhausted and filthy they might be, but they were 'salvors in possession' and also free men. No mean feat under the circumstances.

Setting out again in January, their first task was to pick up the mooring wires, which had been tied together and dropped to the seabed. This was attempted by dragging the sandy bottom with the Z-shaped dredge on the end of the grab. All the positions had been carefully marked on their chart before they had left, and very soon a wire rope was sighted close to the wreck and picked up. Sod's Law! To everyone's great consternation, it could not be brought to the surface despite the thirty ton pull of the main winch. Even worse, the dredge would not budge either way, even though several attempts made at lowering and steaming north-west, towards a relative length of slack. Alec was in the wheelhouse and the rest of the crew were underneath the 'A' frame on the stern.

'There's nothing for it, but to keep *Redeemer*'s head into the sea and bring it slowly to the surface,' shouted Alec. 'You'd better stand well clear in case something breaks under the strain.'

After much labouring of the main engine, the main hoist winch hauled up a thin yellow, plastic-coated cable.

'Wo!! Wo!! Stop!' ordered Rod. 'You'd better come and have a look at this – it's not ours!'

'What the hell is it?' inquired Alec.

'Search me – it looks like a telephone cable, but there isn't one marked on the chart.'

'I know – and it's up to date. It seems to run in a north-east/south-west direction. Where on earth does it go to?'

'North Africa? Perhaps its a trans-continental link?'

'I hope we haven't damaged it. Look it could take ages to get it released, safely. It's getting late and I don't want to make a mess of things by getting it entangled on the wreck. Let's just get the grab in and attach a rope to the cable, so that we can keep it suspended for the night. One thing's for sure, it looks expensive ... I'd hate to be responsible for breaking it.'

Famous last words.

All went well until late the following morning. The strange, uncharted wire was buoyed and let go from the ship, in order that the search for the moorings could continue. After about an hour, one of our wires was caught and hauled in, but with such a weight on it that it parted.

'Bastard!' cursed Alec, as *Redeemer*'s bow plunged deep into the water with the recoil like a bellying whale. 'We must be trying to lift the north-west mooring block, as well. Put the dredge over, again.'

A little later, the strange cable reappeared, this time hanging limp and vertical.

'Uh-oh ... it's broken!', gasped Rodney. 'D'you think it was a new telephone link?'

'I hope not. Come on let's look at the damage. 'Steve,' he shouted through the open porthole, 'see if you can haul in an end. I want to take a look at it.'

On examination it looked most peculiar, as Alec parted the wet glistening inner wires with his thumb. 'That's odd,' he concluded, 'It's a coaxial cable. I've never seen a telephone cable like this before.'

'What d'you think it is then?' asked Steve. 'Here Rod, put your ear to the end of it and see if you can make out what they're saying.'

'Won't be able to understand anyway – it'll be in Italian or Arabic.'

'If it is a telephone cable, I bet the guy had the receiver pulled out of his hand pretty sharp at the other end.'

'I'm not convinced it is a telephone cable, I think it's a hydrophone for monitoring the movement of submarines and the noise of ship's propellers.' 'Military stuff' evinced Rod with a pursing of lips. 'I know the Yanks have got a big base in Sicily.'

'It's probably been laid close to the *Kohistan* for a purpose. Submarines often use wrecks to navigate by.'

'Do you think they'll know who did it, Alec?' worried Steve.

'We're eighteen miles offshore. They may not be able to tell where the break is. One thing for sure is that we can't stay here like lemons with it on deck. Let's bulldog an eye into the fast end and use it as our north-west mooring. It's never going to work again anyway'.

It sounded as reasonable a plan as any. Two days later, an Italian reconnaissance plane flew low over *Redeemer* six times, as she lay tied between the four, newly laid buoys. If it had been a listening device running across the Sicilian Channel, they obviously had their suspicions as to who had wiped it out, but never would they have dreamed to which piece of NATO property, the vessel beneath them was attached.

Had Michael Burgoyne, with whom I had begun dealing at the British Consulate General, known this, I expect he would have laughed in his gentle, husky way and said, 'Good Lord' shaking his head in admiration at the chaos that his fellow countrymen were still capable of wreaking on the high seas. Unconventional and full-bloodied, he too, like us, was something of an anachronism, and a relic of the less hidebound past. From the very first moment I had first spoken to him, he gained my affection.

Following Menzies Campbell's intervention, I had made contact directly with Naples, and as I waited to be put through to the person whose responsibility we had now become, I prepared myself for grappling with someone diffident and effete.

'Hel-lo?' enquired a mellow bass voice.

'This is Moya Crawford from Deep Water Recovery & Exploration.'

'Now, that's a familiar name,' came the response with more than a hint of wolfishness.

'Hmm. All too familiar, if you ask me.'

He chuckled throatily, amused, and I knew I had found a kindred spirit. Being handed over to this consular official, was like being thrust into the protection of a minder with whom one would quite happily go out to dinner. Seasoned and robust, so adept was his flattery that I soon suspected that Vice-Consul was both his title and his warning.

We discussed the case. He explained that he had been on holiday at the time of the arrest. Rather than acting as censor, he made coping with the prospect of Alec's trial so much easier by being my guide. 'You'll soon learn that understanding Italian procedure is something of an art form,' he volunteered, stopping me feeling stupid for walking slap bang into such a mess. 'How are you supposed to know that you need to request permission if this isn't specified in the Admiralty Notes to Mariners. I shall write a note to the Naval Attaché about that, to see if he can get them to put it in. Besides, I understand that it takes five days for the paperwork to be turned round ... in theory that is,' and he gave his throaty chuckle.

In every respect it was as if he had all the time in the world just to go over the facts and sort out our problem. In the process, showing the rare trait of actually listening with such attention, that on occasion, he could recount what I had told him without adulteration of either substance or emphasis. In this seemingly effortless fashion, a bond was created in which I could face Alec's trial. When I asked questions, his answers were always honest, even though he knew I was concerned. Sharing a keen sense of the absurd, he led me through the terrifying labyrinth of the Italian legal system with numerous jokes, much wisdom and no disclaimer. In return I depended on him as wholly and unguardedly as if blind.

In those weeks and at Her Majesty's expense, in amongst evidence and documentation, and his contact with our lawyer in Palermo, we strayed periodically to chat about normal life. I learnt that he had an Italian wife and a daughter the same age as Rachel, and had chosen to make Italy his home, even though he missed his beloved Cornwall. There was something about the panache and colour of this idiosyncratic country, in which he revelled. He enjoyed the vibrancy, the food, the wine. Yet, he was no fool, 'The natives here are born streetwise,' he commented, appreciating much of the downside.

On this manly rock I ventured all my faith and in turn, Alec entrusted his future to me.

His way of proving his innocence was not to fuss, but to persevere in all weathers on the *Kohistan* to begin bringing up cargo from the wreck and show that he was a bona fide salvage engineer. Isolated, both physically and mentally in his position of authority, he was the sole driving force. Day in, day out, he set the pace with early mornings and late finishes, working through most of the night. It was a regime of twenty-four hour seamanship, improvements and repairs. There was never a moment without stress or motion, not even in sleep. A part of his mind never switched off, always on duty.

In the quick, peaked winter swell, the days on site were scant few and on the rare occasion there was a lull, nothing went right. The farce with the hydrophone had wreaked untold damage to the moorings, and consequently the westerly ones were soon lost.

'Three, six, niners,' that's what Noradeen in Bizerta had termed the northerly winds. 'Once they set in, you can guarantee not getting back to work before they had blown themselves out and if this doesn't happen by the third day, then you're probably in for a long wait.' He had been right. This onslaught had been so severe, that it had subsided only on the tenth day. They had returned to the wrecksite in the relative calm, it was to find to everyone's utter disappointment, that the two west buoys had been overwhelmed and sunk.

'Right we shall just have to dredge for them on the seabed, again' commanded Alec, in a tone that hid his own dismal thoughts. Then, as they began searching, the Loran positioning system ceased transmission for essential maintenance, making it impossible to gauge their location with any accuracy.

'Will nothing go right?' demanded Alec, frustrated by the endless slog.

Eventually, by recovering what bits of wire and chain he could and using a spare block out of the hold, he cobbled together one good mooring out of the two that had been lost, but still he was one short. To replace it properly, he would have to steam to Malta or a French port to pick up more materials. Both time and money prohibited this. Desperate to get on, he proceeded to rig a system by which *Redeemer* could be manoeuvred over the *Kohistan*, using just three anchor points. Tired and dejected, after having been back at sea for over a month without respite, it was in this makeshift fashion that they began their attempt to equal the world depth record for commercial cargo recovery.

The strain was beginning to tell. 'This ship would roll on a wet lawn,' Rod, who had come from serving on much larger ships, informed Alec with some asperity. In such circumstances, the thought of having forsaken everything at Kilburns, with its snowdrops and viburnums in flower, for a wrecksite in the Sicilian Channel, was almost painful.

It was towards the end of February. As the camera and grab was sent down in the brief lull, such was the extent of Comex's blasting, that initially it was hard to relocate No. 3 hold, as there were few identifiable pieces of superstructure left. It was a case of edging along the wreck. At last, behind the void of No. 2, the remains of the collapsed bridge was found and explosives were prepared to begin cutting it away.

Alec's feelings were ambivalent as he prepared the first 37.5 kilogram charges for detonation. Like a chain of thick *liverwurst* sausages he strapped the small, grey parcels to a condenser tube, to keep them flat and rigid and primed them with both Cordtex and a pressure resistant detonator. As familiar and necessary a tool as they were, they had caused him such trouble it was almost inconceivable. 'Plaster gelatine! Kilo for kilo, one could probably cause almost as much damage and mayhem with petrol,' he thought pondering the misdemeanour for which he was shortly to be tried, gaining a twinge of satisfaction that at least the stuff was going to be used.

Suspended from two loops, so that it dangled horizontally, the charge was held in the jaws of a pincer grab, and as it was lowered the four hundred odd metres to the wreck, the detonating cable was paid out by hand. Once positioned, the pincers were opened. The lateral control was so delicate, that on one occasion – when the electrical detonating cable had been inadvertently pulled out – the explosives were recovered and relaid.

It was enthralling work. For its short duration, as they consulted the ship's drawings and pursued their salvage plan, all the hardship and self sacrifice seemed worthwhile. Then the barometer fell, and another tempest swept in. There were no other days before the court case on 6th March. In order to go into port the remaining bangs on board had to be destroyed. This precious waste was the ultimate bad joke as far as Alec was concerned.

Michael Burgoyne's parting words had been, 'I'm afraid that nothing can be taken for granted – you may be looking at a custodial sentence, here'.

'I know, that's why I'm going,' I had replied.

'I'll see you there.'

One of my final acts had been to visit Menzies Campbell at his surgery, to bring him up to date with the situation, just in case everything went terribly wrong. Curiously, by finding the courage to face up to the possibility of jail, it was as if I could ward it off. And so it was, with the moral support of these two very different establishment figures, that I had set off from home. I left the children in a waving huddle at the train station, in the care of my parents, like a scene from *The Railway Children*. Having parted with played down emotion and suitably encouraging words, 'I've just got to go way for a few days to give Daddy a hand. He needs me for a while'.

There was no way that I was going to burden them and they knew nothing of the trial. Even as far as the very few people who did know were concerned, I had been equally tight-lipped, and it was 'Just a formality'. I hid my own feelings even from Jonathan Miller, who had been such a support just talking over the situation and going over the legal aspects. For the whole time we had dealt with the matter, I had taken the premise that Alec was innocent of any evil intent and would go free, but found, as the day got closer, that I knew the outcome could just as easily go one way as the other.

On my journey, the arable fields gave way to the industrial coast of East Fife. Derelict factories and empty harbours replaced the well kept farms. The disused pithead at Kirkcaldy stood bleak against the seal grey of the Forth, and the wind blown dust from the aluminium works at Burntisland, stained the surrounding wasteland henna red. As we passed the shipbreakers at Inverkeithing, I looked out of habit to see if they were dismantling anything of interest, stirring further thoughts of Alec and *Redeemer*. We had hardly spoken since he had left Marseilles, just a couple of Radio Link calls that were if anything more upsetting because they were public and clinical. Nothing about us at all.

A night in Gatwick and two plane flights later, the bus that would take me to Palermo wound through cultivated hillside plots, that were lush with spring growth and dappled a shade of soft pink with blossoming peach trees. This rural perfection all too soon gave way to the city, with its blocks of flats and streets thronged with cars. My suitcase had been lost en route and so I walked to the advocate's office, which I found on the first floor of rather a dilapidated street close to the port.

He was a small, dapper man with dark-rimmed glasses and oiled, black hair and he spoke almost perfect English. Again, like dealing with the Intelligence Officer in Bizerta, the whole crisis seemed so absurd, because he and his surroundings were so ordinary. For the whole while that we sat going over the main bones of the case, I steeled myself for Alec's entrance; so that when he appeared with Rodney, the restrained manner in which I greeted this absent and indicted lover, with just a shake of hand, must have seemed very prim to the lawyer, indeed. Not a touch of *Tosca*, no torrid Latin embrace, far more like *Mary Poppins* goes to gangland. Words, looks, touch – each might be among the last for a considerable while. I could not bear for our personal moments to be adulterated by being witnessed by anyone.

'Good to see you,' Alec suggested. We understood each other perfectly.

'Capitano. Capitano. Welcome … welcome. Do sit down.' His arrival held most import and the advocate was duly deferential as he was handed the Ship's Log. A few points were discussed. The defence was that *Redeemer*'s entry into port was an enforced passage. Therefore, as master, he was innocent under the Articles of the Geneva Convention.

'That's fine,' Alec authorised. He expressed no desire to look at the paperwork, dismissing my file gently with his hand. This gesture summed up his confidence in me: that he should come ashore the day before he appeared in court, in the certain knowledge that everything which could be done, would be done.

We left, bidden to arrive at the court at 9 a.m.

In Marsala *Redeemer* sat against the mole that sheltered the port, looking rather dumpy and out of place amongst the local vessels, with their slim lines and tremendously high, flared bows. The colouring of everything around was enhanced against the blueness of the sky and the ivory white buildings. Not just the boats, but the cars and the clothes of people who passed by. Only a fine, wind blown talc toned down the scene. Lying in drifts against the walls, steps and curbs, it merged them into the roads and harbour.

Aboard, we stepped back into our own engineering world. Everyone else was on surprisingly good form, despite the circumstances, simply relieved to be tied up and ashore for a few hours. We ate in the mess, amidst jokes and stories. Only Alec and I were subdued in anticipation of the morrow. Duty, duty, duty, it seemed an eternity before we could excuse ourselves and finally be alone.

Of all the cabins on the ship, Alec's is the most austere and cheerless. An oblong space with a couple of built-in bunks and a table aft of the engine room. Every conceivable space is filled with precious electrical or hydraulic equipment, small fiddly spares that might get lost anywhere else, files and books. Alec never gave his own comfort very much thought and in this utilitarian compartment, that was little more than a store, he took me in his arms. and held me as if we should never let go.

To get to the Palazia di Justicia, the car from the ship's agents transported Alec, Rodney and me through narrow streets, full of picturesque houses with rusting balconies. It stood like a stucco fortress in the centre of town and its security was breathtaking. Each of the few, high windows was grilled on the outside and steel shuttered on the inside. To get in, each person had to enter a bullet proof chamber, one at a time, and be scanned. A system of green and red lights controlled the human traffic. Once inside, guards in black uniforms with tasselled epaulettes and red seams down their trousers, paced the cool corridors with machine guns slung across their chests. All deliberately intimidating and without parallel in any local British court.

Our advocate greeted us. The promise of the proceedings beginning on time proved to be false, and when we made enquiries this was met by a polite shrug. 'It's always the same.'

As we waited awkwardly, an usher brought along Michael Burgoyne who had travelled down especially on the overnight ferry with his chauffeur. Well over six foot, broad shouldered and bearded with auburn hair, he was dressed in a fine tweed suit that leant an air of gentlemanly gravitas to his frame. Conducting himself just as he had sounded, his soothing presence was a boon.

'Good morning, Mrs Crawford.'

'Good morning. I've been wondering what you looked like.'

'There I had the advantage – I'd seen your picture in Simon Martin's book.'

'Doing the washing in the burn!' I exclaimed with mock disapproval, only too aware that our carefree days on Foula could not have been further away. 'It seems a long time ago.'

'You've worn it well.'

I smiled, pleased that our approval of each other had not been destroyed. There was no falter. We stood in a group, Anglo-Saxon giants towering above the mill of swarthy, darkly clad Sicilians, chatting easily as if waiting to go into a very different sort of bar.

Eventually Alec's name was called and he was shown into the courtroom. Everyone else shuffled in, seemingly aware of the form. Only we were none too sure of the procedures and so Rodney was told to remain outside. Alec, as the accused, was courteously led ahead.

The room was akin to a Methodist chapel or Scottish kirk. Hard varnished benches for the onlookers filled the aft section, rising so that those at the back could see and an ironwork barrier, partitioned off what could be deemed to be the altar end. Desks for the prosecution and defence sat elevated, opposite each other. Above them, with the legend, *La Legge e Egale per Tutti*, 'The Law is equal for all', emblazoned on the wall, was placed the Triplenary Bench.

Our advocate stood spreading out his papers as the three judges entered. Everyone in an official capacity rose, including a hesitant Alec. Before the proceeding began in earnest, Michael Burgoyne, who had been standing to one side, discreetly approached the senior judge to ask the Court's sanction to act as translator. This lean, middle-aged man looked severe in his black gown, white necklet and glasses, a trait that was exaggerated as he leant forward to catch what was said. After making sure neither of his colleagues had any objection, permission was granted with a curt nod. Her Britannic Majesty's consul returned to his position and catching my eye, as I sat alone and conspicuous in the front row, bestowed the most reassuring wink of encouragement.

From then on, events were difficult to follow. The charges were read out. Each sentence followed by a hushed murmur as Mike, stooping behind Alec with one hand for support on the back of his chair, spoke confidentially in his ear. When he had ceased I had to try to catch a gesture of the hand or look from the latter, to indicate his answer.

As our advocate began to speak, the Recorder transcribed his words using two biros selotaped together, they had had different coloured inks so that he could differentiate defence from prosecution. Then Alec was examined. I concentrated hard, trying to make some sense of it all, but it was fruitless. In the monotony, time lost its meaning.

After some indiscernible while, Rod was brought in for corroboration, and guessing from the 'Yes's' and 'No's' that he gave as replies, it seemed that many of the questions to him were leading, but it did not seem to cause any concern.

Following this, our advocate gave another lengthy sermon, and then the Prosecution spoke briefly. No further witnesses were called.

The judges went out, and Court was adjourned pending their decision.

We grouped around the advocate's table and waited. Enduring the elapse like kith and kin outside an operating theatre. Until the verdict was given, there was no future, it was on 'pause'.

The limbo lasted a quarter of an hour. The Bench returned and gave their pronouncement – Alec was a free man. The senior judge, immediately reformed in my eyes into a benign character, shook his hand.

As we decamped ourselves and were released out into the street, the mood was one of uttermost relief.

'Uh,' sighed Alec good-naturedly, holding his hand to his chest in mock palpitation, 'thank God that's over and done with'.

'Yes. It will be a great weight removed' affirmed Mike. 'Come on, the *advocato* says that he would like to buy us all a celebratory whisky – and remember to drink up, they don't believe in washing glasses around here. Then I'll treat you to lunch.'

Once the requisite toasts had been dispensed with, we parted from our legal representative with all due thanks. It was only in the back of the Consular Rover, as we cruised for a place to eat, that I could begin to quiz.

'What was the verdict?'

'That it was outside the Court's jurisdiction – I was really quite surprised and am not quite sure that it's right. I thought that they would go for the Geneva Convention, which seemed the sensible course to me' and he raised his eyebrows as if to say, 'but that's Sicily for you – unpredictable'.

'Can you tell us what went on?'

'The evidence which led to Alec's indictment contained a statement from an anti-sabotage officer, swearing that the explosives you had on-board were unsafe and improperly stored. First your lawyer explained at some length that they were of no danger to the people of Mazara del Vallo. The explosives were new, and were in good condition having been stored not only according to British standards, but Italian ones.

'Then he went on to the aspect of Forced Passage, and we heard from both Alec and Rod about not being able to go to Tunisia. Finally, he cited several other cases in which people had broken the same law as you, particularly that of an Israeli ship whom he defended for having guns, which were mandatory under their own law for self-protection.

'The prosecution asked for two years imprisonment, which is too long to be suspended and a million lire fine. So it's just as well they decided they wanted nothing to do with it' and he smiled. It was all Mike's doing, I knew. He had hardly raised his voice above a purr, but his very presence had won the day.

The meal at the waterside restaurant was excellent and the chauffeur came, too. The place was quiet and the ante pasta was laid out on the table like a feast. After weeks of sometimes dubious fare on *Redeemer*, living off mostly rice and tinned meat as the stores dwindled, it provided a most unexpected and piquant ending to a total aberration.

We had coffee on the ship out of stained mugs, as the cook was not very particular, and the Vice-Consul smoked coarse, native cigarettes, like small cigars. Replete and at liberty to go, a feeling of overwhelming bonhomie bound us all and we idled away an enchanted afternoon. Savouring the moment. We had all done our duty and played our roles, now we wished to play hooky.

As the sunlight became golden in the late afternoon, it was time for Mike to return. We said our goodbyes on the quayside and gave our sincerest thanks. He left and the magic was broken. It was back to work for us all, he to his desk and us to our wreck.

Within forty-eight hours, as Mike wound up his consular duties for the afternoon, we were struggling with a strong easterly current on the moorings and poor underwater visibility. Raising the grab, Alec set off in the rubber inflatable to cut the moorings, in a swell that was so steep he often disappeared from sight and we ran for Marettimo, behind which we were now permitted to shelter.

At midnight, with a veering gale, we had to pick up the anchor and shift. In what was now an onshore wind, with the stark, birdless cliffs rising sheer above us, I thought 'This is not the place for both parents of four small children', and felt irresponsible. The following morning, with flans gusting to pick up sheets of water, we had to shift again. Only on my final day did the conditions improve and I was dropped ashore on the island to catch the hydrofoil.

Redeemer returned directly to the *Kohistan* and lifted their first lead ingots.

Alec kicked one of the small, ovoid shaped pigs as it lay on the aft deck, 'Good job I didn't need one of these on Tuesday to prove that we were real salvors ...'

CHAPTER
21

THE *KOHISTAN*

The beaten up 'portakabin', which served as the watchman's home in the container yard at Saumaty, shook violently, imitating a cardboard box with squabbling cats in it. Inside, the diminutive guard and his buxom, unnaturally blonde girlfriend, who usually wore little more than an oversize shirt, were having the most appalling row. Their frantic motion was interspersed with the sound of smashing crockery, which reverberated off the stacked steel crates around us with all the fury of domestic mortars. These volleys were followed by prolonged bursts of Gallic abuse, she hysterical, he angry and defensive.

Neither we, nor the children, had to see the action or understand the vocabulary, to know that the last thing we wanted was for this brawl to spill out and envelop us. Especially since we had been informed that the man's vicious alsatian had just been replaced by a sawn-off shotgun. Alert and with ill-concealed haste, we scrambled up the short bank that separated us from *Redeemer*, dodging through the rusting anchors and concrete mooring blocks that barred the way, heedless to any cuts from the dried out barnacles in which they were covered, and jumped aboard with all the alacrity of reaching 'Den'.

Staying aboard *Redeemer* in a backwater of industrial Marseilles for a week was hardly the average family holiday in France. We were tied up in a basin that had been cut into the hillside west of the city, in little more than a depot. A fishmarket and quay took up where the containers ceased and the waterfront gave way to the docks. From then on, the vast, ugly port went on for miles, its derelict warehouses bisected by a flyover, in a style of town planning akin to Birmingham-sur-Mer.

Difficult although it had been, I had found the money to join Alec as he came in to unload, because it was such a special event. He had just equalled the world depth record for commercial cargo recovery and I did not want this achievement to pass without notice. As if testament to his ability, we shared our dead end berth with the only other vessel to gain this distinction, the huge barge, *Comex II*, with its towering gantry aft. Beside her, *Redeemer* looked like a toy. But with a handful of crew Alec had continued on the *Kohistan*, where she had left off.

'Half Marseilles sailed with her when she went out to the wreck, the yard manager told me,' said Alec, with no very great amusement when I had arrived, nodding across at the great slab-sided hull. 'You know that she used a two wire grab and they guided it with a million pound ROV. It doesn't bear thinking about. And she needed an anchor handler to lay her moorings. The costs must have been horrendous. Totally uneconomic and to think that we've dug right down into the bowels of the *Kohistan*, at the cost of £13,000 a month.'

'I know – you've done really well.'

'But it's been so hard, Moya. So desperately hard. Sixty-two days at sea on *Redeemer*, with the only break, if you can call it that, being when the Italians arrested us, again.'

'At least we managed to sort that out, this time.'

'All to your credit. What would I do without you,' and he caught hold of my hand. 'Often, if it weren't for the thought of you and the children, I'd give in. Everything's been such a slog. It comes with just using second hand equipment all the time, nothing's ever quite right, and O.K., I get it to work in the end out of sheer perseverance, but it takes so much time and I'm just exhausted. I feel such a failure at times ...'

'No not at all, Alec. I'm very proud of you. No one else could have done it. Removing three decks and digging out all of that overburden in over 400 metres of water, using a salvage vessel that was once a wreck, herself. It's staggering when you think about it.'

'But progress is so slow without a stowage plan. I feel as if I've let everybody down.'

'That can't be helped and besides – you can lift anything you want from the bottom of the oceans, it's just a question of money. You say it yourself. The goal is to develop an economic recovery system and you're getting there.' My words were not conciliatory, I was genuinely impressed. 'Come on, old man. Cheer up' and I pulled him along. 'The children are desperate to go fishing.'

In the strong July heat, we dipped over the gunwales with our hooks on short lengths of line, trying an assortment of bait from the galley, ranging from bread to baked beans. The hills rose gauntly behind, dusty, ivory-tinged rock that shimmered in the heat. Whilst we dabbled for the scavenging mullet, capturing the greedy ones in a bucket, particles of grit blew around us, borne on the warm dry wind from the interior.

With only half an eye on the sport, I thought of Alec and what he had said, all too aware of the toll the *Kohistan* had taken on him. His letters home since the court case, in which he recorded the happenings of each day as he kept his night watch, had been graphic. They went on for pages in his distinctive, unflowery hand and in their typical mix of personal thoughts and mechanical news, it was just as if we were together. From mid-May onwards, the calendar of setbacks had been relentless and he had been stoic:

'I've just stopped now at two o'clock on the afternoon of Monday 21st, as the westerly swell is bearing onto us and the ship is rolling badly, preventing us from taking the grab aboard safely. We lost five bags of wolfram out of the last lift – and nearly the camera too! The underwater visibility has been very poor the last two days and so I've just been grabbing generally in No. 3 hold to complete the removal of rice. So far, we've shifted hundreds of tonnes. I can hardly see, but as long as we get ingots of lead in the grab, I know I'm in reasonably the right place. Unfortunately, we're dragging our north-west mooring and so I've eased the wires, while we wait for the weather to improve. Besides the swell, we've heavy rain and thunder and lightning.

'We had some real drama, this morning, when a large, red Panamanian ship, carrying a deck cargo of timber came heading straight for us. It wouldn't alter course, however much we blasted the foghorn, nor would it answer our radio call. I got Steve and Rob, the new cook, to quickly prepare the rubber inflatable in case we had to abandon ship. Rod got the vessel to turn to port at the last moment, missing us and just clearing one of our mooring buoys. What a relief.

'We continued grabbing after nearly being run down – in fact we never stopped – and my intention was to carry on all night if the forecast at 9.50 p.m. was bad, but life never follows a predictable pattern. Just before the forecast was due, the pipe from the sea valve to the Lister engine was discovered to be fractured. Water was just pouring in and so everything had to be stopped as soon as we had the grab safely onboard. To stem the rising flow, we started the main engine and got its bilge pumps in motion. This stabilised the situation. Working under the floor plates in the oily water was arduous, but we soon found that a section of pipe had corroded right through by electrolytic action, even though it was less than a year old. With some fumbling and a lot of swearing I managed to remove the offending section and replaced it with flexible hose. In the end, the weather forecast turned out not to be too bad, and so I had a shower, did my watch 1200–0200 hours – and went to bed.

'The following morning, the weather still did not look good with a south-easterly swell. We've been working in up to three and a half metres of swell and so continued in probably only two metres. The grab wasn't recovering its usual quantities and then later, it failed to close. By the time we opened the pod and located the fault, which was just a loose solenoid, the weather had deteriorated so much, with very short, steep waves, that we decided to slip our moorings before we dragged or parted one of them. Gale warnings were by then being issued and so we steamed to Marretimo to anchor on the north side. We had to weave our way through floats and nets to get to our anchorage, as the small fishing boats had seemed to concentrate their efforts in the lee.

'On Wednesday, with the wind still freshening, we set to work on the pod, not just to tighten up the solenoid, but to improve on what had been a hasty, but effective job of manufacture at sea, when the coupling for the electric motor had gone. A fierce, squally wind interrupted us, as it forced the ship to drag. We lifted the anchor and dropped it very close in, not only to get a hold, but to get enough shelter to do the modifications on the pod. It was only a temporary measure and so after tea, we prepared to shift *Redeemer* a little further off before nightfall. This should have been a routine job, but things started to go wrong very quickly. The anchor had become fast and would not come up. Then the wind suddenly veered, shifting us over the anchor buoy rope, and this got caught in our propeller. From being perfectly safe, we were now attached by both ends and rolling alarmingly, totally immobilised. The main anchor chain then snapped, leaving us only a stone's throw from the rocks in gale force winds, held by a rope attached to our propeller.

'I hastily put on my wetsuit, fins, weight belt and mask. There being no compressed air left, there was no point in using a diving bottle, and so I just went over the side. As her transom stern was facing into the wind, it kept on slamming down and shooting water in all directions, like a bellying whale, making it quite hard to time catching my breath. It also didn't help that for some reason I thought I had a demand valve in my mouth and inhaled underwater.

'Like all these incidents, one's only concern is to get the job done and you really don't worry about the conditions, although the rather tasty curry we'd just eaten was probably the cause of the severe cramp I got in my legs. I managed to secure another rope to the anchor buoy line and then cut the section entangled in the propeller and take it off. We then started the main engine and got some sea room. In this little more relaxed situation, we pulled the anchor out using the buoy rope and lifted it on board. The wind by this time was severe, with salt spray covering the ship.

'We relaid the anchor, but then after a couple of hours, it dragged and so we had to lift and relay it, again. This time it held, but now it was nearly my time for watch-keeping and so I just stayed up. Another night with little sleep.

'To be prepared for emergencies when I go to my bunk, I slacken all my boot laces to make it easy to put them on, and lay my clothes out in order, just in case.'

24th May: 'Today, I didn't get up until after eight and work is progressing slowly on an extension to the orange peel on the grab. This will help hold the ingots in, so that they won't get washed away in a heavy swell, when they come to the surface.

'I am trying to have an easy morning, undertaking a few small jobs, writing this letter and doing some washing. I am down to looking through my dirty clothes, to see if they are cleaner than the ones I'm wearing. Some of my shirts are now in such a bad state, that they are being relegated to the much needed role of engine room rags. Morale is fairly high, now that we are making substantial recoveries, but I'm finding life on the ship very hard. I just wish we could complete loading and head for Marseilles for some real rest. I'm so desperate to see you, my heart lifts with the very thought. We just seem so close to winning and yet small breakdowns or the weather snatch it away from our grasp. I know I must just push on. It's now just a matter of perseverance because the system works well, but summoning the energy at times is a major effort, although so far I have always managed to achieve it. I sometimes think it's an endurance test between the ship, the crew and the moorings, to see which breaks first!'

31st May: 'The last day of another month; it seems unbelievable how fast the days fly by. We lost the whole of the 26th just lying on a mooring at the wrecksite waiting for the swell to drop, which it fortunately did that night.

'On the 27th, we tied up in a strong current coming from the North and put the grab down. I always aim to position the ship on the boiler room side of No. 3 hold, and then I can orientate myself, but, this time, the grab went down probably opposite the engine room, or near No. 4 hold. In the lights of the camera, I could see what looked like cheese-shaped ingots lying on the seafloor, shining brightly. I stopped manoeuvring the ship and scooped some up, knowing that this might be my only chance to recover them, as they would be hard, if not impossible to find, again. The slow hoist to the surface began and we all waited expectantly, to see what valuable objects we'd recovered.

'All seemed fine at first. The grab spewed most of its contents on the deck and then suddenly, the whole area above the explosives store burst into flames, giving off a thick, white smoke. Rod, Steve and Rob were all outside and so I shouted for them all to keep clear, just in case the fumes were toxic and immediately returned the grab to the sea. This quenched its flames, but the aft deck was still ablaze.

'Everyone by now was in the accommodation. After a few minutes pause, just in case there was an explosion, I ventured aft on the smoke-free side, wielding a shovel. The "ingots" were melting and the flames running everywhere. The only real way to kill them was to shovel the stuff overboard, as the fire was made worse if buckets of water were thrown over it. We removed all the largest bits and just had to leave the lesser ones to burn out, as we listened to a cacophony of alarms, as the smoke and gas detectors went off.

'Five hours later, small fires would still suddenly flare up as we were working. My conclusion is that they must have been phosphorous, which spontaneously combusts when it comes into contact with air, and I suspect they were incendiary bombs from the First World War. To think they've been there since 1915. Although the flames scorched the paint off our steel plate aft, there was no other damage; just a bit of hair-raising astonishment and a slight delay.

'We continued grabbing in a new corner of No.3 hold and cleared out mostly rice, as well as some steel plating, beams and so forth. We were well into the non-ferrous cargo by the evening, so that by the next day we had a clear view of the neat rows of small, hessian sacks of wolfram, which was very encouraging. These are separated by wooden beams. There are also bits of steel appearing through them, which I can only conclude are the pillars that supported the 'tween deck. If so, these will descend to the bottom of the hold and I'd normally, put down a small charge to loosen them up, but I can't do this as it will burst the hessian sacks. These obstructions are proving a curse, because the grab catches on them, as it closes, allowing much of the wolfram to drop out.

'The machinery has been working well with all our modifications and I just hope it stays like that. Three times we've had a problem with dirty fuel and I think it could be with us for quite a while. Twice I've been up in the middle of the night to change fuel filters on the Lister generator.

'On Tuesday 29th, we got off to a good start in reasonable weather conditions, although for some unknown reason I had a terrible headache. The wind and swell gradually increased until lunchtime, when it became unworkable. The weather continued to deteriorate all the time and I was violently sick. It was midnight before I had shaken off feeling ill, and the ship was taking a tremendous punishment, with the sea on her stern. We stayed on the moorings, but slackened all the ropes.

'Wednesday was awful, the whole boat shaking, even the old VHF radio fell off its bracket. I was reluctant to leave, but by 4.30 p.m. the conditions were so bad that we had to let go and headed for Marretimo. On the way in , the main engine started to overheat and I discovered that the thumping vibration of the sea had shut off the main sea valve to its water cooling system. That's the first and last time that will happen, because I have tied it open now! The Lister sea valve has also closed by three turns.

'Today, in the calm of Marretimo, we are slightly licking our sores, after we catch up on some sleep and renew our energy after three days of continual pounding. The last of the fresh water is being pumped from the barrels in the hold, into the fresh water tank and I have a number of maintenance jobs to cover, before attempting some improvements. If I have time.

'Now after thirty-five days at sea, all our stocks are starting to run down and I think we'll have to go in somewhere soon to take on fuel, fresh water, lubricating oil and food. If we get a good spell of weather, however, we'll postpone until we're desperate. I've dipped the tanks and we now have 1175 gallons of diesel left, which will cover a trip to Marseilles and ten days work. Rod has emptied all but two of our water barrels into the main tank, which guarantees us eight days plus. The meat supply will last six days and then we are onto the last of the tins from Dundee. We are also getting very low on Shell Rimula X30, mainly because of an earlier problem we had with the main engine.

'Rod has stowed all the lead and wolfram recovered so far in the hold and I can see no problem with regard to volume because its so dense. This is a bonus, because we are carrying so many spares, that there is only one third of the cargo space left. We've just got to get it all up now. If we do not require the rest of the explosives for No. 3 hold, I will use them to cut the deck of No. 4 at the engine room bulkhead, because I am sure that is where the rest of the wolfram will be, if we do not find it all where we are digging now. It is so very arduous, working without a stowage plan. We look to be into a great quantity of full sacks, but I do not know how deep it is and so it's impossible to estimate a tonnage. There is probably a day's work cutting the deck of No. 4, but it will make good use of the remaining explosives.

'The weather here does seem very unsettled at the moment. It is a very long time since we had anything like a calm day. We've a continual swell from one direction or the other, which seems too heavy to be generated by the winds we're getting. All very mysterious and annoying. We're presently attached to one buoy on the wrecksite, with the ship rolling somewhat, and so I'm consuming books at a tremendous rate, but I'm hoping that the conditions will moderate overnight and let us get on tomorrow.'

3rd June: 'There was no such luck. We moored up on Friday above the wolfram that we had exposed. Unfortunately, the slope towards *Comex*'s hole was getting too steep and the grab kept on toppling over and so we moved to one side to clear more rice and debris, in order to make the area level. We first went to the south side and dug everything out, except for some coal, which appears to be pouring out of a bunker in No. 3.

'On Saturday, we moved to the north-side and recovered about two and a half tonnes of lead and wolfram, in amongst the dross, lifting the total aboard *Redeemer* to over twenty tonnes.

'Today is Sunday and the swell has increased all night, making it marginal to work. I put the grab down in nil visibility and came up with nine bags of wolfram. Unfortunately, the swell became so bad I thought I'd damage the camera and so I removed it and blanked off its cable. We continued grabbing, but the ship heaved and pitched so much, that we damaged the pod and the camera cage; not seriously, but it took a few hours to repair them both. I am now waiting for the swell to moderate. What has happened to our summer weather?

'We have run out of coffee and sugar now. The latter in a disastrous fashion, as Rob, the cook, did not notice until there was none. Since we have also run out of oatmeal and cereal, breakfast is beginning to look grim as this means no fresh bread. That would really make for hard rations and so I suggested using the syrup from the tinned apricots to feed the yeast and so far it has worked well.

'The weather calmed off after tea and we managed to get grabbing again and recovered half a tonne of wolfram and half a tonne of lead. The grab does not seem to be picking up the wolfram very easily. I am beginning to think that we'll have to move to where the rice stow in No. 2 meets the wolfram in No. 3, and catch the edge of the wolfram with the grab. The top layer of bags is rotten and we tend to lift out a sort of black mud, made up of wolfram, rotten bags, rice and general debris, including wood and steel.

'Morale is slipping badly as the weather encroaches in on us. We seemed to be doing relatively well and everything looked good, but now it's all slowing down. I feel just dead beat, just so very disappointed that we cannot get on, and even when we do get on I feel frustrated at how slowly the cargo is coming up. What a struggle this wolfram is compared to an ingot cargo, just because it is in bags and can neither stand blasting nor is it easily picked up. When you are in piles of metal, they tend to fall down giving a reasonably level surface all the time, but the wolfram stays stacked and is nearly always covered with a thin layer of rice. Thank goodness I've still some books to read, or the worry would tear me apart.'

And so the salvage work went on, in a round of dragged moorings, modifications, swell and repairs.

By the time I turned up in Marseilles, it was a month since that last sentence was written, but I had had little need of the postman to keep me up to date recently, as I got all the news from Alec himself, when I flew out to get him 'unarrested', as our ship's agent in Trapani would say.

Even I wonder how it all happened again, especially as I had tried so hard to keep everything in order and we had been applying for permission to enter Italian waters with explosives on a monthly basis, ever since the trial.

Vince had just joined ship. Even though the provisions were very low, they had picked him up from Marretimo, instead of going into Sicily, because the weather was so good, and they wanted to get back to the *Kohistan*. After a brief period of lifting wolfram and lead, the grab stopped gripping and they hauled it up to find that the coupling to the hydraulic pump had broken. They dug out a replacement amongst the spares and connected it to the opposite end of the electric motor round, because the shaft they had been using had been bent. This involved cutting by-ways in solid stainless steel, using nothing more than a drill and a file and all sorts of clever things. They had hoped to be able to carry on, but the weather began to deteriorate, so the moorings were slipped and *Redeemer* went back to the north end of the island.

Vince was put ashore the next morning and kindly bought some food to keep them going and Alec returned to the ship. Everything was working by tea-time and he was just replacing the lid on the electro-hydraulic pod, when a small coastguard launch turned up and ordered him onboard with all the ship's papers and passports. There he was until eleven o' clock at night. At which point they were ordered into Trapani the next day, as soon as they had finished an engine repair they had already started.

They steamed into the Roads just after lunch and could rouse not a soul. In the early evening the Harbour Master called up on the radio, saying that they must take on stores and bunkers and then leave immediately. That was fine until the harbour tug, which was halfway through pumping fresh water aboard, was ordered to stop and return to port. Not a drop of fuel oil was delivered.

A horrible sense of *déja vu* had already overtaken me by this time and I was on my way. Which was just as well, as by 7.30 a.m. the next morning the ship and the explosives were sequestrated, again. I knew as soon as I arrived in the bus from Palermo a couple of hours later, that the situation was not good, when I saw our distinctive little ship lying off, about half a mile from harbour.

'Uh oh' I thought, 'if things had been sorted out, she would've been against the harbour wall by now.'

It took a day for me just to be allowed on board and during this time, I happened to be in the agent's office, as Lieutenant Vitale, who seemed in charge at the Commanderia di Porto, arrested Alec over the VHF. After each sentence, read out in slightly halting English, Alec repeated the words with deliberation, as he wrote them down; and when the officer had finished, he was thanked politely and asked with typical aplomb, 'Now, have you got any good news for me?' The staff around me broke out into a ripple of applause, in typically Latin fashion, being appreciative of the sense of style. Crazy, crazy world.

I took a room in a cheap *pension* for the night and tried to get Michael Burgoyne on the telephone. Unfortunately, he was in Sardinia ministering to the British soccer fans at the World Cup. The evening was hot and sticky and I was unable to open the heavy metal shuttering that shaded the window. I could not face going out to eat alone. I just lay on the bed in the gloom, in my loose silk underwear, despondent.

Making my way to the port office as soon as it opened. I found Lieutenant Vitale very decent about the whole thing. Had I not caught him off duty the day before, in his emerald green tee-shirt and jeans, I might have been afraid of him, dressed in his chalk white uniform, with all its gold tassels, but his cover had been blown. He entertained me with glasses of chilled coffee and showed me photographs of his young daughter on whom he doted, as we tackled the problem of *Redeemer*.

'The trouble in the beginning,' he explained, 'was that your permission to enter Italian waters with explosives had not come back from Rome, even though your ship's agent sent it off by courier five weeks ago. This happens' and he shrugged philosophically. 'but now it appears that you don't have a valid export licence for the explosives, like you did before and therefore your ship's papers are not in order. This is very serious indeed.'

'How could this be so?' I implored. 'We bought them entirely legally in Marseille.'

'I really do not know, but the matter is going up to the Procuratore Generale. It is now out of our hands. I'm very sorry.'

'Can I go onboard now?'

'The harbour master has given his permission. You can go when we bring the crew in to take their statements.' He added, 'do you know?' as if ashamed that such reasonable people should be so inconvenienced, 'when we first went onboard, we thought you were Dutch and that there was going to be a fight – but then we found out you were British.'

I laughed gently, accepting the compliment. What Dutch mariners had done to deserve such a reputation was never explained, but that they should intimidate Naval personnel who were armed with not only pistols, but machine guns, rather amused me.

The crew were taken ashore one by one, and after they had all been interviewed, I stayed with Alec. We sat alone in the mess, he with his head in my lap, as I stroked his forehead and listened to all his woes. I had never seen him so unhappy and this arrest was just the final straw. It was one of those pivotal moments in our relationship, when I knew that I could either sit, giving him my sympathy as his wife, or leave him alone and depressed to do my job.

I felt so awful as Rod took me away in the rubber inflatable. Not least, because I did not have a clue, where we had gone wrong. I simply could not figure it out and it was only when we were practically at the harbour steps, that I realised.

'I think I can fix it,' I told him animatedly, not wishing to explain, in case I was wrong.

Hurrying up to the office of our ship's agent in Sicily, I asked for a telephone, so that I could contact Saunier, our ship's agent in Marseilles.

It was a nerve wracking wait until the documentation I had requested arrived by fax. Vittoria, the helpful secretary, hurriedly ripped it off the machine. 'There you are,' I explained in triumph. 'The reason why we have no export licence, is because these explosives came from France and Nitro-Bickford, the manufacturers delivered them freight on board. They have the export licence, not us, because they filled out all the forms. Here's a copy – look!'

'Well done Signora Crawford. The capitano has a narrow escape.'

With much hassle, visits to the Procuratore and 'tuts' from our Palermo lawyer at being supposedly caught for the same offence twice, the whole of the next day was spent in getting the legal proceedings dropped. I was put ashore at 4.30 a.m. the following morning, by the light of a torch, long before the dawn rose over the domed churches that dominated the skyline. Kitted out in my smart summer dress, because I was going to call into the relevant government offices in Rome and make sure that our next permission was all in order, the salt water in the bottom of the rubber inflatable lapped over my blue leather shoes, leaving a permanent tide mark.

'The trouble is Alec, I am starting to worry that we've lost touch with reality. Look at us here, you and me We're the only ones about. You're in your boiler suit and I'm dolled up to the nines, having just stopped you being charged with being a terrorist, for a second time. This whole event's been so incredibly outlandish and yet it seems perfectly normal.'

'I know,' he agreed with a rueful smile.

It had taken another couple of days after I had gone, before Alec and *Redeemer* were finally released. Even this could not be simple, because the agent called up the ship urgently late in the evening, saying 'You're free to go, but you must take bunkers onboard and leave straight away. The problem is that your old permission to come into Italian waters expires at midnight and the new authority does not come into force until 8 o'clock tomorrow morning. The Captain of the Port assures me that if you stay here a minute longer than you should, he'll have to arrest you again.'

'I knew it,' Alec told me as we discussed these events in Marseilles, sitting in his cabin aft. 'I just knew it. The consul who was standing in for Michael Burgoyne said that nothing so ridiculous could happen, but I took on bunkers and got the hell out it, simply not taking the chance.'

'You've had a ghastly time.

'I know. I really don't think I can stand much more. We just don't seem to be getting on as fast as we should. The grab and the underwater power pack works well now, and we have knocked all the wrinkles out of them, but the trouble is we're just not getting the time onsite. *Redeemer*'s not the right shape of ship.

'I've been thinking a lot about working down to 2200 metres, whilst we've been onsite. There seems no reason why we can't extend the recovery system. The real problem is the motion of the surface vessel. *Redeemer*, although she has a good sea-keeping hull, is simply not the right shape, and so I've been considering whether we should go to a barge, like the *Comex* one, or a large supply boat, or a semi-submersible. But do you know, I believe that the shape of hull we need is like this,' and he picked up a large manila envelope, that had been lying on the table, and using a blunt pencil outlined what looked like an asymmetrical egg-timer.

'It's very simple,' he explained. 'It steams to the site in the horizontal position, and when you want to lift, it turns up like this.' He turned the drawing through ninety degrees, so it was now vertical, with the smaller bulge at the top. 'The narrowing up here at the waist means that there is less buoyancy at the waterline, and this, coupled with the new 'bottom' of the hull being well beneath the main action of the waves, helps to reduce heave.'

In the time honoured fashion of novel ideas being expressed on the back of the fag packets, I understood immediately. He was right. It was so obvious and this was why I admired him so much. In amongst all the other competing philosophies, he could ignore what everyone was doing and come up with a breathtakingly original approach.

'Yes. It's certainly radical.'

'I'm convinced it will work.'

'I don't see why not. How much do you think it would cost to design and build?'

'Millions.'

We did not have millions. In fact I worried how we were going to pay all our bills. There was only one wreck of which I knew that would justify such an investment and that was the *François Vieljeux*.'

CHAPTER

22

COMEX

Somewhere up the back of Marseilles, the rain grey ingots slipped out of the back of the tipping truck with the rumble of overhead thunder, forming a leaden heap in the scrap merchant's yard. As with game, the excitement had been in their capture, and now, wrenched from their hiding place on the *Kohistan* and in a mound, they were surprisingly lack lustre. Not so to their purchaser, who stood beside them to have his photograph taken, the archetype of the great, white, metal hunter. The spoils from our expedition had been quantified and we were soon to be rewarded and he handed me the weighbridge slips for the loads with a flourish.

I had accompanied the dark, olive-skinned lorry driver on each of the runs and suggested, 'I'll just walk back to the ship. It's not far,' wishing to save him the detour through the high rise flats that filled the hinterland to the port.

'If you walk, you'll get your throat cut,' he replied, drawing his finger across his throat, 'Queeech!' in vivid mime, just in case I did not fully catch his meaning in French. Hardly one of those handy phrases taught in the BBC linguistics series, but I understood perfectly, thanking him cordially when he dropped me off just outside the container base at Saumaty.

At last there was the prospect of some money. To get paid, I would have to travel to the other side of town to visit the cashier at Comex. Essentially, this was incorrect, as the lead I had just sold in the insalubrious migrant quarter had been the British Treasury's property. Strictly, it should have invoiced the scrap merchant, in order to pay Comex as per the percentage in their salvage agreement, and they in turn should have given us our cut.

In practice, however, this being France where the chances of raising a speedy government invoice for commodities sunk in 1915, were regarded quite accurately as being nil, Comex acted as banker and the paper trail went in reverse. We could have waited months to get some cash otherwise and I collected the much needed cheque before returning to Scotland with the children, leaving Alec to return to his soul destroying work on the wreck.

In many respects, Comex had been very good to us, for even the use of the private facilities at Saumaty were entirely due to them and so I always felt bad about what I had to do next.

We were concerned about the future. Alec had shown me his idea for STEADY and I knew that there was only one wreck within our grasp that would pay for it, the François Vieljeux. We were equipped with the vaguest of details about the wreck, such as her estimated cargo valued in millions of pounds, but knew she was deep and lay off the Atlantic coast of Spain. The only trouble was, the salvage agreement lay with Comex Deep Sea Salvage Ltd.

As their barge, Comex II, loomed large opposite Redeemer, the merits of our relative ways of tackling the Kohistan, were a frequent topic of conversation between Alec and myself. In particular, we had discussed whether it would be a prudent business decision to give up our independence and combine forces with their company, as good wrecks were far and few between, and if we could use our innovation to make them viable, they had the size and collateral to relieve the burden of funding. When I had had a meeting with Henri Delauze, their president, this was a possibility that I kept at the back of my mind.

There are some people to whom one warms immediately, such as this engagingly modest man who in his own way had done as much for the development of mixed gas breathing, as Cousteau had achieved for SCUBA diving, before him. Ageless, in both physique and enthusiasm, he had an attractive lop-sided smile and treated me whimsically, with a gentle paternalism that I found disquieting. Not because it offended my pride. In not appreciating our ambition and determination, he was put at a considerable disadvantage, and that made me feel underhand.

'We have very different business philosophies,' he observed in English with his attractive accent. 'Yours is the small family approach and ours is the large, industrial one. I sometimes think that you are right, but I'm out voted, here.'

Without me having to say a word, he had told me what I wished to know. There would be no easy route for us. We may have equalled his company's world depth record for commercial cargo recovery on a fraction of the budget, using far less equipment and a crew of four, but we were still on our own. Ours would continue to be a lonely path. So be it. Henri's only real mistake in the meeting, was to be wrong footed by our lack of resources and not perceive us as rivals. Had he done so, he could have eliminated us within months, simply by delaying payment. We were on our uppers.

I was downcast, that they regarded our technology as being so insignificant. We had invested so much of our lives into it, that it was hard not to take his remarks as a personal snub, but by the time I had got back to *Redeemer* my resolution was firm. We had achieved too much to give in now. We had to press on and quite literally, if we wished to continue in marine salvage, it was the *François Vieljeux*, or bust. Consequently, as soon as I got back to my desk in Fife, I picked up the telephone to the cargo department of the Salvage Association.

I had dealt with Peter Edwards in the Cargo Recovery Department off and on over a long period and knew that confidentiality was all important in his work. He would never divulge a scrap of information about a wreck, unless one specifically declared an interest. 'That's a coincidence,' he remarked, 'because we haven't renewed Comex's agreement since it ran out in March. They've had it for five years and haven't really done much about it, apart from conduct an underwater survey, and we're getting pressure from the underwriters. There's an American outfit that's keen, too.

'What you're going to have to do is confirm in writing. Then we'll ask you all to submit salvage proposals, indicating what sort of award you would be prepared to accept. At that point, we'll have to discuss the matter here and make a recommendation to our principals.'

I simply could not believe our luck and could hardly wait to contact Alec, who was by this time back onsite in the Sicilian Channel, 'Good news. It looks as if we might have a chance with the wreck off Spain. Over.' 'Aah,' his voice brightened measurably, 'that's great. I've been working on the new deep water system, whenever I've had time. What depth is she – about 1400 metres? Over.'

'I'm not too sure. I'll have to get a chart. Over.'

'What sort of timescale are we talking about? Over.'

'We have to put in our proposals before the end of August, for a decision by the end of September. Over.'

'That's fine. Look, things aren't going too well here. We've done a lot of blasting from aft of No. 3 bulkhead. It's been a lot of work and yesterday we lifted out a heavy steel beam, about fifteen metres long, to get down to the double bottoms, but there's no sign of any more wolfram, at all. Just a few more ingots of lead. I'm going to have to shift to No. 4 hold and search there. Over.'

'O.K. I know you'll do your best ... good luck. Over and out.' Nobody could have pushed themselves more than Alec, but it was all to no avail. Blasting his way through the aft saloon house, bridge house, spar deck and main deck, the debris and overburden were all cleared away with the grab. In the better weather conditions he worked an eighteen hour day as routine, removing even the tunnels that housed the propeller shafts and the steering gear, but not one grain of the remaining four hundred and fifty tons of wolfram was found. This was the forfeit of working without a stowage plan. A week later, bitterly disappointed after his valiant effort, he placed a radio link call. The defeat was thick in his voice.

'We've got absolutely nowhere. I'm just shattered. What do you think we ought to do next? I could dig down to have a look in No. 2 hold, but we'd need more explosives ... Over.'

I knew him too well. This was a question about giving up on the *Kohistan*, and I measured my words, carefully. 'I can't see any point, Alec. It just means a whole lot more expense and we don't know if the wolfram's stowed there. And even say it is, if it's spilled into all the other cargo, like in No. 3, we'd get so little that we'd probably only just break even, anyway. It's not going to solve our problems. Our best chance is to get the new salvage agreement. We've just got a little over a fortnight to put our proposal together. Why don't you just come home? Over.'

This was a plea every bit as much as a question. Encouraging him to return, was to ask him to admit defeat and I was aware of that. His self confidence had taken such a hammering.

'That's what I think, too.' There was an audible sigh of relief. 'I'm glad we agree. We'll lift the moorings and I'll phone from Marseilles. Over and out'. *Redeemer* had become his isolated prison and I felt like a Home Secretary, who had just commuted a sentence.

After shutting off the sea valves, switching off the gas, padlocking the watertight doors and other numerous chores, he left his trusty little ship tied up in the basin at Saumaty without a backward glance; sick of the constant duty, the dirt and grease, the motion, the deprivation and total lack of anything pleasurably sensual. During the past fifteen months conditions and experiences onboard had frequently been as close as you could get to being at war, without actually getting fired at. Akin to all who have endured hardship, Alec came back to us vulnerable and drawn. When I met him off the train at Leuchars, his smile was wan and his normally upright frame sagged. Numbed with fatigue, beaten both physically and mentally, I collected a shell. Only rest and succour would deliver the proper man.

'It's been a long haul, Moya.'

'I know. Welcome home.'

Having now experienced many such reunions, I find it hard to see they can be anything but an anticlimax, the expectations are so high on all sides. During his absence, Alec had constantly dreamt of the happy hustle and bustle of home, but an hour or two after he came back he realised what chaos it really was. Worn out, all that he wanted was our affection, its amenities and a little peace.

Rob, Drew, Patrick and Rachel, aged, eleven, eight, six and five years old, frequently chatted about their father and longed to use up masses of their young energy with him on his return. As he sat in his chair, they clustered on his knee and in a chorus babbled out their news and various requests.

'Dad, come and play rugby in the garden, I want to try my tackle on you' ... 'Dad, do you want a spin in my new white van? I got it as scrap. It needs the brakes fixing' ... 'Dad, can you take us swimming in St Andrews on Saturday?' ... 'Dad, will you read our bedtime story tonight?' 'Dad ...' 'Dad ...' 'Dad ...'

For my part, I wanted to be transported by a soulmate from my hours of drudgery and cherished. Only devotion prevented me from saying, 'Right, it's now your turn to hold the fort. There's food in the fridge. I'm off.'

Friends and family, also wanted to see Alec and called by. Yet his experiences had been so intense, and his absence so long, that many common bonds had been severed, and he found the effort of conversation wearing. His mother would ask him, how it had been and he would dissemble, with a smile, 'Oh, a bit rough at times' and lead her on to tell him what she and his father had been up to. Simon, always came by and as content as Alec was to sit over a cup of coffee and recount some of his more alarming tales to their mutual laughter, he never complained even to him. The simultaneous process of giving him succour, and reabsorbing him into the family unit and society of friends was particularly complex. To cap it all, we had only seven days left to complete the salvage proposal on the *François Vieljeux*, during which time school would begin for all four children.

They and business were the first priority. He and I fitted in around them both, if not around each other, as it took almost a month to fully relinquish our roles of salvage master and single, working mother, and make all the compromises of being man and wife. During this period, Alec gradually stopped instructing me explicitly in simple tasks, as if one of the crew, and I got used to having my comings and goings monitored, ceasing to resent the inquiry, 'When will you be back?'

The one subject on which we totally agreed from the very start, was the necessity to get the new salvage agreement.

At the beginning of October, when we still had not heard the outcome, *Redeemer's* winter berth had to be arranged in Marseilles. This was how I found myself having a breakfast of dry toast and apricot jam, in a canteen-like dining room, the only white female in an hotel, full of North African construction workers. My timing could not have been worse. I had arrived late the previous night at the main railway station and had phoned eagerly to get the long awaited news. My mother had answered the phone.

'What are you doing there?'

'Alec's been invited out to dinner by his cousin, but he's left you a message. It says ... wait a minute,' there was a rustle as she picked up the note to read the precise words, like announcing an Oscar winner. 'We've got the agreement. Love, Alec. I'm so thrilled for you, my dear.'

I could not quite take it in, strangely upset not to share the moment with Alec himself, after all the bad tidings he had given me over the past year.

I had prayed for this agreement to ward off financial ruin and had always envisaged sharing this glorious moment hugging and kissing with joy. Reality was being washed out after almost twenty-four hours of travelling by the cheapest means possible, and standing alone amongst litter in a squalid corner of the Gare St Charles. 'Marseilles!' I thought to myself. It was tantamount to being *Comexville*, the company's presence in the city was so high profile, 'Why couldn't I have been anywhere else!'

Any pleasure I felt was negated by the duty of having to do the decent thing and face up to Henri Delauze. 'Oh Alec, how can you do this to me?' I grumbled making my way up the steep hill to locate my bed in the Colbert District, close to the agent's office in the Rue St Cannat.

Neither did things improve with a night's sleep. Skimming through a discarded local newspaper as I ate, I found a large article on the back page praising Comex's specialist diving facilities, as a group of Soviet Cosmonauts were using them for training for weightlessness in space. My heart sank, as I knew that they had been trying to raise twenty-two million dollars to begin their industrial recovery programme, with the *François Vieljeux* as the gateway to all the deeper wrecks. We had just rent these plans to shreds. The closer I got, the bigger the disparity between their massive organisation and our minnow outfit seemed to grow, making the prospect of their outrage and indignation at being beaten seem all the worse.

Plucking up my courage, I went along to the agents as soon as they opened, so that I could begin making appointments, feeling as sneaky as a spy, as they happened to work for Comex, too. They gave me the use of a phone and I braced myself for curtness as I was put through to Henri Delauze's personal secretary. To my astonishment, she was as friendly as ever.

'Madame Crawford, I am sorry. I have spoken to him and he apologises that he is busy all day with visitors, but he says that he can see you this evening at six p.m. at his house, if that's convenient. Shall I give you the address?'

Above left The lost hoist umbilical finally secured.

Above right Henry Cumming flexes his muscles straightening the kinks.

Right A 'cat's cradle' of expensive hoist umbilical.

Alec operates the entire underwater system from his position in the wheelhouse.

One of the *François Vieljeux*'s hatch beams, lifted from 1250 metres – as deep as Ben Nevis is high.

Above Usual weather conditions on the wrecksite, 45 miles south-west of Cape Finisterre.

Left Some of the sisal overburden from the *François Vieljeux*, including 'tubeworms' (centre).

Below Orders of the day. (*Paul Cleaver*)

Right Copper wirebars, in No. 3 hold of *François Vieljeux*.

Below The team which tripled the world depth record for commercial cargo recovery. *From left* – Moya, Alec, Vincent Snell, Frank Gallacher and Henry Cumming. (*Paul Cleaver*)

Right Six-tined grab deposits copper cathodes on aft deck, with the grind of metal on metal.

Below left The gentler side of salvage – Henry's painting of *Redeemer*.

Below right Roughie-toughie salvors – Henry paints Frank when it is too windy to work.

Bayona, our port of shelter on the *François Vieljeux*.

Crossing the Bay of Biscay, returning to Scotland with our first load of copper.

Above At Corpach sea lock, beneath Ben Nevis, on the final leg of our journey home to Dundee.

Right The passing of the years – Rob, Drew, Rachel and Patrick, all growing up, 1993.

Right Wrecksite of the *François Vieljeux* – the loads mount up.

Below left The eight-tined electro-hydraulic grab, with 200 tonnes closing force, 1996.

Below right Progress – the recoveries become an unremarkable event.

I was stunned at the reception. To invite me to his home, after what we had done. Surely, this was something strange and the invitation puzzled me all day, as I travelled along to Saumaty to complete my other tasks. I had expected searing wrath, like a fireball which would burst down the streets from the Boulevard des Oceans and sear me to a crisp, wherever I was in town. There was not even a cautionary message from Alec, when I got back to my hotel room, to say that Henri Delauze' assistant, Daniel Simoncini, who was in charge of the salvage projects, had rung up in high dudgeon. He was younger and more volatile and I had anticipated a major scene from him – perhaps he would be there, this evening ... I dreaded the thought.

Purposefully dressing in the most feminine outfit I could muster, to look as defenceless as possible, I was so nervous that I simply had to get out and caught a seven franc bus in the direction of Pharo. Arriving half an hour early, I found my destination and killed the remaining time by sitting in a small garden dedicated to fallen partisans, overlooking the sea. Twilight fell rapidly and the oil paint colours of the day were succumbed into the charcoal of the night. The temperature was pleasant, but I felt hot and cold in turns and the palms of my hands perspired. As the street lights began to glow yellow, there was no putting off the showdown much longer. I consulted my watch. Five minutes past six ...

The high wall kept out the world. Prickling with adrenaline, I rang the bell. Henri Delauze answered the intercom himself.

'Ah come in.' Not a detection of anger in his voice.

The security lock was released. I made my way through the unknown secluded garden, down a short stretch of path. He came out to met me himself. An articulated diving suit, stood guardian by the veranda and he gestured past it as we ascended the steps, as at ease and hospitable as ever.

'I'm afraid that Daniel Simoncini could not join us, as he has another meeting, but do come into my study. We may talk, there.'

I was shown into a discreetly lit room. Built into the cliffside, the view was spectacular and the outside world pressed close against the sweeping window with the night. Shimmering lamps across the water, at the narrow entrance to the Vieux Port, flicked serpents' tongues across the inky void of the channel, and the illuminated Fort St Jean blazed a foil of liquid gold.

I caught the movement of an isolated figure beside a sleek diving vessel, that was tied to the wooden jetty, directly below.

'That's the *Minibex*,' he commented as he made his way to the other side of a large desk that was covered with papers and the odd piece of sunken treasure. An encrusted amphora rested on the floor. With the workspace so intermingled with the sea, there was no doubting that it was Henri's room and that he took pleasure in it. Unassuming as he was, it felt a privilege to be there. He indicated for me to take a seat.

I slipped off my shawl, outwardly composed and he regarded me benignly, with his quirky smile, 'What can we do for you?' The question was kindly intoned.

The whole event, the setting, the circumstance and particularly his relaxed attitude seemed incredible. I knew that the Salvage Association would have informed his company that they had not been successful in retaining the agreement, at the same time as they told us we had won; but reading his tanned, open face across the other side of the desk, there was no agitation, no acrimony. His whole manner was genuine, this was not acting. As unbelievable as it seemed to me, there was no other explanation. He simply did not know.

Of all the eventualities for which I had prepared myself, contempt, ire, even violence, his lacking this vital piece of intelligence had never entered my head. Slowly, gently, the bearer of dreadful news, I broached the subject as if it were death. 'Monsieur Delauze. I've come here today, because, I wanted you to know that we've been given the salvage agreement on the *François Vieljeux* ...'

His jaw dropped, and for a moment he was shocked.

I watched, concerned. We both sat stock still. The content of my sentence had been catastrophic. The atmosphere intense and there was total silence. It was excruciating. I, managing director of a penurious salvage company and mother of four, had just informed the president of one of the largest diving companies in the world, that we had whipped one of the most lucrative recovery agreements out from beneath his nose. Had this been a flashy American soap opera, I would have been pacing the room in my power suit and bird's nest hair, as he cursed 'You damn bitch ...!' pulled out a gun and shot me.

Slowly he gathered his thoughts.

I broke the peace. 'I'm sorry ... but I thought you knew. We found out yesterday.'

'N-no ... I had ... n-not ... been told,' he stammered out his English, it was such an effort. 'The managing director of our salvage company is not in his London office. He's here in Marseilles.'

Chivalrous to the last, there was another long pause, as he mastered himself. It would have been less painful had he been angry. Eventually, he spoke. 'Naturally, I am very disappointed, but I wish you the best of luck.'

I felt awful. 'That's very good of you' and I made as if to go.

'Look, I have to make a few phone calls, but you must stay and have a drink. Would you wait for me in the meeting room, next door?'

I owed him this at least and sat patiently, as bidden, with a glass of cold beer, gazing out across the amazing view, as the sound of him talking came muffled through the wall. I could not hear, but I did not have to, I knew to whom he would be speaking and after what had seemed some considerable while, he returned, more composed. 'I understand that you have a meeting with Daniel, tomorrow. He wants to speak to you.'

I gave him a wry smile, thinking 'Grab me by the throat more like!' but my mouth replied, 'I have to speak to him about the paperwork for the *Kohistan*.'

'Before you go, can I ask what percentage you agreed?'

There was no harm in telling him, for it was considerably lower than his – the one he had presumed would be renewed. We knew what it was, because despite his workforce being sworn to secrecy and using code names for all their wrecks, they had let slip some of the most pertinent facts.

'How can we compete against that!'

'I'm afraid you can't. We've designed our system to have extremely low running costs and so can accept less.' With this knowledge, he became visibly dejected again, and I suspect that his last faint hope of using his influence to reverse the Salvage Association's decision, expired. He knew why he had been beaten.

The bell in the wall rang again, releasing me, but the ordeal was not completely over. Down the garden path, whom should be coming in the other direction, but the still oblivious managing director of Comex Deep Sea Salvage Ltd. I found out later that the pertinent fax, informing Comex that their salvage agreement on the *François Vieljeux* had not been renewed, was lying unread on his machine in the London office. With him was a merchant banker from the United States to invest in their portfolio of salvage projects.

What a mercy we were introduced in the shadows, for neither of them noticed Henri's concealed fury, he stood ramrod straight and positively bristled, and they both blithely ignored me.

'What an honour to meet you, Sir,' greeted the American to Henri Delauze.

How true his words, and how mean I felt in leaving him in such a ghastly position, even though the best thing I could do was just go. Closing the door, I ran up the road as fast as I could, laughing and swearing at the mischief I had caused.

The meeting with Daniel the next morning, did not bother me half as much, because we did not like each other. Slightly taller than me and extremely good looking, we were almost exactly the same age. It was his mannerism to be humourless and treat people with a purposeful disdain. I was not remotely his sort of woman, nor was he my kind of man and so, thus well matched, we were at liberty to be unscrupulously combative.

I was put in a conference room beside the main door to wait for him. He burst into the room, peremptorily, but with great flare. 'So. This is not very friendly of you!' he accused.

'What do you mean, *not very friendly?*' I was deliberately obtuse, even though I knew full well what he meant.

'To take our salvage agreement away.'

'I understand that it expired several months ago.'

He sat beside me and pulled up his chair close, as if to intimidate, 'You know,' he threatened softly, 'that we shall turn up onsite'.

Despite his proximity, his body language was not that of a physically aggressive man, and so I risked shrugging dismissively as I had expected this. Even so, I worried what he might do next.

'I see that does not bother you!'

It did. In fact, it was our main concern that Comex might try to become 'Salvor in Possession', and oust us that way, just as Alec and Simon had done to Nundy on the *Oceanic*.

I shrugged again, even more diffident.

He changed tack, 'How can you expect to do anything with that toy?' This was how he always referred to *Redeemer*.

'I'm sure that Alec will find a way.'

By now I had the papers pulled out for the sales on the *Kohistan*, as I just wanted to escape and changed the subject. 'This is the receipt from the company who bought the wolfram. and these are receipts for the haulage costs. You, I think, have the documents for the French customs,' and before we could continue, the receptionist knocked on the door and called him away for a moment.

This brief respite released me. The copies he required were on the table, I gathered my affairs and with an air of inarguable finality, snapped my briefcase shut as he walked back in.

'I don't think there is anything more to be said,' I declared, knowing that nothing could be further from the truth and pressed my exit. I had defied him and with a look of wonder, he let me go. We parted at the entrance.

'Tell Alec,' he called after me from underneath the porch, as I marched off into the bright Provence sun, 'That if he gets anything from the *François Vieljeux* I shall give him my admiration.'

I twirled on my heel, swinging my briefcase with light abandon at the pleasure of getting away in one piece and teased, provocatively, 'Daniel, I should have that in writing' and gave a parting wave. To his credit, for the first occasion in all the time I had known him, he laughed and waved back.

We had been so broke before I had arrived, that I had to pay for my ticket by withdrawing two hundred pounds from the farming company account. That evening, I returned to Britain with a cargo recovery agreement worth £10.3 million, sleeping fully dressed on a plastic covered mattress in a cabin full of five strangers, male and female, in a second-class couchette.

Who says salvage does not have it's glamorous side?

CHAPTER

23

THE FRANÇOIS VIELJEUX

Very occasionally, for people who live and work on dry land, the elements will effect their lives. The roads will be blocked by floods and travel will be disrupted, or the wind will blow, stripping slates off roofs, tipping over caravans and uprooting trees. On the news, there will be shots of high seas lashing harbour breakwaters, with the odd yacht plunging in the swell, unreachable and beyond hope. The bulk of the population watch these scenes from the security of their armchairs. Draughts may sneak up under the doors. At worst, the electricity might go off, an interruption which is frequently borne with bad grace.

There is a different outlook. On hearing the elements beating against the window pane, anyone who has had anything to do with ships or boats, casts an anxious eye into the rapidly moving clouds and pities any soul at the whim of the ocean. Far worse, on occasion some of us pray for at least one particular person.

The *François Vieljeux* met her end on just such a night with the loss of twenty-three lives.

The hell. The terror. The noise.

The overwhelming, merciless power of towering waves, fifteen metres high, which curl in the air and tumble in a force of ice white energy. The thrusting, plunging motion. Up on a peak one moment. Down in a trough the next. Always rolling. Pitching. The list shifting ever to starboard; so that disorder and chaos is added to fear, as cupboards burst open, plates crash and items tumble from shelves and drawers. Nowhere to balance and keep foothold, as the floors become part walls. The pain of being thrown and tossed against hard, unyielding surfaces. The retching sickness and physical exhaustion.

Ordeal by water. Such torture, until sheer dispassionate physics takes over and the last of the ship's buoyancy is exhausted. The flimsy shield of steel, which is the hull, is claimed by gravity and hopeless souls are swallowed up to fare as best they can. Their own strength and capricious luck will divide them into those who will live and those who will die. There is no fairness. No justice. It does not matter who you are, or how many needy dependants you will leave behind The elements are indifferent, cruel even. 'Mayday! … Mayday! … Mayday!' 'Help me! … Help me! … God Help me! …' There is no dispensation for simply being in the wrong place at the wrong time; just shockingly cold, violent, muscle-cramping liquid, powering in every direction. Crashing. Sucking. Swirling. Dragging.

Drowning. 'They cry unto the Lord … He maketh the storm a calm, so that the waves thereof are still.' If only it were so.

On the 14th February 1979, the 11000 ton, French cargo/container ship, *François Vieljeux*, foundered in the winter Atlantic, forty-five miles south-west of Cape Finisterre. To reconstruct her last moments with any insight is harrowing.

Just over a fortnight before, this unremarkable vessel lay against a wharf in Mombasa, Kenya, completing her stowage of coffee and adding fruit concentrate to the copper and zinc already loaded in Dar es Salaam. The total weight of cargo she was carrying increased to just over 14000 tonnes. Seven times the length of *Redeemer*, there would have been nothing to pick her out from any other inter-continental trader. She had four holds and a pair of square masts amidships, that stood sentinel like rugby posts. Her bridge and accommodation were aft. Once the steel hatch covers had been secured, rolled out in strips mechanically like vast garage doors, the bulk of the hundred and twenty-three containers she was transporting could be seen on deck, giving the appearance of a shopper peering over heavily laden arms.

On board there were twenty-eight crew and three wives.

What began as an ordinary trip, deteriorated as the *François Vieljeux* cleared the Suez Canal and began encountering heavy Mediterranean seas on 8th February. The ship pitched severely heading into the force nine gale and the deck was awash.

At 0100 hours on 9th February, the bilge alarms rang in holds 2, 3 and 4 in which the copper and zinc were stowed. Water appeared to be breaching the hatch covers and pumping was frequent, as she fought her way to the Gibraltar Strait. A slight list had appeared to starboard and the aft ballast tank was filled to improve the ship's trim, before she set out into the Atlantic on the night of 12th February. Heading on a course of 293 degrees to pass Cape St Vincent, she encountered a westerly wind and swell.

Cape St Vincent was skirted around at 1300 hours the next day. By this time the swell had become very heavy from the west-north-west, and the ship's rolling had become accentuated, which was causing concern. The aft flume tank was filled with 250 tonnes of salt water to restore an acceptable trim. Water continued to breach holds 2, 3 and 4, and the Captain gave orders for them to be pumped at each alarm, and twice a day at 0800 and 1700 hours.

During that night, the winds, always from the west, freshened and reached force nine or ten by dawn. At 0800 hours on 14th February, the speed of the *François Vieljeux* was fourteen knots and around an hour later, the Captain reported a list to starboard. Now, ominously, the ship's goal post masts did not return past the vertical when she rolled and the starboard gunwales were being submerged. Ballast and diesel were shifted, but despite these measures, the list got worse.

As Cape Finisterre was neared, the sea conditions deteriorated, producing pyramidal waves, five storeys high. There was no shelter close at hand. No respite. In the most awful conditions he had ever experienced, the Captain decided to head west into the gale, in order to protect the *François Vieljeux*'s hatch covers from taking in any more water. It was to be of no avail. Shortly after the manoeuvre, the list lurched abruptly to twenty-two degrees to starboard. The accompanying shift of every movable object, signalled the end.

At 1025 hours an S.O.S. was broadcast.

Several ships received the message, including the cargo ship, *Saint Dominique* and the tug, *Abeille Nomandie*, both French. They headed to assist their compatriots on the now stricken *François Vieljeux*, which was being tossed savagely and inundated.

In a last desperate attempt to save their lives, the Captain ordered full speed to port. They would try to make for Vigo. Broadside on, with her low gunwale exposed to the full onslaught of the Atlantic, a number of containers were washed away. More water poured in the holds.

Now, it was just a question of time.

Pray that the rescuers arrived soon. The crew and passengers assembled, prepared to abandon ship, although it was impossible to launch the lifeboats. No one panicked. Heeled over as she was, more containers broke loose and the starboard life-saving equipment was swept away. This loss was academic.

Then the main engine stopped. Its silence was a death knell. The winds gusted up to storm force twelve.

Inching ever over, filling rapidly with water and in her final throes, the *François Vieljeux* capsized to starboard. The position was thirty miles offshore. The *Saint Dominique* witnessed the devastating end, as at the last moment she sank by the stern. Searching the area for over two hours, she picked up nine survivors one of whom died onboard. The *Abeille Normandie* then took over and recovered ten bodies. The other twelve were never found.

Without doubt, this is the tragedy of cargo recovery. At times people die when a ship is lost. It is a reality that one learns to accept.

Curious to think that at the time the sinking occurred, we knew nothing about it. We were still on the *Argyll* and had not even lifted *Redeemer*. When eventually we were awarded the salvage agreement on the *François Vieljeux*, her wreck had lain on the bottom for eleven years; so far beyond the reach of commercial technology, that she was not even located for nearly a decade. The task of lifting the six thousand six hundred tonnes of copper and seven hundred tonnes of zinc cargo that she had taken to the bottom, had waited for us.

During that November in 1990, we had a brief spurt, in which the development of our salvage business seemed to really come together. Alec was working hard arranging the building of his new lifting system; Vince had arranged the finance for the *François Vieljeux* project and I was about to go off to Vigo, to begin sorting out the logistics of turning up onsite. All was going fine and it was just a question of hard work … when the letter came.

It was Saturday morning. Kilburns is built into the rock, with the kitchen on the first floor. Alec had gone down to pick up the mail, which we had heard being put through the bottom door. Recognising a Bank of Scotland envelope, he had opened up it as he came up the stone stairs.

'Here,' he said, 'as he entered the kitchen. 'You'd better read this,' his voice was hollow.

I had been making pastry with the children, and in my haste wiped my floury hands on my thighs to take it from him. It was from our local bank manager, addressed to Kilburns Salvage Company and concerned *Redeemer*'s overdraft. A glance at the opening sentence told me all I had to know. Skipping hastily though the paragraphs, I found the crux over the page, 'The Bank requires your £340,000 overdraft to be paid back within one month'.

For the first time for as long as I could remember we had been contented. The family were thriving. We had a salvage agreement on a valuable cargo that was in a modern ship, for which we had plans and a manifest. After a prolonged and chronic bout of risk taking and self-sacrifice, it seemed that our striving had been worthwhile and our destiny was under control. Happiness. Relaxation. Ease. Joy. The letter reinforced that these sensations were not meant for us. They were forbidden, impermissible. We had been reckless and foolhardy to enjoy them, and now this was the tab.

'This is serious ...' I commented, collapsing on the wooden barrel that sat by the back door. Gutted.

'Just as we seemed to be getting somewhere ... and after all we've been through.'

'My thoughts exactly ...'

'What on earth do we do now?'

'We can't let it all be for nothing.'

In an instant, everything that was hopeful turned rancid; and carefree minds that had been engaged in enjoying a family weekend, stalled at the prospect of imminent bankruptcy. There would be no more levity, today.

Alec and I discussed the problem endlessly. There was no way we could reimburse the whole sum. If the Bank thought it would be possible to clear our debt on the back of the *François Vieljeux* agreement, they were sorely deluded. We were going to have to triple the world depth record for commercial cargo recovery merely to pick up the first ingot. Nobody had salvaged in that sort of depth before; let alone with a vessel they had lifted from the seafloor. Given this scenario, the gamble was steep enough, as it was and Vince had done marvellously to raise the funds at all. There was nothing spare.

'How are we going to turn the situation around, Alec?'

'There's no point in dealing with Cupar. We won't get anywhere, there. What about writing to the Chief Executive in Edinburgh?'

' Go to the very top, you mean? We've nothing to lose.'

'We could send a telex. It's more likely to reach him that way.'

It is humbling how one's priorities get rearranged. I had been looking forward to a meeting with the Minister of Aviation and Shipping in London on the Tuesday, about the Department of Transport's policy on competitive tendering. I was going with Menzies Campbell. Suddenly reimmersed in worry, Lord Brabazon of Tara and the vagaries of government seemed hardly important at all.

Practically the whole of my Sunday was spent in the office, composing a dispatch on which our livelihood, ship, home and farm would all depend. Alec looked after Robert, Drew, Patrick and Rachel and meals, and every so often I would go through, for reassurance that it was what he wanted to say.

The thrust was plain.

We had given our all, overcoming almost insurmountable obstacles including imprisonment and being held by gunboat. Nothing would have been easier when *Redeemer* was sequestrated in Sicily, than to have abandoned her, simply run away; but we had stuck to her; withstood all the aggravation; behaved properly and seen everything through; to the point of beating off major, international competition to win this new agreement and give ourselves a future. To have it all dashed from our hands, now, when we had come so far, seemed unthinkable. Not only was it unjust, but it did not make business sense. The monthly charter that was coming in for *Redeemer* backed this up.

First thing in the morning, after obtaining the correct number for the Bank of Scotland's impressive headquarters on the Mound, the telex machine was set into motion.

FOR THE ATTN. OF MR BRUCE PATULLO ... DEAR SIR ...

We did not even send a copy to the local branch. Now, all that could be done was try to soldier on and wait for the response.

It was a clear November morning in Westminster, as Ming and I walked the half mile to Marsham Street. I had been wondering ever since we had met in the Lobby, if I should mention that things were not all good with us, and Deep Water Recovery & Exploration Ltd, whose interests he had allied, could be going bust at this very moment, but surmised that he would prefer not to know. The meeting with the minister would pass and be forgotten. Ignorance was best.

I was grateful to him for arranging this audience, even though he never let me get away with much and I had had to produce the evidence to substantiate our case. The basis for argument was contained in one of the Department of Transport's own bulletins. On it I had highlighted the sentence:

> In the case of a wreck which has lain on the sea bed apparently abandoned for many years, persons will be entitled, irrespective of contract, but with due observance to the rights which may have accrued to other salvors by virtue of prior possession, to dive and locate it if they can and having done so to recover which parts of the vessel and its contents as they can.

'How,' I had asked him, 'Can you competitive tender for a right?'
'Arh,' like 'checkmate' had come the reply.
After all the trouble they had given us, I was disappointed with the calibre of the civil servants who sat round the table to advise the minister. They obviously did not appreciate the unique legislation under their control and were too eager to implement dogma to realise that salvage, with or without a contract, was a reward for services rendered. It was salvors like us, who conferred the benefit on owners like them, and not the

other way round. If we did not want to recover their cargo, they could not make us. The War Risks Insurance Scheme may have paid out hundreds of thousands of pounds, but if we did not take risks and exert ourselves to bring their assets ashore, they were as good as lost.

Far from helping us as a British company, they had cost us a fortune and set us back months. 'Fools,' I reflected, 'You think you've all the cards. What you don't know is that we have the *François Vieljeux* agreement. Her cargo is worth millions more than the *Glenartney*'s and we did not have to competitive tender, nor be arrested nor tied up in port to get it. You've been left behind. Keep your cargoes. We don't want to confer our benefit on you, any more!'

Ming had warned me that we would not get any definite response...and certainly would not get an apology. Leaving behind a document that put forward an alternative approach, we wandered back to the House of Commons, talking about this and that. I told him about the *François Vieljeux* and how I was flying out to Spain that afternoon.

When we got to Parliament Square we took our leave. I thanked him for everything. He had seen us through some of our of lowest points and had been a good friend as well as a good MP. 'I hope I did not embarrass you in any way?'

'No,' he chuckled, perhaps remembering how cross I had been at times. 'It's been fun ... The best of luck in Vigo.'

We went our separate routes. The goodbye was a watershed, cutting off all to do with the Mediterranean that had been so awful; the Department of Transport, Sicily, Tunisia and *bangs*. That whole terrible episode was finished. Before me lay the future.

And in the very first instance, that meant the Bank.

24

VIGO

I walked to Victoria Station, where I had left my luggage, and called Alec from a payphone.

'Have you had any word?'

'Yes,' he breathed rapidly, almost bemused, 'a telex has arrived from Bruce Patullo and it says:

THE BANK OF SCOTLAND HAS LENT YOU MORE MONEY THAN A PRUDENT BANKER MIGHT DEEM FIT. BUT WE SHALL CONSIDER THE MATTER. YOU MAY MAKE AN APPOINTMENT TO SEE YOUR AREA MANAGER.

'What do you think it means?'

'I really don't know ... it could be worse. What do you think we ought to reply?'

'I haven't a clue. Look, I don't want to miss my plane. I've got to get out to Heathrow, I'll have a think about it and ring back from there.'

Mulling over a response on the interminable Piccadilly Line, I knew that courage was the only virtue that would pull us through, and wrote a riposte in capitals on the back of a piece of paper, to dictate as soon as I had checked in.

In the years since the *Parthenia*, Alec still had not managed to conquer the telex and had to be given instructions above the noise of flight arrivals and departures in Terminal Two. 'Right, press Store'

'Store ... O.K. got that. It says Message Number 5.'

'Type FROM ALEC CRAWFORD. New Line.'

'F-r-o-m A-l-e-c C-r-a-w-f-o-r-d', he repeated searching for the letters and using only his forefingers. 'How do I do New Line?'

'Press Enter.'

'Yup. Found it. Carry on.'

And so it went on, until after DEAR SIR (comma) New Line', we got to the crux, WE KNOW THAT THE BANK OF SCOTLAND HAS LENT US

MORE MONEY THAN A PRUDENT BANKER MIGHT DEEM FIT (comma) BUT THAT IS WHY IT SEEMS QUESTIONABLE FOR THEM TO GIVE UP NOW (comma) WHEN IT IS LIKELY THAT BOTH THEIR FAITH AND THEIR FUNDS ARE GOING TO BE REPAID (full stop) I WILL MAKE AN APPOINTMENT TO SEE OUR AREA MANAGER (full stop) New Line. YOURS SINCERELY (comma) New Line. ALEC CRAWFORD.

There was nothing to do now, but for me to perform my duties and wait. I hated killing time like this. Life was so full of uncertainties that one felt almost dishonest pressing ahead. It was the showmanship of launching oneself off a trapeze, doubting whether the catch could be made, or not. If it was, one kept one's bargain with those involved and few were any the wiser, never knowing what nerve it had taken to leap into oblivion; but failure meant a crash, no safety net and everyone being shocked and upset.

Madrid for a night. A morning at the British Consulate, and then a flight to Santiago de Compostella in north-west Spain. As the taxi driver wound his way down through the flats to the railway station, cutting a sharp hair-pin bend, I wondered to what sort of place I had come. The Atlantic breeze, laden with moisture and a gossamer mist filled the air, giving the deserted low, stone building a slightly eerie feeling.

The place was so lifeless, that I was almost surprised to find someone behind the counter, but speaking the few words of Spanish I knew, I eventually made it clear that I would like a single ticket to Vigo. The cost in pesetas was rattled back so quickly, that I had no way of deciphering the amount and so handed over a big note, from which the cost could be taken. My ear was so completely untuned to both the language and accent, that the rolling r's, the ya's and sybillic th's, sounded a mystery. There was no way I could ask, 'Where does the train go from?' and so had to find a timetable on a board, leaning against the wall. It sent me off to search for Platform Two. On its flat surface was erected a gaunt corrugated roof on stilts, a couple of metal benches and some lamp posts. Looking up and down the line, it disappeared into ethereal gloom in both directions, and I shuddered in the damp.

'Half an hour to go ... Have I got the right platform? Will there even be a train?' I began to wonder, as I waited for ages, alone.

Eventually a group of women turned up and it was like a time warp. Obviously fishwives, some old, some surprisingly young, they carried enormous wicker panniers covered with check cloths. Pulled tightly around their waists were black and white striped aprons, which hung over long skirts and rubber boots. Striking in appearance, joking and chattering, they could have stepped straight out of the pages of *National Geographic*; an image of contented traditional labour against a landscape of stark industrialism, wreathed in mist. This heretical thought and their company cheered me up. Slowly, one or two more people began to arrive.

When the train from La Coruña pulled in, the brown carriages were quaint, ancient rolling stock with hard, slatted seats. These were practically full and moving along to find a space, I noticed the varnish peeling off the woodwork and worn linoleum floor. It was not like Intercity at home at all, with its plastic tables and fabric covered seats. In particular there was an unusual noise, totally unfamiliar, and for a moment it took me a while to work out what it was. Everyone was talking, and animated voices rise and fell above the slow thrum of tracks, like the chirruping in an aviary of birds. Looking round, there was not a sullen face and no commuters hid behind the evening newspaper, for fear of having to converse. The plump teenager opposite was eating sunflower seeds out of a paper bag, cracking them with her teeth and spitting the husks onto the floor. She leant across in a casual, friendly manner and offered for me to take some. I gestured, 'No thanks', but already I was taken with this out of the way corner of Spain.

As we wound along the narrow track, through the rocks covered with brambles and heather, the flora gave the illusion of the west of Britain. A notion that was immediately dispelled by the eucalyptus trees, or scattered villages with their red tiled houses; each with its small pagoda-like store, an *ahorra*, and citrus trees around the back door and vines. 'I would like to work here,' I mused. It was cool and temperate, not like the searing heat of Sicily, but would we ever get to the *François Vieljeux*, I still did not know.

The journey was ponderous, with frequent stops. This station a timber yard, this one a grand, almost colonial building in the centre of a town. Derelict mills with chimneys like obelisks, baroque churches that are miniature copies of the great cathedral of Santiago, a modern coat hangar bridge; all was foreign and new, as we wound our way to the coast, where we skirted round the inlets. Finally, the city drew near and we began cutting through a *mêlée* of flats, and squat houses. Washing bedecked the balconies and a few isolated flowers bloomed in hardened back yards.

Vigo is built on a steep hillside, like San Francisco, with a view over her great river, or *ria*, which has been the secret of her wealth. She rises from the water, overcrowded and higgedly piggedly, a huge car-manufacturing conurbation and Europe's largest fishing port.

The terminus is high up and so it was another taxi to the Lloyd's Agent down on the waterfront. I found the office, set back across the main road from the Transatlantic Quay. Outside was the hustle of modern streets, but once up the steps into rather a splendid turn of the century building and through the double door, it was like putting the clock back to an age of solicitous calm, when maritime trade was king. A high wooden counter lined the room making it look like a banking hall, with its brass grills proclaiming departments, like *Encargos*. A model of a long, sleek steamship, took up most of the near wall, and with a gallery above and a bronze bust of the founder, the hushed and purposeful interior had a respectful, library air.

'May I speak in English? I'm here about the *François Vieljeux*. I believe the Salvage Association informed you I was coming.'

After hours of travelling I felt exhausted and dirty, as if blown in on the wind and yet my arrival was met with that eager anticipation that a deviation for the norm brings. Salvage is always intriguing and I was greeted by a smiling face.

'Ah, Señora Crawford. My name is Henrique Duran. My cousin, our managing director is expecting you. Come through to his office' and I was ushered into a small room with red leather furniture and oak desk covered with paperwork. As Consul for Norway, the picture of their Royal Family sat atop the wooden dado, alongside that of a state photograph of King Juan Carlos of Spain. Soon I learnt that not only were they a long-established family, but Alberto was also one of the local MPs and so it seemed that I had swapped a Scottish Liberal for a Spanish Conservative. They were about the same age, but as different in build and manner as in dress and politics. In his coloured shirt and autumn suit, Alberto was as openly suave and continental as Ming was reserved and British. His English was perfect.

The wreck of the *François Vieljeux* lies in the Spanish Exclusive Economic Zone. This two hundred miles zone gave their authorities a certain measure of control over our activities on the wrecksite and after our crazy dealings with the Italians, in Rome as well as Sicily, I had feared the worst. This is why my briefcase was so heavy. Sensitive to trouble, I had come armed with translated documents about our company and every relevant piece of legislation I could find; laying aside three days out of my schedule for plodding around offices and establishing our rights. I might even have to go back to Madrid.

'No problem. I have spoken to the authorities. All they require is for the Salvage Association to prove their title to the cargo and then you may begin.'

'That's it?' I wanted to demand. 'Nothing more?' I could hardly believe it.

Seeing my surprise, he added. 'As you find , we are very efficient here.'

All there was left for me to do was arrange a base.

'Vigo is very expensive,' Alberto declared. 'As you just want a mooring, except for loading and unloading, I suggest you use Bayona, a small fishing village fifteen kilometres down the coast. The anchorage is good, as it is very sheltered.'

Everything was accomplished. It should have been a cause for celebration, but I had still to find out whether we would be able to arrive in the spring, or have to sell *Redeemer*. That evening, lying on the flowery counterpane of my bed in the Hotel Bahia de Vigo, I waited for Alec to ring and tell me our fate.

'It's all going to be O.K., Moya. I knew it as soon as I walked into the meeting that it had all been agreed. We can turn up on the *François Vieljeux!*'

I felt hollow, wrung out under the strain of having to pretend. It had by no means been a foregone conclusion that we would be able to carry on. Plenty of more conventional companies had had their throats cut for less. For once, it seemed, in amongst all the cynicism and bean counting, enterprise still had some value. The Bank of Scotland had stood by us. Without this, we would have been moribund.

CHAPTER

25

DEEP WATER

The sleepy, deserted port I had surveyed in the winter, with its empty streets and shuttered shops and cafes, could not be compared to the fair to which I returned in early July. Cooler than the cities, and not so commercialised as the Mediterranean coast, Bayona was an indigenous tourist resort, and its population swelled by tens of thousands in the summer months.

After completing a colossal refit in the berth at Saumaty, Alec had steamed round through the Straits of Gibraltar and had been anchored off the former fishing village for six weeks. The Clark Chapman winches had been removed and an impressive, shiny white new one stood in their place. It had been fabricated by Lebus Engineering of Sittingbourne to Alec's design, as their grooving was essential to maintain the life of the new 1850 metre hoist umbilical. He had spent hours at his drawing board in the kitchen, in amongst manuals of hydraulic motors and brakes, and data on electrical cables, establishing exactly what he wanted. He was self-trained, but checking over his drawings and calculations, they had been intrigued to find that the only error he had made was to be half an inch out on the diameter of the drum. Alec understood the determining factors, torque, tension, power, pressure, voltage drop and flow; making compromises in his requirements for high hoist speed and big lifts to get around such problems as excessive drag, synchronous oscillation, overheating of the cable, and the squeezing of the drum.

When he had been at a loss at some specific aspect or other, he had either looked it up in a book or phoned up a technical department and asked. Always, he tackled the issue from the same angle, analysing what he wanted to do on the seabed and leading this back to the ship. Never did he start with *Redeemer* and work things out the other way round. In many respects, he appreciated her motion and stability characteristics so well, that she was incidental to him and he altered and adapted her, just as if she were a workshop, afloat.

'Anyone can lift anything they want from the bottom of the oceans' he would reiterate. 'It just depends on how much money they want to spend. Look at the *Glomar Challenger* funded by Howard Hughes.' It had lifted part of a Soviet submarine for the US Navy, from 5000 metres of water. The exercise had cost millions, if not billions of dollars, but the achievement had been made over twenty years previously and had not really pushed technology forward at all. The same sort of drillship was still in operation, today, but its operation was uneconomic for little but the oil industry. 'I want to create a cost-effective system, that would be a *railroad* and open up a hidden continent, to which, at present, access is purely restricted by cost.' It was this pioneering dream that had long since driven his imagination and now he had the chance to begin putting it in place.

In amongst all the specifications, the diameter of the hoist umbilical was the most crucial, as this dictated the size of everything else. Even an extra millimetre in its girth would translate into kilograms more steel and much greater operational costs. It would have been easy to have been sloppy and let the whole thing get out of proportion, as the size/weight ratio shot up on an exponential curve. Quizzing himself, looking at the winch from every angle in his head, Alec sat in his chair in front of the dresser and worried, viewing the underwater system as a whole; making a radical decision, here; easing a little there, until he got it right.

The experience he had gained with the underwater pods on the *Kohistan*, had been invaluable, enabling him to produce a balanced layout for the electrical core, that would send power to signals and bring back video images from the grab. For the first time, the camera would not be on its separate support and supply, but would be built in so that it looked down between the tines. Limited by the quality of insulation around the conductors to the amount of current that could be passed through them, and the voltage drop over the umbilical length – which was over a mile – batteries had to be placed in the body of the grab to provide a constant energy source. These would be trickle-charged from the surface, to prevent them going flat. This arrangement was not perfect, but it was certainly an improvement on the Preussag system for sampling, in which the batteries had to be changed after every few open and shut operations. With its three layers of wire strands, to make it as rotationally stable as possible, the resulting thirty-two millimetre rope, as they are termed, had an all important safe working load of twelve tonnes.

Alec, so easy going about his own personal requirements, could not have been more exacting in his technical demands. It must be right. Now that we were breaking depth barriers, and not just equalling them. It was uncharted territory we were entering and with we had been able to utilise far fewer second-hand pieces of equipment. The cost of the winch and hoist umbilical alone was over £100,000 without any design cost. Every so often we were swept by a sensation of pioneering, which made the undertaking exciting and frightening, at one and the same time.

When the day came in February for the twenty-six tonne artic lorry to take all his spares and requirements for Saumaty, the contents of its load, which had been accumulated from the farm steading over weeks, were so densely packed that it could take hardly another spanner or tin of grease. With its departure, our frenetic winter together came to an end.

'I'm sorry that I have not had more time to spend with you, Moya. Everything has just been so busy.' It was always the same way. I had got used to it by now.

Only Alec, after all his years of working around remote island piers with so little back up, would have thought of taking a handful of new men, to begin a major engineering job in a container port in Marseilles. Charlie Marsden, a friend of the late Charlie Butterworth, who had just recently upgraded his Deck Officer's Ticket, was to be our new First Mate. Frank Gallacher, a welder who had trained with Yarrows on the Clyde, was to help with the mechanical work, and Dave Rossiter, an ex-marine who had fought in the Falklands Islands, was the cook. Between them, they had the old winch dismantled; the new winch craned into the hold and bedded in; the extra hydraulic pumps that were required, fitted; the moorings on deck and the ship provisioned and ready to set sail by 25th May.

Vince joined *Redeemer* for the voyage, as down on her loadline, but freshly painted and tidy, she quitted the Mediterranean and headed for Vigo. On her arrival, although we did not know it at the time, the Harbour Master was so astonished by her size that he bet Alberto Duran she would never lift anything at all from such a great depth. Many people remembered the *François Vieljeux* sinking and knew how treacherous the conditions could be there. Silently, and in Spanish, the lines were drawn in the port between believers and non-believers. Not to make our chance of success seem any more far fetched than it was, Alberto discreetly omitted to mention that we had raised *Redeemer* from the seabed. As he put it, 'That would be too much for them to take in'.

So much is usually unknown when one turns up onsite, but in the case of *François Vieljeux*, we had seen a promotional video that Comex had produced, which showed she was lying upright on the seabed. This took a tremendous element of the risk away, for had she been upside down, there was no way we could blast our way through a modern hull in over a kilometre of water and expect to make any money out of it. It would have necessitated the use of liquid explosives, simply to withstand the pressure at that depth and this would mean a whole new learning curve, as we had never used them before. They were also expensive and we would be hidebound by regulations that would limit all our movements. Besides, as far as I was concerned any form of *bang* was a dirty word, and I was prepared to resign, get a divorce, even, rather than have anything to do with them, anymore.

Alec found the wreck on the first day's search. Which even though we had got an accurate position was no mean feat, considering we were equipped solely with an echosounder. As they had steamed slowly backwards and forwards in a grid over the co-ordinates, the pen traced a jagged line that shot up and down like a fluctuating economy, denoting an extremely uneven bottom that declined steeply, as the continental shelf disappeared into the Iberian Abyssal Plain.

'That's her. I'm sure it is,' he declared to Charlie who was at the controls. 'You can see her, there,' and he pointed to a minute blip on the paper which seemed indistinguishable from any of the others.

'If you say so.'

'Look you can see, even though it's very small, the echo's hard. One thousand two hundred and fifty metres to the bottom. It certainly is a hell of a way.'

'What's that in feet – around four thousand, one hundred. Just about as deep as Ben Nevis is high.'

They both raised their eyebrows, as thinking back to the mountain that overshadowed Fort William, the force of this analogy came home.

The next step was to survey the surrounding contours, so that the best place for each of the four moorings could be determined and for a second time they had good reason to think of a Scottish landscape. Within the immediate vicinity, the slope was so severe that it fell away by seventeen per cent, in some places plunging in sheer cliffs.

'This is going to give us problems, Charlie. It's going to be like anchoring a hot air balloon to the side of a glen. The east buoys are going to be high and they'll want to pull out, all the time; and the strain on the west buoys is going to be immense, especially given the predominate direction of the swell.'

'Getting them in exactly the right position is going to be critical, too. The length of the rope is going to have to be exactly right.'

'I know and we're just feeling our way. Nobody else has laid a four-point mooring system so deep, let alone in such conditions. They're going to be the deepest in the world. Crazy, isn't it!'

It was, but even at this stage we had not fully appreciated how bad 'such conditions' really were. It was not until the beginning of July that work could begin, because there had been a particularly long inclement spell. 'It was just pure bad luck,' we had thought. 'After all, this was summer.' We gritted our teeth and pressed on.

Every day that had not been spent in preparing or laying a mooring, was used to complete the underwater electrical pod. This complicated unit contained most of a battery charger; the power unit from a gyro; the innards out of an underwater vehicle, including solid state relays and a handful of components from an Arbroath scrap yard, so that even Alec admitted, 'Quite a mix'. With minimal clearance, the fantastical array with all its wires was squeezed into a heavy duty container. This was topped up with oil, so that the walls could take the pressure of nearly 2000 pounds per square inch, the weight of a family car pressing on an area the size of a man's thumb. It had to be brim full or else, at depth, the steel would be squeezed, as easily as pressing into dough.

So much of the development was breaking new ground, that for most part Alec was inventing as he went along. 'It should work,' he would say about a new development, but to make alterations, the electro-hydraulic pods were secured to the body of the grab with rope and their protective guards were left off, for ease of removal. The resulting array of thick hose going in all directions and coiled in great loops, here and there, looked like Medusa's hair.

Nevertheless, it was a tremendous day when *Redeemer* tied up and it all worked, sending our first images back from the *François Vieljeux*.

'I don't want to drop the camera directly onto the wreck, in case it gets caught amongst the goal post masts and top hamper,' he told Charlie, as he paid out the winch and they viewed the monitor.

'How many layers is that on the winch, Frank?' he queried, shouting out of the open window – once they got established, he would really have to put a closed-circuit camera up, so that he could see for himself.

'Six and a half …' came the reply.

Head down, again. 'O.K. We must be getting near the bottom, now. I'll slow down, gazing intently, he and Charlie peered into the screen.

'Look … there's the seabed' and his hand instantly stopped the winch. 'Now let's see … In which direction do we need to go?' Looking at the buoys, which were now pulled much closer in around the ship, each on a long length of polypropylene rope, he used the satellite position system, to gain his bearings. 'We need to go west …'

'Can you slacken the brake on the forward port winch, Frank?' he shouted through the open door and there was a drone of hydraulics and creaking of the strained fibres, as the turns were made.

'What's that?' asked Charlie, pointing to a great, long box. 'It looks like a container …' After a pause … 'There's another one, there …' and suddenly the shadow of the hull loomed up, a flat steel wall.

Alec let *Redeemer* settle, before beginning to manoeuvre along its side. 'There are letters painted on her, S…N…C…D…V. Societe Navale Chargeurs Delmas Vieljeux. They had owned the *François Vieljeux*, 'We've got the right wreck. Let's have a look at the holds'. Easing gently, first this way and then that, to get the grab down through the top hamper of rigging, they began to explore. 'We must be careful not to touch anything, some of this steel will be like a knife. It would cut through the hoist umbilical just like that, all £30,000 worth.'

Everything was going so well … and then the wind blew. We might be overcoming the physical difficulties of providing power and lift, three times deeper than ever before, but what we had not bargained for so far south, was the constant bad weather.

Soon a pattern emerged and we were in and out of the wrecksite like a fiddler's elbow. The day in Bayona would be mirror calm. The sun would be shining on the yachts moored in the lee of the parador, with hardly a cloud in the sky. 'Finisterre Traffic is giving up to seven off Cape Finisterre, with a rough sea – that surely can't be right?' Alec would say, as they steamed past the Cies Islands. Twelve miles off and the wind would begin to freshen and the north-westerly swell would kick in and by the time they got to the moorings, it was a different world. There would be crests on the waves and the decks would be awash. All they would be able to do was count the vast, soft yellow buoys, as they floated over a kilometre apart, to make sure they were all still there, and return to the stillness of port.

In.

Out. Too rough.

In.

Out. Get tied up, which takes four hours. Get the grab down. There would be a fault and the grab tines would not close. Twenty minutes would pass, as it was lifted up and caught. The fault would usually be traced to the silver box in which all the electrical wires met, so called because it was made out of stainless steel. This would be removed; the oil drained off and each connection checked. Alec would get out his diagrams to make sure that the arrangement was correct, 'Red to blue' and touch both ends with his avometer, 'Green to brown, white to black …' and so on, until the problem was eliminated and everything could be restored. The grab could then be tested on the surface, where it would open and close like a dream.

'That's fine,' he would declare, 'we'll get it over the stern and lift a few more of these hatch covers before the evening.'

Down the grab would go to the bottom to everyone's relief – only to not work again. Heavy sighs all round, and some swearing to himself from Alec. 'Right, we've got to take it up, again.' It would be lifted and fixed. Once ready to put down, the wind would blow and the forecast would be gales. The moorings would have to be released whilst there was still a little light and there would be an uncomfortable passage in heightening seas to take shelter until the weather passed, which seldom took less than three days.

Out, again.

And so it went on. And on.

Soon, we began to realise just how much the weather was dictated by Cape Finisterre. It stuck way out into the Atlantic and whether it was a high or a low tracking across the ocean, half of the system would escape into Biscay and the balance would be squeezed against this promontory, so that the isobars would tighten and the winds intensify. The same happened with the current and swell and this is why the *François Vieljeux* had foundered, where she did. It had not been inevitable, just a matter of time. It was the spot. Which had now become our spot. The Shipping Forecast even broadcast its own monotonous lyric, 'South Finisterre, north to north-west three to four. Occasionally six to eight around Cape Finisterre'. For weeks on end, a groundswell would be blown from somewhere in the mid-Atlantic. We might as well have told everybody that we worked three thousand miles off the eastern seaboard of America, as thirty miles off the coast of Spain.

By the time the winter weather chased us off the site in late October, we had cleared away the aft end of No. 3 hold and dug down through the containers and dross to find absolutely nothing but sisal, tins of pineapple and a handful of tubular creatures, a metre long, the likes of which we had never seen before. Scientists later identified them as *Vestimentiferans*, which are a genus of invertebrate normally associated with sulphide deposits and cold methane seeps. A most remarkable discovery, as they had never been found in the eastern Atlantic before. Papers were written and a letter appeared in *Nature*. We were hailed as great achievers, pushing forward understanding of the unexplored deep sea world. This made us feel a little better about ourselves, but it did not pay the bills.

'What are we going to do, Alec, the copper should be there? The First Mate's stowage plan put over three thousand tonnes split between the main hold and 'tween deck. Where's it all gone?'

'I really don't know. You can see from the videos the grab biting into the double bottoms. There's absolutely nothing covering them now, except this layer of silt from the rotted coffee beans.

'Eye witnesses stated that when the *François Vieljeux* sank, she capsized to ninety degrees and sank by the stern and yet we find her lying absolutely upright on the seabed. How did she end up like that – perhaps under the water she continued to roll, or even turned completely upside down and the cargo fell out of her holds. It's impossible to tell. All I can say, is that we have done all this bloody work and I can't find a copper wirebar, anywhere.

'We'll just have to scrape through the winter somehow. I know now what alterations I would like to make to both the battery system and the moorings so that they are both more efficient. And when we go back, before we dig some more, I'm going to have a look in the surrounding area, in case her cargo is on the seabed, like the *Renate S*. It would make it a much easier job, if it were . . .'

In 1992, ease was not what the gods had in store.

The salvage season started badly with the Spanish authorities tying us up in Vigo. Apparently, our permission to work the *François Vieljeux* had to be given on an annual basis, and in our enthusiasm to begin our search, we had sailed straight to the wrecksite from Penzance. We were in theory entirely within our rights to do so, as this was salvage which was outwith international convention, but with the trend towards countries exercising increasing amounts of extra-territorial jurisdiction and the harbour still run by the military, we were on a hiding to nothing.

'This isn't a requirement of the United Nations Law of the Sea,' I had complained to Alberto, exasperated with the bureaucracy that seemed to be stretching ever further from the shore, it seemed, wherever we worked in the world.

Ten years out of dictatorship, he was pragmatic. 'Moya, this is Spain. We are a young democracy, here. If the authorities ask you to do it. You do it.' We buckled under and complied.

Eager to begin searching with the sonar Vince had procured, Alec could not get out to sea quick enough and his heart got a lift as he heard me speak on *Woman's Hour*, on Long Wave radio, as he steamed out to the wreck. I was about to leave, to give a presentation at the Twelfth International Tug and Salvage Conference in Genoa, their first female speaker in the twenty-five years that these reprobates from around the world had got together. It was quite something for me to have been asked and he smiled, encouraged at the sound of my familiar voice over the airwaves.

When I spoke in Italy, the reception from the audience was fantastic. I was very proud, but within another fortnight things could not have been worse. I received a call.

'Hello,' said a woebegone voice.

'Alec! How are you. I've been wondering how you've been getting on.'

'We've had a slight problem with our camera.'

'What's that?'

'It's on the bottom with the hoist umbilical!' and he gave one of his troubled laughs.

It was one way of breaking the dreadful news. He did not volunteer much about how the accident had happened, and I knew better than ask. The details would come out in time, as they did in his next letter.

The sonar had to be abandoned after only its second run, as *Redeemer* had taken on a big wave when it was mapping the east side of the wreck that made everything bang and rattle and the readings went. The problem seemed to be in the control unit in the wheelhouse, as the light which flashed every time a trigger pulse was sent to the towfish, stayed permanently on. It was taken onboard and examined. The electronics were found to be completely dry, so with manual in hand, Alec turned his attention to the printed circuit boards, but was unable to pinpoint a fault without an oscilloscope. There was nothing for it, but to put the camera on the sonar frame and tow it behind *Redeemer* on the umbilical, and this job was completed during the following five days of gales.

On Friday 29th May, they left for the wrecksite around 0600 hours and started the search with the camera. The knack was to keep the forward speed just high enough to maintain the frame flying about five metres above the seabed. In this way the image was perfect, especially as Alec had eliminated the interference that had periodically flashed across the monitor the previous year. Working though the night to 0200 hours, they were finding a lot of debris, but not what they were looking for. Containers, winches, railings, derricks, tins of pineapple and sisal, were scattered like the pieces of crashed spaceship across an open, rugged moonscape; embedded in a fine powdery silt, which puffed into the air if caught in the camera's slipstream as it passed overhead. Tragic, haunting images, caught on video, of contents and fittings, broken free and emptied out, as wantonly and haphazardly as plastic promotions in a cereal packet. There was a definite trail down the east side of the wreck.

The work carried on through Saturday and Sunday with hardly a break, not even stopping for meals. Up early, to bed late, only four hours sleep. Once, a hydraulic hose broke and the camera hit the bottom. Alec quickly fixed the problem and got it working again, until late on Monday, after another day's scanning, the camera picture began to go.

Another setback. A day to fix the damage caused by the camera frame catching on the debris on the seafloor and then out again before dawn. Determined not to lose the good weather Alec flogged himself on and, tired, he yawned as he lowered the camera for the first run of the day. Just as he did so, the observation camera, which he had newly installed to watch the main winch, went on the blink and the picture went fuzzy. Fiddling with the connectors, he continued to pay out the winch, as he knew how long it would take for the camera to reach the seabed.

He could not locate the problem. Should he stop and climb into the hold to see if the fault was there, he wondered. No, he would press on. There was no time to lose. He knew how many turns were on the drum, anyway, even though the hoist umbilical was almost out to its full length, as instead of working vertically, they were towing the camera some distance behind.

Then everything went wrong at once. The light went out on the seafloor and the camera snagged. Alec, paid out a little more thinking that there were still enough left. When the tension went tight and before he could slam on the brake – the whole thing came off the drum. The end snaked up from the end of the hold, over the aft pulley sheave – and was gone.

'Oh no!!' shouted Alec in anguish. 'No!!!'

Keeping his head, he noted down the exact position from the satellite navigating system and leaping down the ladder and through the watertight door, raced to the stern joining Frank and Henry Cumming, the new cook. There was not even a ripple on the water to show it had gone and for several minutes life did not seem worth living. He considered following it overboard.

Lost for words, he returned to the hatch to sit in a collapsed and dejected heap.

'What are we going to do now, Alec?' Henry asked at some length.

'I think we'd better put the kettle on,' came the broken hearted reply.

He had long since considered the 1250 metres beneath *Redeemer*'s hull as an irrelevance. It had been just like working in a fraction of that depth. Now with his lifeline lying that far below, and presented with the Herculean task of getting it back, the depth seemed as profound as the problem was unfathomable.

CHAPTER

26

COPPER

The next few weeks were a nightmare of toil, injury and despair. The hoist umbilical lay concealed, as if it had never existed and only the empty winch barrel, proved that it was not a dream. A weaker personality than Alec's might have broken under such circumstances, but determined, commanding, a born leader of men, there was no exertion he would spare to get it back.

The 'Z' dredge with which they began dragging was not up to the job and did not catch a thing, as they steamed backwards and forwards for a whole day, with it trailing along the seabed.

'Why won't it foul?' demanded Alec bitterly in the wheelhouse, as *Redeemer* wallowed languidly in the heavy swell. 'I don't see how it's not snagging on the hoist umbilical! We're in the right area. Everything seems to have gone wrong this year ...' More than anything he was cross with himself for losing it in the first place.

The atmosphere onboard was oppressed, but resolute. Frank and Henry, in particular, were staunch. 'How's it going, Alec,' Henry inquired rhetorically, as he handed over a mug of coffee late into the night. He was Alec's nephew, his sister's eldest boy and had come to join us to get some practical experience. He was talented in many ways and had risen to the challenge. Now, he was concerned that his uncle had not ceased working in eighteen hours. 'I thought you'd like a hot drink.'

His solicitude was unheeded, Alec was figuring out what to do. 'We're just going to have to go in and make up another grapple out of the new Danforth anchor. It will take a day's work, but it's the only way. This 'Z' dredge is too light and just an utter waste of time.

'We'll steam in. I'll turn the ship around.'

The fabrication was carried out in the lee of the Cies Islands and it was to be a full thirty-six hours before *Redeemer* was back onsite, again. The forecast was poor and there were gale warnings, but Alec was cast iron in his will to push on. The longer the hoist umbilical was on the bottom, the less likely it was to work again, given the eventuality that it would be retrieved. Without the benefit of video images or sonar, it was a mission that was all the more impossible.

They began once more to search blind. 'Right lads' Alec ordered after several runs, 'I want to get the grapple back on deck to see if any of the tines are bent. We'll know if it's been on the bottom, or not, by whether there's any mud on it.'

In the now lumpy sea, the grapple was hoisted to the stern and lashed with a rope, for Alec to examine. Swaying instinctively in the rolling motion, a rogue wave appeared broadside to the gunwale, and the deck simply disappeared from under their feet as *Redeemer* lurched to starboard in its wake.

'Look out!' Henry shouted as the tines of the grapple swung towards Alec's head. Ducking, he lost his balance and splayed across the deck, his right knee taking the full force of the blow on a piece of steel channel. It sliced hard into the flesh. Supported back into the mess, his trouser leg was cut off to reveal a wide, diagonal wound that left the whole cartilage fully exposed. Blood poured everywhere. A clean rag helped stem the flow and Alec swore, more in fury than in pain, which had not yet set in. 'It will have to be sewn up … We'll have to go in. Let's get a bandage on it and I'll call up Moya on the radio.'

By this time it was eleven o'clock at night.

With the kind help of Alberto Duran and an ambulance to the Centro Medico, forty-two stitches later, the Vigo pilots ferried Alec back to the ship with one incredibly sore and rigid limb. Posting him back on board with all the inelegance of a cumbersome parcel.

'You must be careful. Take it easy,' they remonstrated in Spanish.

'Thanks very much. No problem,' he assured them with a wave and not the slightest intention of so doing. By evening they had new extensions welded on the tines and they were ready for sea.

For two and a half days, leg swollen and throbbing, they trawled backwards and forwards without any luck. It seemed that the grapple was getting caught, but was tripping at the last moment, so that it released their quarry. The problem was analysed and more alterations were made. This time surely, they willed and the very next shot they had success.

'Yes! That's it. It's caught. We've got it!' Alec exclaimed, overjoyed.

Slowly, tentatively the main winch hauled in the minesweeper wire. Every noise, every movement jarred the senses. Faces so taut and tense, it was as if each body were personally taking the strain. One thousand metres. Five hundred metres. Two hundred metres. One hundred metres. Closer. Closer.

'Come on ... come on.' They could now see the shackle joining onto the chain of the grapple as it appeared over the stern. Gently ... gently ... Henry and Frank, were sheltering in the aft funnel for protection, in case something broke and there was a backlash. A piece of minesweeper wire giving way under load would cut a man's body in half.

'Have you got all those wires ready so that we can begin securing it?' Alec shouted to them. As he spoke, there was a dull bang, like the discharge of a shotgun and the wire recoiled, having snapped at the aft block. *Redeemer* settled in the water and Alec shut his eyes in disbelief as the hoist umbilical tumbled to the bottom, again.

Every day that went past made his responsibility for losing the umbilical harder to bear. It had been such a disastrous mistake. He had just tried too hard and been too tired and felt that in pushing himself to the limit, he had let everybody down. Only the thought of the family gave him the courage to carry on. Vince, realising how badly Alec was struggling, went out to give him physical as well as moral support. A new stimulus, fresh enthusiasm, a positive outlook; all these things he brought and more.

'You rest a while, Alec, give your knee a break, I'll work on deck with the lads.'

More wire and more chain were robbed from the supply for the moorings in the hold. More fabrication undertaken to replace the lost grapple. Another dawn in which weary, dispirited bodies awoke to face another eighteen hours to be spent trawling up and down over the position of loss, to no avail. And then another. Where would it all end?

Early on the morning of 15th June, when everyone was still hazed with sleep, miraculously the hoist umbilical caught for the second time.

'I don't want to risk lifting it to the surface and losing it, again,' Alec instructed Vince. 'We'll drag it into shallower water, so that it is still supported by bottom, which will reduce some of the load.'

Steaming at a slow rate of knots, they headed for the coast of Spain. At 350 metres, water depth, the trailing bundle snagged on the seabed and they were caught. Easing gently forward, they applied a steady force to free it, but it would not budge. They tried at various angles, but still it was held fast. After three hours of patient diligence, the lift wire snapped and the weight was gone.

A groan went up over the ship. Hands were placed on brows in incredulity.

Alec, physically exhausted, his shoulders sagging, and his skin grey and deeply shadowed beneath the eyes, limped his way on deck. His voice was drained and without emotion when he spoke. 'Frank, can you put the welder on, we'll have to make up another grapple. We're running out of steel. You'll have to use some of the heavy threaded bar that's in the hold for tines. Henry, we need to get another reel of minesweeper wire out, too. So if you can begin taking off the hatch beams, I'll use the derrick to lift a new drum out.'

Even before the repairs were made, the wind had blown up and it was back to the shelter of the isles. Another day eaten up by bad weather – and the next.

When the conditions abated and they finally did manage to return, the seabed beneath them was so rocky that the tines were being torn from the grapple. By now they were so low on metal stock that the ship had to be raked for likely pieces, and some heavy duty hydraulic pipe was sacrificed to make the necessary stays. Over the stern went the modified tool and eventually, on what was going to be the last run of the night, it caught.

'Let's see if we can begin creeping inshore again ...' Alec asserted.

The revs of the engine gave a low, gravelly rumble as it was put gently ahead.

'No ... we're not getting anywhere. Let's hoist just a little more ... No? Bastard! Why aren't we moving? The seabed must be incredibly steep here, like cliffs ... I'll lift a little more and try, again.'

They persevered, but when 0300 hours came without any progress, Alec gave in for the night. 'It's no good. I'm just too tired. I'm going to make another mistake.' The self blame was always there.

After a couple of hours of profound sleep, his head was a little clearer and on taking over the watch, he announced 'The only way is to go south-west, into deeper water'.

Eyes flashed a semaphore of surprise to each other. It seemed crazy, but if Alec said so ...

With another hundred metres beneath their keel, the umbilical came free. *Redeemer*'s stern thrust a little deeper in the water, as she took the weight and they turned almost imperceptibly eastwards, to attempt a more gradual slope. The progress was so slow. Every second of every hour was enervated by anxiety. At one dreadful moment, the individual strands of the minesweeper wire began to ping apart, as if burst.

Frank pointed it out, 'Alec! That's the wire going to break, again!'

'Stand well back everybody! Off the deck.'

Slackening the tension immediately by paying out, he knocked *Redeemer* out of gear and hearts beat fast until the damaged section was safely on the winch drum. A narrow escape.

By nightfall, they had achieved ninety metres of water. Here, the seabed became very rocky according to the chart and they called a halt to prepare all the wire strops and chain stoppers that would be necessary for the last crucial stage of heaving the hoist umbilical onboard. Caught as it was on the bottom, once more, Alec, as pragmatic as ever, used it as an anchor overnight. They would need all their energy in the morn.

Laboriously, the six tonnes of steel wire and electrical cable were reclaimed, inched out of the water with the chain stoppers, which could be wound around a promising section for it to be hauled in and belayed. It was twenty hours of non-stop toil, before the mile long cat's cradle of thick wire rope, hung in great whorls off the 'A' frame; snaking its way across the whole aft deck in knots and kinks and curls.

'What a wonder, we got it back Alec – but do you think it will ever work, again?' Vince asked.

The first step was to carry out some tests. Surprisingly, the Osprey underwater camera still worked, despite being submerged for a fortnight and being dragged across thirty miles of seabed. The hoist umbilical, however, was a different story. It had been so badly mangled that the central electrical core had been broken in a number of places. Not a single individual cable remained intact, and so that it was as useless for passing power and signals as a severed spinal cord. This was a disaster and not solely in monetary terms.

It was a specially made product, our own creation at the leading edge of technology. There was not another to be bought off the shelf, or picked up second hand and the lead-in time for a replacement was twenty-two weeks. Five months! By that time, the salvage season would have ended. There was no way that we could not go through another winter without finding the copper and this meant only one course. The damaged sections would have to be cut out and the wire rope rejoined. Nobody had done this before and the chances of making, what inevitably would be weak links, take the weight of the steel wire, let alone any load, would be very slim. but there was no other option. An expert was flown out from the UK to identify exactly where the breaks had occurred.

When he saw the tangled skein of steel armouring and electric cable, Mick Lloyd from Draka Calflex, just shook his head. 'Where to begin?' so little was accessible and the heavy muddle had to be prised apart with a crowbar to trace the tortuous route it took. The work was dirty and heavy. Using a line meter to pin point the damage, he marked off the good sections and the decision had to be made where to make the cuts. The measurements were made, checked, and checked again, for once the deed was done there would be no going back. With a shower of sparks from the Stihl saw, we had a lesser hoist umbilical that was not long enough to reach the wreck, a dud contorted middle, and a short, sound tail. The good ends were bound with insulating tape to stop the wire strands from unravelling.

They protruded out of the jumble, four diminutive stubs. The only job now was to free them.

A week of backbreaking exertion began. They sweated in the Spanish sun, covered in underwater grease with which the wire armouring was impregnated. A chain gang could not have slaved harder, or undertaken a filthier, more thankless labour. First, the ruined 400 metre middle section was prised out, by threading it through backwards and forwards, literally tugging it through the knots. Finally released, it was coiled up and dropped into the hold. Now there was only 1400 metres to go, three and a half circuits of an athletics track.

These 'laps' still hung from the 'A' frame, and once they were pulled off, there was hardly a section of the hatch or aft deck on it which was possible to tread. They wound in a huge bights, making it a struggle to clamber anywhere.

The short piece, which was eighty-eight metres long, had to be disengaged from both itself and the main length. Even with this chore complete, the enormity of the remaining task seemed undiminished. Our hoist umbilical still looked as if it had come from the bottom of my mother's knitting bag.

Sometimes there would be considerable strips that lay loose and could be coiled to one side. At others, the knots were so tight that winches and tackles had to be applied, in order to wrench them apart. There seemed no obvious conclusion, the process was never ending as the liberated section was woven in and out at all angles, whichever way it went. Soon, literally kilometres had gone through everyone's gloved hands; to the next village, Ramallossa and back; then to Vigo and back – to Madrid and back, so it felt, everyone's arms were so tired.

Muscles ached and bulged with the exercise, but still only a third was free. As a repetitive action, it got more arduous as the proportion that was clear became greater; until it took all morning simply to pull the wire rope through once, a two tonne piece of metallic spaghetti that went on, and on, and on; and as soon as it was manhandled through, the whole bundle had to be turned, so that the end could be found and forced back though, again; so that the whole process could be repeated. Heavy rain made the task more onerous, as everything became slippery and movement was hampered by oilskins. Alec was just about to give up and attack the bundle from underneath, when they hit a lucky patch and loops began to peel away.

'About a thousand metres – one kilometre free. Thank heaven!' he declared, trying to straighten up, 'My back feel's as if will it never bend again'. Exhausted, he had to continue setting the pace and in response,

Henry and Frank strove beyond the call of employment or duty, both aware that they were on the final strait.

The other end was extricated. After shoving it through and hauling it out once, the scribble disentangled and the two huge figure of eight coils which they had so painfully made pronounced that order had been made out of chaos.

Slumping down, wherever they had stood, the men's forms lay prostrate and motionless.

'That's it. Stage two over ... Thanks chaps. We're all so knackered, I think we'll feed it onto the winch drum tomorrow.' The other two exhaled, welcoming the respite. With Alec, one could never bank on these things.

Frank had made up a wooden clamp out of two sturdy batons, through which the hoist umbilical could be pulled under tension. This squeezing effect took out some of the more minor deformities, but the result was by no means perfect. Sometimes, a kink would be too bad to reel on, and the process had to be halted. The hoist umbilical on the drum would be secured to the hatch combing, so that it remained tightly wound, whilst the offending birdcage of wire strands were attacked with pipe wrenches and bulldog grips, to persuade them back into some semblance of a sheath.

The result was never very successful and the layers which had formerly run off and on with spectacular precision, now wobbled this way and that, with all the deviations, great and small, of an infant learning to master a bike. Two extremely severe jack knives each took a day's efforts to correct. Had this not been done, the section would have come out of the groove of the aft pulley, and been thrown straight off the rim.

Only once they had finished, could Alec permit himself to think about continuing the search for the copper.

He had been feeling better since he had begun taking antibiotics for a deep seated infection that had taken root in his wounded knee and his former enthusiasm began to return, as he pored over the chart he had made of the search area. For weeks, he had not even bothered to listen to the Shipping Forecasts, they were so academic. Now, finding the frequency on Long Wave, he heard the *The Archers'* distinctive signature tune, followed by another all too familiar refrain – 'Force five or six, possibly seven around Cape Finisterre'.

'It doesn't matter, we'll still have to go out. Even if it's a question of hanging around until the conditions calm down.'

They had almost completed their survey down the east side of the wreck, when they had been so rudely interrupted. This now seemed an eternity, before, but Alec was nothing, if not methodical. He would finish this area inshore, before continuing to the south, not least because both areas were shallower and still within their reach. The days passed, and the squares on his grid were eliminated. 'Where are these elusive wirebars?' he pondered, going over the details of the *François Vieljeux*'s loss and the underwater videos, again and again, as if to hit on any missed clues. Even so, it was impossible to piece together what had happened to her in those final moments, as she tumbled to the seafloor. Had she gone over completely, turning upside down, perhaps floating submerged? Had she tipped over backwards if she had gone, as witnessed, down by the stern? Silent and inanimate, her wreck gave nothing away.

They had plotted numerous containers, and their scattered contents but nothing that could be mistaken for copper or zinc. There was nothing for it, but to add on another length and begin scanning to the west. More bad luck, it was deeper than marked on the Admiralty Chart and what could be saved from the damaged 400 metre section, had to be cut out and a second joint made. It was around this all-time low, that I went out to Spain. Alec's sister, Ann, had kindly offered to take the children to her home in Devon for a fortnight, and this holiday allowed me to get away.

Staying in the wheelhouse until well after dark, when the windows silvered by the night became mirrors and reflected the interior, our presence was multiplied fourfold. Four wives, with their arms on their husband's shoulders, each staring into a television monitor and captured from a different angle. Four sets of red warning lights and engine room controls.

The seabed off Galicia passed beneath our mutual gaze and Alec was bolstered by the companionship. 'The Flemish eyes I've made to join the wire are holding and I think I've got the electrical connections right now. It's cost us a lot of time sorting them out, but they seem to work. There's only interference when they go over the pulley sheave and get a bend, but otherwise there have been no more shorts. What a hassle, Moya.'

'I know.'

'After we've looked here, there's just the northern sector to go. It's unlikely that the cargo is there, but we'll have to rule it out. I'm beginning to think it could still be in the *François Vieljeux*, but heavens knows where. It's ironic, really, what should have been a simple procedure to eliminate a possibility, has ended up wasting our summer by ruining our hoist umbilical and giving us over a month of work. It might even make us run out of money and lose the wreck.'

'Don't be too hard on yourself'.

'Who else is there to blame? I feel such a failure at times!'

Anyone who witnessed the clear black and white images that from over a mile of water, through a hoist umbilical with two joins in it, could not have believed that for one moment. Here we were examining parts of the planet which lay hidden to all but a handful of scientific institutes and defence funded companies at the cost of £13,000 per month. That was not failure.

'No, Alec,' I disagreed. 'Anything, but that.'

I was fascinated by what I saw, humbled even. The deep ocean was by no means a dead world, cold and sunless though it was, it was very much alive. As the camera traversed the bottom at a speed of one knot, the lights disturbed the inhabitants. Dogfish were common and we would come across whole groups of them; similarly eels, which lay in round coils on the bottom until they were startled and they would metamorphose into ribbons and flutter away. Henry identified the grotesque creatures, with reptilian heads like lizard dragons, as angler fish, so ugly that they lost none of their menace despite their distance away. Starfish were by far the most numerous. Their anaemic white colour would reflect back, making them shine and take on rather a ghoulish appearance; stalked crinoids, too, had established large colonies, animals like miniature palm trees, they wafted as if bending in the breeze as our intrusion swept past. The silty sand was pitted all over with hundreds and thousands of burrows, hinting at a plethora of clandestine and subterranean creatures of which we were totally ignorant.

Then we would spot a man made object that would cause a flurry of excitement; a piece of metal structure here; a rubber fender, there. Hopes were guardedly raised, when we happened upon a trail of split and broken coffee sacks a quarter of mile wide, lying to the south-west and avidly the monitor was watched as they became thicker and thicker. 'Let this be it,' prayed Alec, but just as they had appeared out of nothingness, they petered out.

A few days later, when we were alone and working into the early hours of the morning, the umbilical fouled, again, and the picture went. Alec slammed on the brake, and buried his face in his hands, his voice shaking, 'I can't bear it if the joints go and we lose the camera'. As he tentatively turned the winch controls to hoist, the needle of the pressure gauge, which quantified the load, crept round to 1500 psi and stayed there for several moments until there was a thump. The hoist umbilical leapt on the pulley as the weight came off, and the needle jerked right back.

Utter defeat set into his look. 'It will take a while to reel it in, because of the deformities, but when we get to where the joints ought to be, I want you to go out aft and tell me when you see the end coming out of the water.'

Redeemer was rolling, but looking up at the clear dark sky, it was as if the stars were being agitated from side to side, and I was still. Illuminated in the deck lights, I watched the water drip away from the distorted wire rope as it writhed out of the inky brine. Foreboding stifled my breathing. Could any of us stand much more of this punishment? The first joint appeared and I signalled a thumb's up to Alec in the wheelhouse, and after what seemed an eternity, the second. 'Just the camera, now,' I thought. Ten thousand pounds' worth ...' The orange cage came into sight. Hanging vertically, initially it was impossible for me to see and there was a dreadful pause. No, we were all right. It was there and we took comfort, even though the electrical connections in the joints had been broken.

'I'll have to get my tools to repair then. One thing though, Moya, at least the strain has taken some of the kinks out of the wire!' I laughed, because it was true.

Finally, the weather blew us offsite. It always staggered me how quickly the conditions changed from being unpleasant to frightening. Cutting across the breaking waves, the journey into Bayona was wet and rough.

It was not long before I had to return to my duties at home and consign Alec once more to his lonely vigil. By the end of the month, with the whole area around the *François Vieljeux* thoroughly searched, there was no alternative, but to lay the moorings around the wreck, and begin a second, even greater excavation.

Everyone was totally depressed, our money was dwindling and everything, including repairs and maintenance, took much longer because of always having to make do. When Alec phoned to give me updates, I always willed myself to take on a calm, positive voice, when the weekly toll of bad weather and damage was revealed.

'We're moving forward from the aft end of No. 3 hold. There are containers and fallen hatch beams that are giving us a lot of trouble. I keep on having to cut back the hoist umbilical and rejoin it to the grab, because of the damage we're getting – that wastes twenty-four hours each time, for the resin to cure. The conditions are really pretty atrocious, but we're getting there ...'

September passed and October, until the patient process was more than I could bear. It seemed irrelevant that we were operating remotely in 1250 metres of water; dangling our grab into sections of a hold that were 14.5 metres long by 5.5 metres wide. We were operating on No Cure/No Pay and to date, this precision was not paying the bills, and I wanted to yell down the receiver, 'How on earth am I supposed to run a business and bring up a family, like this? When are we going to get some money in? I've had enough. I simply hate it!' Such a lash, however heartfelt, would have been weak as well as totally unproductive. My life might be tough and stressful, but Alec's was physically dangerous. There was an onus not to be self indulgent, for him, the crew, even Vince.

This particular call from a Spanish call box had begun much the same as any other and my spirits sank. The generator was on the blink. The junction box had been repaired and the tines of the grab had had to welded. To all this I showed polite, informed concern, until he said, 'We had got the grab into the forward, starboard corner of No. 3 hold and Henry who was watching the monitor with me, said "What's that, Alec?" I could see sort of fingers sticking out beneath a wide steel plate and it's the copper ...'

'You mean you've found it!'

'Yes.'

'Why didn't you say!'

He laughed apologetically. 'I've got used to it, now. Obviously, we were ecstatic when we found it, but now we've got to concentrate on getting some of it before the winter breaks.'

'All that wait finally come to an end. I can hardly believe it.'

'The batteries are giving me a bit of a problem. I know what changes I want to make before next season. We'll have to see about a new hoist umbilical, this one is on its last legs. I don't know how much longer it's going to hold out. Let's just hope our luck lasts and we even get a few tonnes up before the winter forces us back to Scotland ...'

27

WORLD RECORDS

It did not. We updated the underwater system in the winter, and by the time Alec had his moorings laid and his new underwater pods working properly, it was late June, the following year. This was typical of Alec, to take whatever opportunity he had to push our technology forward, even at the expense of time.

'It's taken longer than I had anticipated to power the system, with current from the surface, but there's no point using batteries, if I can operate the grab, this way. It will give us so much more power. We've got to keep on developing the equipment, it's what will make all the struggle worth while in the end.'

I have to admit, I agreed, but as the days passed with sticking relays and shorting wires, and the electrical unit, with its transformer and motor being manhandled in and out of its container, all I wanted was a quick fix. The problem was the wirebars themselves. Nearly a metre and a half long and weighing over 121 kilograms each, they were wedged together in such a tight pyramid in the corner of the hold, that the grab was having the greatest difficulty in teasing any out. They were locked solid.

I had the children out with me, and we had taken a flat up one of the back streets in Bayona, to provide Alec with some semblance of home, on the odd occasions that he was in. Frank and Henry had returned for another season, even though we seemed to be going through a succession of First Mates. After Charlie Marsden had gone to the oil industry, the challenge had been to find a good replacement.

On this particular day, the boys were away swimming and Rachel and I had made our way down to the small cove beneath the parador for her to await a Spanish friend. As Calvinistic as ever, I could not sit down for an hour without doing anything and so had settled down to read Alan Bullock's *Hitler and Stalin, Parallel Lives*, when *Redeemer* steamed rapidly round the end of the breakwater and dropped anchor. To Rachel's complaints, at having to quit the pleasures of sandcastles so precipitously, to meet whoever came ashore, I simply replied, 'It's our job.'

'What's gone wrong now?' I wondered, as laden with our belongings we walked the gauntlet of bikini-clad sunbathers and waved from the end of the wooden pontoon. The rubber inflatable had been put into the water with such alacrity, that I confided, 'This must either be extremely good news, or an absolute disaster'. Even when Alec raised his hand in a friendly wave, I was not convinced one way or the other, as sometimes his buoyant mood was nothing but a ploy to prepare me for something awful.

'It's bad news. It's bad news. It's bad news,' I told myself, so worn out by all the false hopes, that I could not bear to be encouraged, simply to be downcast. How many times over the last month had I tentatively asked, 'Got any yet?' only to be met with a heavy sigh and a sorry explanation.

In the end I did not have to ask. As the boat zoomed ever closer, Alec smiled and gave the thumb's up signal.

'How many?'

'Just five and then the cylinder head gasket on the Gardner went, we had put such a load on it, but that's it Moya, we've lifted some wirebars at last. We've tripled the world depth record for commercial cargo recovery.'

The embrace I gave and words of congratulation seemed so banal, considering not just the achievement, but all the endurance it had taken to make it. 'I'm so proud of you.'

The rubber inflatable motored the short distance back to *Redeemer* and I viewed the cause of all our struggle. Already oxidising in the sun, and turning from a bright strawberry blond to a dull auburn, the long dense fingers of metal lay in a neat line on deck and were so unremarkable that I smiled as if at a whimsical joke. They had been so tardily delayed on their journey from Africa to Europe. 'All that effort for those.'

'Not exactly gold ingots, are they, but there are eight and a half of them to the tonne, that's over a thousand pounds worth. Just over another ten million quid, to go!'

'Shall we get the champagne now, Alec?' inquired Henry.

'Why not,' and alone, a small team as we had been for months we celebrated with a bottle that Vince's friend, John Dare, had provided when we left Marseilles. Far from exuberance, the atmosphere was happy, but subdued. No great whoops and slapping of palms, just pleasure at having been vindicated. It had been a difficult struggle developing our equipment under such severe, uncompromising conditions, but our cost efficient technology was now unequivocally proven to work and our risk would be repaid as the copper came up in increasing amounts.

'Well done Alec.'

'Well done everybody.'

'To us and wha's like us ...' cheered Henry in the well known Scottish salute.

'Guy few and they're all dead!' came the retort.

The toasts were short and to the point.

'I'll go ashore and call Vince and the Salvage Association to let them know.' Considering that throughout the years most of our business has been conducted from public phone boxes, it was an apposite forum from which to broadcast our breakthrough. I spoke to my mother and Sukey Roxburgh who helps me in the office, as well.

'Mum, Alec's got the first copper up off the *François Vieljeux* ... I know, it's been such a battle, I can hardly believe we've got there ... He's overjoyed ... Can you ring round and let a few other people know, it's so difficult from here? Alec's mother, Simon and Alison, Tommy Clark, Jonathan Miller. I would like them to hear before it is in any of the papers ... Sukey's going to deal with the press release. I've asked her to phone John Noble of Murray Fenton's and Chris Belton at the Ministry of Defence. They've both been very supportive as well ... Just a meal for everyone in the flat tonight, we're too poor and all too exhausted for anything else ... I'll give him your love and congratulations ... Bye.'

And essentially, that is the story over. Every salvage tale ends with the first recovery, for that is when much, if not quite all, of the uncertainty ends.

The copper wirebars and cathodes, so elusive for so long, certainly did not give themselves up as hostages, and the grab continued to struggle to break them out from what was almost a solid mound. Catching days here and there, often lying on one of the buoys for days, just to tie up for a few hours of lifting weather, we had thirty tonnes by the time winter seas took hold. *Redeemer* crossed Biscay in awful conditions and continued up through the Irish Sea on the west coast, to the Caledonian Canal.

I was early to meet the ship and caught a glimpse of her as she steamed into Loch Linnhe, cutting through the still, sheltered waters of an icy December morning, as I drove along the road to Fort William. Standing by the car at the sea lock at Corpach, watching her progress under the all dominating summit of Ben Nevis, which has its head in the clouds and its base in the sea, I felt a mixture of emotions. Pride? Patriotism? Sentimentality? Call it what you will, its austerity and harsh beauty caused a lump in my throat, as I knew its stature represented our conquest in the capricious element of the Atlantic, almost metre for metre. The rugged windswept coast of Scotland and its islands, especially Foula, had founded the experience to make our achievement. Coping with the hostility of its shores had given us the grit to endure; and the affection and practical support of many of its inhabitants, had fuelled the tenacity to carry on. I knew we could not have tried harder to acquit any of our obligations, in any way.

The rest of the journey completed the series of touchstones from the past. Through Loch Ness, where we had tested the second generation system to the *Glenartney* – a wreck that has never been worked to this day, and the Department of Transport has long since given up its policy of competitive tendering. Around Rattray Head, inshore of where the *Guido* was sunk, the wreck on which we had failed so miserably with our first cargo recovery attempt and finally to Victoria Dock in Dundee, *Redeemer's* home port. How apt that we should unload our spoils in the very berth to which she had been towed by the *Valorous* as a burnt out hull and Alec had confided his dreams for working in 330 metres of water. How impossibly crazy these had seemed then. How incredibly they had been surpassed.

* * * * *

That triumph was five years ago. In the interim we have gone on to lift ever increasing tonnages by improving our engineering. Bigger hydraulic rams on the grab tines took the haul up to one hundred and fifty tonnes for 1994, a figure which was subsequently tripled to four hundred and fifty tonnes in 1995. We were looking towards a similar increment the following season, when a faulty hoist umbilical we were sold took away every material advance of the new eight-tined grab with two hundred tonnes closing force, which Alec's had designed and built – and like Snakes and Ladders, we slid right back down the board.

The irony was that before the problems set in, we lifted fifteen tonnes on its very first day on the *François Vieljeux*, almost half the total of our entire first year; but such an anomaly only serves to mark our progress like a milestone along a tortuous journey; and so it was, resorting to the mettle we had forged over the years, that we limped over the 1000 tonne watershed, despite being so badly let down. Risdon Beazley, our old rivals, had set the limit for this quantity of metal at 136 metres. At 1250 metres, this was a second world record for cargo recovery to our credit, and with it, the lifting system which had so long been a prototype, could be claimed as a reliable and commercially viable unit having lifted over £1.5 million in value.

I am glad to say, our aspirations do not end there. I am sitting, finishing this account in a pleasant flat which over looks *Redeemer's* anchorage at Bayona knowing that her days are numbered and soon, we shall be heading for a new wreck, lying even deeper in 3500 metres of water.

The new winding mechanism on her stern has given us all sorts of problems over the last few months, bringing back old memories. These are now solved and with its unique ability to replace steel with man-made fibres, we are now planning to take it and our underwater units down to 11000 metres, full ocean depth, for scientific survey work. This will not be with *Redeemer*. Scarred, rusting in places and beginning to show her age, her leg of the race will soon be over. Already, two universities, Cranfield and Newcastle upon Tyne, are helping with the research work required for her replacement, *STEADY*, which has been so long in the wings, the innovation of which does her retirement no disservice at all.

With approximately a fifteen million pound investment, and a hull that transfers from the horizontal steaming mode, to a vertical operating mode, when it arrives onsite, I have not the slightest doubt that this final element in our *railroad to the seabed*, will give us as much anguish as some of our previous leaps of the imagination in the past. So be it.

I have few complaints. As a woman in a man's world I have been privileged enough not only to get to the top and follow my own specific interests through being on the Steering Committee of BRIDGE – the British Initiative to Study the mid-Ocean Ridge – as well as being an elected council member for the Society for Underwater Technology; but have had the good fortune to be loved, married and bring up four healthy, spirited children. The two who were born before we lifted *Redeemer*, are now blossoming out into the world in their own right; Robert, with a Trinity House scholarship is off on a BP tanker, somewhere in the Pacific, beginning his training as a Deck Officer. Drew is in New Zealand, driving fast cars as is his passion and earning his keep on a sheep station – still sixteen years old he has got a march on his mother by several months in 'running away' from home; Patrick and Rachel are with us here, but it will not be long before they go, too. In all, despite the hardships, I believe they have appreciated the trials and tribulations of their unorthodox upbringing.

Certainly, we have packed in much during the years. Long may our resolution to withstand the pace continue. There is still so much more to achieve.

INDEX